IMAGINARY PORTRAITS

IMAGINARY PORTRAITS

with

The Child in the House

and

Gaston de Latour

WALTER PATER

Introduction by
BILL BECKLEY

ALLWORTH PRESS
NEW YORK

School of
VISUAL ARTS

A E S T H E T I C S   T O D A Y

Editorial Director: Bill Beckley

The Aesthetics Today series includes *The Laws of Fésole* and *Lectures on Art* by John Ruskin and *Uncontrollable Beauty* edited by Bill Beckley with David Shapiro.

© 1997 Bill Beckley

All rights reserved. Copyright under Berne Copyright Convention, Universal Copyright Convention, and Pan-American Copyright Convention. No part of this book may be reproduced, stored in a retrieval system, or transmitted in any form, or by any means, electronic, mechanical, photocopying, recording, or otherwise, without prior permission of the publisher.

Published by Allworth Press

An imprint of Allworth Communications

10 East 23rd Street, New York, NY 10010

Copublished with the School of Visual Arts

Cover design: Douglas Design, New York, NY

Book design: Sharp Des!gns, Holt, MI

Front cover: *Portrait of a Young Man* by Bronzino (1503–1572) is reproduced by courtesy of The Metropolitan Museum of Art, bequest of Mrs. H. O. Havemeyer, 1929. The H. O. Havemeyer Collection. © 1989 The Metropolitan Museum of Art.

Page xx: From "Esthetique du Mal" in *Collected Poems* by Wallace Stevens. © 1947 by Wallace Stevens. Reprinted by permission of Alfred A. Knopf Inc.

ISBN: 1-880559-77-3

Library of Congress Catalog Card Number: 96-79665

Printed in Canada

CONTENTS

Well! we are all condamnés, as Victor Hugo says: we are all under sentence of death but with a sort of indefinite reprieve—*les hommes sont tous condamnés à mort avec des sursis indéfinis*: we have an interval, and then our place knows us no more. Some spend this interval in listlessness, some in high passions, the wisest, at least among "the children of the world," in art and song. For our one chance lies in expanding that interval, in getting as many pulsations as possible into a given time. Great passions may give us this quickened sense of life, ecstasy and sorrow of love, the various forms of enthusiastic activity, disinterested or otherwise, which come naturally to many of us. Only be sure that it is passion—that it does yield you this fruit of a quickened, multiplied consciousness. Of this wisdom, the poetic passion, the desire of beauty, the love of art for art's sake, has most; for art comes to you professing frankly to give nothing but the highest quality to your moments as they pass, and simply for those moment's sake.

Walter Pater, *Studies in the History of the Renaissance,* 1868

INTRODUCTION
ROCKET MAN

by Bill Beckley

He who is ever looking for the breaking of light he knows not whence about him, notes with a strange heedfulness the faintest paleness in the sky.   —*from "Diaphaneitè"*

Philosophical Fictions—Whiter Shades of Pale

ONE LATE NOVEMBER, DURING A VISIT TO AN ANTIQUARIAN BOOKSTORE IN NEW Haven, I came across a charming little American edition of *The Child in the House* published in 1895. It was no more than a pamphlet, a quarter of an inch thick, with a fragile, gray paper cover protected by a clear plastic jacket and numbered 1/350. I skimmed it in the bookstore, then wrote out a check. By the time I stepped outside, I couldn't stop reading it. As I sat engrossed on the doorstep of the bookstore, a townhouse on a tree-lined street near Yale, my little son waited impatiently in the car. It seemed a trade-off—a bit of guilt, anxiety, and compassion in exchange for (though quite similar to) the pleasure of reading. In that winter light, the house of Pater's story fused in my mind with a house I had known as a child. My childhood mixed with Pater's fictional childhood and that of the child in the car. *The Child in the House* opened a path of experience I had forgotten for so long a time.

Though the body of his writings is small compared to a contemporary like John Ruskin, Pater's dominion and influence is just as far-reaching. In his brilliant biography, *Walter Pater: Lover of Strange Souls,* Denis

Donoghue writes that Pater's afterlife "is the first act of so many literary careers. Pater gave modern literature its first act."

Pater foresaw the modern movement in prose and poetry. In Harold Bloom's words, "He fathered the future." Echo after echo of Pater can be found in the prose of Oscar Wilde, F. Scott Fitzgerald, James Joyce, Marcel Proust, Evelyn Waugh, Tennessee Williams, Vladimir Nabokov, Joseph Conrad, Virginia Woolf, Jorge Luis Borges, and Samuel Beckett as well as in the poetry of T. S. Eliot, Ezra Pound, Wallace Stevens, and John Ashbery.

For Walter Pater, the end is not the *fruit* of experience, but experience itself. Through that idea, Pater's fictional works and characters embody his aesthetic philosophy, expressed so beautifully in the "Conclusion" of *Studies in the History of the Renaissance*:

> Experience, already reduced to a swarm of impressions, is ringed round for each one of us by that thick wall of personality through which no real voice has ever pierced on its way to us, or from us to that which we can only conjecture to be without. Every one of these impressions is the individual in his isolation, each mind keeping as a solitary prisoner its own dream of a world. Analysis goes a step further still, and assures us that those impressions of the individual mind to which, for each one of us, experience dwindles down, are in perpetual flight; that each is limited by the time, and that as time is indefinitely divisible, each of them is divisible also; all that is actual in it being a single moment, gone while we try to apprehend it, of which it may ever be truly said that it has ceased to be than that it is. . . . It is with this movement, with the passage and desolation of impressions, images, sensations, that analysis leaves off—that continual vanishing away, that strange, perpetual weaving and unweaving of ourselves.

Pater's fiction begins with *The Child in the House,* which he called "the germinating, original, source, specimen, of all my imaginative work." *The Child in the House* describes the aesthetic awakening of a little boy. There are different opinions as to how closely it may be autobiographical, but I don't think the matter is too important. The story is about acquiescence and consent to experience, transgressing personality and allowing for penetration of the thick wall adulthood so often constructs. Pater describes this process of "brain-building":

> For it is false to suppose that a child's sense of beauty is dependent on any choiceness or special fineness in the objects which present themselves to it, though this indeed comes to be the rule with most of us in later life; earlier, to some degree, we see inwardly; and the child finds itself, and with unstinted delight, a difference for the sense, in those whites and reds through the smoke on the very homely buildings, and in the gold of the dandelions at the road side, just beyond the houses, where not a handful of earth is virgin and untouched, in the lack of better ministries to its desire of beauty.

Pater originally sent off *The Child in the House* to *Macmillan's* magazine in April of 1878. Although he said he intended it to be complete in itself, as well as the first part of a series, he didn't include it in *Imaginary Portraits,* which was published on May 24, 1887. *Imaginary Portraits* was a collection of four stories that had been published separately: "A Prince of Court Painters" (October 1885), "Denys L'Auxerrois" (October 1886), "Sebastian van Storck (March 1886), and "Duke Carl of Rosenmold" (May 1887). "A Prince of Court Painters" is a poignant story about the French painter Antoine Watteau, who died in 1721, told through the correspondence of a diarist who is in love with him. The portraits, including *The Child in the House,* the four *Imaginary Portraits,* and *Gaston de Latour,* are stories of lives in times of cultural and aesthetic change. In a sense, *Imaginary Portraits* is a continuation of *Studies in the History of the Renaissance,* which consists of stories about the lives of Renaissance artists, including Botticelli, Michelangelo, Giorgione, and da Vinci. In writing about the lives of these historical figures, Pater did much to fill in the blanks, so there is a very thin line between his real and imaginary characters.

Gaston de Latour was likely meant as a follow-up to Pater's only novel, *Marius the Epicurean,* but Pater did not finish it. The actual life of Gaston de Latour is recorded in one of the latter works of Michel de Montaigne, the great French essayist of the sixteenth century. The real Gaston de Latour married Léonore, the daughter of Montaigne, not to her father's complete satisfaction.

Like all Pater's stories, *Gaston de Latour* describes an age of transition when the old fabric of belief is breaking apart. According to Charles Shadwell, who prepared the text for publication in 1896, two years after Pater's death: "The interest would have centered round the spiritual development of a refined and cultivated mind, capable of keen enjoyment in the pleasures of the senses and of the intellect, but destined to find its complete satisfaction in that which transcends both."

Contributing to Gaston's spiritual development in Pater's fictional account were Montaigne and two other literary figures of the late Renaissance: Pierre de Ronsard (1524–1585), the great poet of the Pléiades movement in France, and the Italian philosopher Giordano Bruno (1548–1600).

The life recanted in *Gaston de Latour* is a life more mature than that of *The Child in the House*, but is still the life of a mind in transformation and influenced by the ideologies of its time. In an interesting juxtaposition, the ideas of the young man are coming together as the conjunct constructs of his age are falling apart. He can either give in to the new value system, seek some kind of balance, or find a set of values that rises above the fray. Though Gaston's times were fraught with political and religious strife, this, as any revolutionary or historian knows, makes for change. If death, for Wallace Stevens, is the mother of beauty, sorrow, for Pater, is the rival of beauty:

> The great passions, the fervid sentiments, of which Gaston dreamed as the true realisation of life, have not always softened men's natures: they have been compatible with many cruelties as in the lost spirits of that very age. They may overflow, on the other hand, in more equitable natures, through the concurrence of happier circumstance, into the universal sympathy which lends a kind of amorous power to the homeliest charities. So it seemed like with Gaston de Latour. Sorrow came along with beauty, a rival of its intricate omnipresence in life. . . . The beauty of the world and its sorrow, solaced a little by religious faith, itself so beautiful a thing; these were the chief impressions with which he made his way outwards, at first only in rambles, as physical

strength increased, over his native plains, whereon, as we have seen, the cruel warfare of that age had aggravated at a thousand points the every-day appeal of suffering humanity.

Through avenues of experience chaotic or calm, beauty was Pater's greatest concern. *Beauty* is a word frequently used in nineteenth-century poetry and prose, and, of course, we can argue that it functioned as an authentication or guarantee as well as mere description. The word turns up less frequently in the twentieth century, as Dave Hickey, one of the most provocative critics of our time, observes in "Prom Night in Flatland." Progressive flattening of pictorial space in painting, for example, created an impenetrability of the picture plane and a preference for masculine descriptive terms like *strength, singularity,* and *autonomy.* In the concluding paragraph of the same essay, Hickey speaks of the *generosity* of beauty. It is through this generosity that there "lies a richer reality, a better language, a more complex sense of community, and a more courageous art."

Beauty's Back

With the reemergence of beauty in contemporary discourse, it is natural that attention should turn to Pater, a central figure in beauty's equation. Pater pursued beauty without apology. He was the father of the aesthetic movement that blossomed in England at the end of the nineteenth century. Though *beauty* may have been defined differently at that time, the word is not irrelevant today. It has returned in contemporary writings of psychologists, poets, and critics alike.

Peter Schjeldahl writes in "Notes on Beauty":

> There is something crazy about a culture in which the value of beauty becomes controversial. It is crazy not to celebrate whatever reconciles us to life. The craziness suggests either a stubborn grievance— an unhappiness with life that turns peoples against notions of reconciliation to it—or benumbed insensibility. The two terms may be one.

A clear-conscienced pursuit of beauty has long lain dormant. The psychologist James Hillman writes, in an essay called "The Practice of Beauty,"

> We want the world because it is beautiful, its sounds and smells and textures, the sensate presence of the world as a body. In short, below the ecological crises lies the deeper crisis of love, that our love has left the world; that the world is loveless results directly from the repression of beauty, its beauty and our sensitivity to beauty. For love to return to the world, beauty must first return, else we love the world only as a moral duty: clean it up, preserve its nature, exploit it less. If love depends on beauty, then beauty comes first, a priority that accords with pagan philosophy rather than Christian. Beauty before love also accords with the all-too-human experience of being driven to love by the allure of beauty.

I do not mean to suggest that Pater is the predominate influence on these comments. In the words of the poet David Shapiro, "No one owns beauty." Certainly Pater does not. It is because of this renewed interest in beauty that we are drawn to Pater's extraordinary writings.

* * *

AFTER A CENTURY OF CULTURAL RELATIVISM, BEGINNING WITH THE WRITINGS of Nietzsche, there is no clear path back to the high Romantic absolute as defined in Keats's lines from "Ode to a Grecian Urn,"

> 'Beauty is Truth, Truth Beauty,'—that is all
> Ye know on earth, and all ye need to know.

As early as 1862, in her poem numbered 449, Emily Dickinson grappled eloquently with the equation,

> I died for Beauty—but was scarce
> Adjusted in the Tomb
> When one who died for Truth, was lain

In an adjoining room—

He questioned softly "Why I failed"?
"For Beauty", I replied—
"And I—for Truth—Themself are One—
We Brethren, are", He said—

And so, as Kinsmen, met a Night—
We talked between the Rooms—
Until the Moss had reached our lips—
And covered up—our names—

Whereas earlier English poets of the Romantic era, as well as the critic John Ruskin, associated beauty with the absolute Good. Pater unlinked this association throughout his work, particularly in the "Conclusion" of *Studies in the History of the Renaissance.* His student Oscar Wilde would then take beauty and run with it. Wilde linked beauty with evil in works like *Salomé* and *The Picture of Dorian Gray.*

Beauty, however defined or linked, is the object of aesthetics. Though he was writing from the filter of late nineteenth-century thought, Pater did much to define aesthetics in the twentieth-century sense. We should remember that *aesthete* is derived from the Greek word *aisthetes,* which means "one who perceives." In Pater's time, the term already had turned from this meaning and the more common understanding of "one professing devotion to the beautiful" to the unfortunate debasement of the term as "snob." Pater wrote from the Greek perspective, and was concerned, as we see particularly in *The Child in the House,* with the nature of perception and experience as a child grows to adulthood. We can see in art of the modern era successful attempts to "make strange," to see past the prisons of cliché that cultural convention and the mere repetition of form place on perceptive experience.

The use of the word *aesthetics* in the sense of "a theory of the beautiful" originated with the German philosopher Alexander Gottlieb Baumgarten. In *Aesthetics,* published in 1750, Baumgarten writes,

Aesthetics (the theory of the fine arts, the theory of the lower kind of knowledge, the art of thinking beautifully, the art of analogical reasoning) is the science of sensuous knowledge. The end of aesthetics is perfection of sensuous knowledge as such. This is beauty.

Baumgarten's writings provided a textbook on aesthetics for another German philosopher, Immanuel Kant, who wrote *The Critique of Judgement* in 1790. For Kant, there is a difference between "determinant" and "reflective" judgments, the former being in the realm of physical science and the latter, the realm of the aesthetic. This difference is the distinction, for example, between the understanding of the various elements of a flower and their functions through biology—the pistol, the stamen, the petals—and finding beautiful the arrangement of flowers in a bouquet.

The objects we experience appear to us through faculties that we have in common to perceive them. In judgments such as "fire melts wax," the imagination unites sensations through form, time, and causality, and constructs our understanding of the phenomenon. But in a judgment such as "that is beautiful," any perceived harmony is the result of free play, not of subordination to a law presupposed as necessary. To call a thing beautiful is really to assert that it seems designed for no other purpose than to unify our imagination and our understanding. Our faculties are stimulated without being obligated. The pleasure in beauty is an end in itself, but Kant also suggests that our pleasure arises from the belief that people's faculties, when put to use in the same sensuous undertaking, can harmonize in the same sensuous ways, like they do through belief in scientific fact. With aesthetic judgments, this happens, however, in a more free-spirited way. We are thus confirmed by our indulgence and corroboration in beauty.

The aesthetic order of Pater's time, influenced by the writings of Baumgarten, Kant, and Winckelmann, had its beginnings in a discussion group called The Old Mortality, which Pater joined in 1862. Its members were mostly agnostics. On one rainy evening in May of 1866, Pater gave a lecture that was an early example of his developing aestheticism as well as an appeal for young people to remain free in mind. The talk was later published as an essay called "Diaphaneitè," meaning "the diaphanous" or "pervious to light."

In understanding Pater's fictional characters, it is useful to be familiar with the three character types that he defined in this lecture. This division was influenced by the cultural critiques of Matthew Arnold, but Pater applied Arnold's classifications to his own ends. Pater's first group of people has success in material things. It includes the people who govern. The second type consists of the artists and saints of the world who relate to the first group by way of being a conscience. They are allowed to be heard, but if they ever pose a serious threat, they are consequently repressed or eliminated. They are useful to the world in that they understand and point out its sickness. The first type lives in the world and controls it; the second type lives by the irony of rebuking it.

Pater's third type, the diaphanous, describes a much rarer sort of being in whom the "elements of our moral nature refine themselves to the burning point." The diaphanous type, according to Donoghue, is not concerned with the world in assertion or contradiction, but looks to the higher consideration of "eternal worth." The diaphanous nature is something one is born with, not something one can acquire. It issues from a kind of grace, without any effort at all. The first two types of character are in continual conflict, as we have seen throughout history. The third rises above that conflict in a spiritual way through "evanescent shades," nuances and veils that refine and fill in between the first two contrasting types of character. But when conflict between the first two types becomes painfully evident in the community, it is often the diaphanous who are sacrificed. An example is Blanche DuBois in Tennessee Williams's *Streetcar Named Desire.* Fearful of the penetrating capacity of light, while attracted to the penetrating capacity of Stanley Kowalski, she is trapped and sacrificed because others in her small world cannot deal with the fact of their own shortcomings. In the final scene, she gives up and tears down the thin curtains, the transparent veils of the room.

In *Pater: Lover of Strange Souls,* Donoghue draws an analogy between Pater's three character types and three ways of seeing. In the first, the eye is brought to rest by seeing opaque, definite objects. This is the rhetoric of realism, an attitude that is legitimized by its referent. In the second, the eye sees an object, but equivocally: the relationship between the object and light around it is indeterminate. This is the rhetoric of irony. It establishes itself as a superior to what it sees, as so many artists claim superiority and find disgust in a culture they often so rightly reject. Irony does not find pleasure in what it sees, but rather in itself. In the third experience of seeing, writes Donoghue, "The mind's eye is gratified by seeing things that offer little or no resistance. The eye sees through them: air, blue sky, crystal, clear water. The mind returns to itself after seeing such objects and feels that the world is permeable." The history of avant-garde art in the twentieth century reads on the whole like an exchange between the first two ways of seeing. But an artist like Andy Warhol might represent the third type. Warhol does not criticize popular culture. He simply holds it up to light. I remember an early work, a dreamlike room of floating silver pillows.

*   *   *

BY THE TIME OF THE PUBLICATION OF *STUDIES IN THE HISTORY OF THE RENAIS-sance* in 1878, Pater had become the center of a small but interesting circle of disciples at Oxford that had evolved from The Old Mortality. The Pre-Raphaelites were among his friends. When *Marius the Epicurean* appeared in 1885, Pater's many disciples hailed the work as gospel.

This small group of people with an aesthetic disposition grew to a larger band of writers and artists that included Dante Gabriel Rossetti, craftsmen and poets like William Morris, and Pater's most famous student, Oscar Wilde.

Oscar Wilde, a student of both Ruskin and Pater at Oxford in the 1870s, was the aesthetic movement's major proponent in literature. Wilde, in some part because he was the more charismatic speaker, took aestheticism from being the Pateresque cult that it was and translated it into a movement. In the process, he charmingly vulgarized his teacher's ideas. So much in Wilde's lectures and writings came from the thoughts of his teacher Pater. His lecture titled "The English Renaissance" was obviously taken from the "Conclusion" of Pater's *Studies in the History of the Renaissance*. Wilde succeeded in his lectures on a popular level because of his charisma and wit. He went on an extensive lecture tour in the United States, delivering lectures that could be taken as a manifesto for the aesthetic movement as well as a homage to his teacher, so saturated were they with the thought of Walter Pater:

> Love art for its own sake, and then all these things shall be added to you. This devotion to beauty, and to the creation of beautiful things, is the test of all great civilizations. It is what makes the life of all great civilizations. It is what makes the life of each citizen a sacrament and not a speculation; for beauty is the only thing time cannot harm. Philosophies may fall away like the sand; creeds follow one another; but what is beautiful is a joy for all seasons, a possession for all eternity. . . .
>
> We in our Renaissance are seeking to create a sovereignty that shall still be England's when her yellow leopards are weary of wars, and the rose on her shield is crimsoned no more with the blood of battle. . . .

With lines like these, Wilde sowed, like so many apple seeds, the future of aestheticism in America. His fancy dress and manner of speaking made him a curiosity in the still largely puritanical country. But he was not always met with New World gawking or naïveté when it came to the subject of beauty. A high point of Wilde's tour in America was his meeting Walt Whitman. The dialogue that took place between the older Whitman and Wilde was a defining moment in the ageless debate on beauty, concerning the methodology of creating it: whether consciously to pursue beauty or to allow it to come as a natural by-product of other concerns. Wilde ventured, "I can't listen to anyone unless he attracts me by a charming style or by beauty of theme." To this Whitman replied, "Why Oscar, it always seems to me that the fellow who makes a dead set at beauty by itself is in a bad way. My idea is that beauty is a result, not an abstraction." Wilde responded, "Yes, and I remember you have said, 'All beauty comes from beautiful blood and a beautiful brain,' and after all I think so too."

* * *

MORE THAN A CENTURY AFTER THIS EXCHANGE, AESTHETICISM IS EMBRACED BY a disorganized minority scattered throughout the various peoples of the world. We can include ourselves as long as we listen, touch, and stare when we rummage through yard sales and flea markets, tend gardens, plant turnips and vineyards, visit galleries and museums, or soak orchids in sinks. The character of Maude in Hal Ashby's wonderful comedy *Harold and Maude* is a member of the club. So are the darker figures of Gustav Aschenbach, Humbert Humbert, and Claire Quilty.

Aestheticism is finding pleasure in words that we say or read, as in Wallace Stevens's "Esthétique du Mal":

> And out of what one sees or hears and out
> Of what one feels, who could have thought to make
> So many selves, so many sensuous worlds,
> As if the air, the mid-day air, was swarming
> With the metaphysical changes that occur,
> Merely in living as and where we live.

These sounds and images are the sensual and erotic life of our culture, remnants of the fact that all language—whatever we say—has evolved from the mating cries of animals.

In the last section of *Gaston de Latour,* "The Lower Pantheism," as published in the 1896 edition, Pater foresaw the coming century by looking to the concept of plurality that was the basis for Stevens's "Esthétique du Mal" and so much of the work of our greatest contemporary poets, writers, and artists:

> The world was even larger than youthful appetite, youthful capacity.
> Let the theologian and every other theorist beware how he narrowed
> either. "The plurality of worlds!"—How petty in comparison seemed
> those sins. . . .

Pluralism's focus is on the layering and depth of meaning in a synchronic way and the possibility of peoples' different ideas coexisting side by side. Pluralism can also be applied to the concept of self. The current tendency to define oneself through ethnic and sexual identity might be a basis for pride (itself a complicated emotion), but it also limits more subtle and personal possibilities in presupposing type, style, and demeanor. The basic tenet of Pater's passage in *Gaston de Latour* is expansive. The purpose is not to found a clique of elite aesthetes, but to point out the subtleties of fulfillment through aesthetic pleasure in any person who desires it.

There is a little country cemetery in The Springs on Long Island. Jackson Pollock is buried there, so are Lee Krasner, Ad Reinhardt, Stuart Davis, and Hanna Wilke. Among the stones of varying size and color, there is a flat marble slab in the lawn several yards below the rough stone of Pollock's grave. It is the marker for Frank O'Hara. Inscribed on the marble are the words "Grace to be born and live as variously as possible." Pater's acknowledgment of the many selves within an individual lives through O'Hara's poem *In Memory of My Feelings*, a fragment recorded here:

> Grace
> to be born and live as variously as possible. The conception
> of the masque barely suggests the sordid identifications.
> I am a Hittite in love with a horse. I don't know what blood's
> in me I feel like an African Prince I am a girl walking downstairs
> in a red pleated dress with the heels I am a champion taking a fall
> I am a jockey with a sprained ass-hole I am the light mist
> in which a face appears. . . .

Secret Ingredients

IN HIS IMAGINATIVE WRITING, PATER UTILIZED FEW OF THE CONVENTIONAL devices that carry a reader through a story. The elements that carry you through Pater's fiction are more like those that convey you through a poem. Character development, an enigma about a character or place that will later be revealed, and establishing expectations of an act to be completed are means of guiding the reader through to a narrative's close. Roland Barthes calls these devices "readerly" because they direct the reader through the story. He opposes "readerly" to "writerly," where the reader "writes" the text through the discovery of different combinational possibilities each time the text is read, something like listening to a symphony. Though a device like suspense was a viable ingredient in early narrative poetry and, of course, is still a powerful ingredient in contemporary storytelling and film, it is hardly present in modern poetry, and certainly not in Pater. There is nothing, either, of the intricate plot development of a contemporary like Thomas Hardy. Pater did, however, note to an editor that he hoped the reader might wonder what ever became of the child in the house, and I do wonder what happened to him. But the character development in Pater's fiction is personal and interior, hardly exterior. No one wins in a shoot-out.

Many modern painters have been accused of not being able to paint because they did not employ traditional elements of painting—perspective, pictorial space, proportion, and figure-ground relationships. With Cézanne, van Gogh, Kandinsky, as well as Newman and Stella, who both began as abstract painters, we have to decide whether the respective styles embodied in their work are a result of a deficiency in traditional rendering or of genius. So much is a result of trust in their, and our own, aesthetic judgment. Certainly John Ruskin made this mistake with Whistler. And Brancusi's *Bird in Flight* was accused of lacking necessary sculptural ingredients when it was first exhibited in this country. The customs service considered it scrap metal and therefore dutiable—unlike original art, which was not.

If Pater's stories lack traditional storytelling ingredients, it is because his concerns were elsewhere. In this, Pater's fiction is very similar to another of my favorite books, Joris-Karl Huysmans's *À Rebours* (*Against Nature*) published in May 1884. *À Rebours* also influenced Oscar Wilde; so much so that he referred to it in *The Picture of Dorian Gray* as "The strangest book I have ever read." Much of the book describes the meticulous consideration of furnishings for his home undertaken by the main character, Des Esseintes. The most vivid image is that of a tortoise. Des Esseintes bought a tortoise to habituate one of his rooms in hopes that its drab colors would balance the brightness of a particular carpet. The opposite effect took place: the carpet seemed even brighter; so he sent the tortoise out to be bejeweled. Thereafter, the carpet paled in comparison.

Very little actually happens in *À Rebours*, or in any of Pater's portraits. When there is action, it is likely to happen "off-screen." What carries Pater's fiction is his philosophical viewpoint penetrating softly and beautifully throughout the narrative—in short, his aestheticism. By contrast, when something actually does occur in his stories, it seems wilder than the wildest carriage chase.

The poetic circumstance of Pater's prose provides rich material from which poets like Wallace Stevens drew and which younger poets can still embrace. As much as the effervescent Oscar Wilde has eclipsed his master, he is far less intellectually stimulating and less likely to influence. Wilde remarked upon hearing of Pater's death, "Was he ever alive?" In death, Pater lives through his continuing influence on successive generations of artists and writers, an influence that has not waned. Walter Pater was a crystal rocket with a gemlike exhaust, blasting off like a sparkler on the Fourth of July. Stage after stage still bounces to grass in a hiss, as the pale corpse the rocket carries floats on a silver pillow through uncharted and limitless transparencies.

NEW YORK, *June 16, 1997*

THE CHILD IN THE HOUSE

The Child in the House

As Florian Deleal walked, one hot afternoon, he overtook by the wayside a poor aged man, and, as he seemed weary with the road, helped him on with the burden which he carried, a certain distance. And as the man told his story, it chanced that he named the place, a little place in the neighborhood of a great city, where Florian had passed his earliest years, but which he had never since seen, and, the story told, went forward on his journey comforted. And that night, like a reward for his pity, a dream of that place came to Florian, a dream which did for him the office of the finer sort of memory, bringing its object to mind with great clearness, yet, as sometimes happens in dreams, raised a little above itself, and above ordinary retrospect. The true aspect of the place, especially of the house there in which he had lived as a child, the fashion of its doors, its hearths, its windows, the very scent upon the air of it, was with him in sleep for a season; only with tints more musically blent on wall and floor, and some finer light and shadow running in and out along its curves and angles, and with all its little carvings daintier. He awoke with a sigh at the thought of almost thirty years which lay between him and that place, yet with a flutter of pleasure still within him at the fair light, as if it were a smile, upon it. And it happened that this accident of his dream was just the thing needed for the beginning of a certain design he then had in view, the noting, namely, of some things in the story of his spirit—in that process of brain-building by which we are, each one of us, what we are. With the image of the place so clear and favorable upon him, he fell to thinking of himself therein, and how his thoughts had grown up to him. In that half-spiritualised house he could watch the better, over again, the gradual expansion of the soul which had come to be, there—of which indeed, through the law which makes the material objects about them so large an element in children's lives, it had actually become a part; inward and outward being woven through and through each other into one inextricable texture—half, tint and trace and accident of homely colour and form, from the wood and the bricks; half, mere soul-stuff, floated thither from who knows how far. In the house and garden of his dream he saw a child moving, and could divide the main streams, at least, of the winds that had played on him, and study so the first stage in that mental journey.

The *old house*, as when Florian talked of it afterwards he always called it (as all children do, who can recollect a change of home, soon enough but not too soon to mark a period in their lives), really was an old house; and an element of French descent in its inmates—descent from Watteau the old court-painter, one of whose gallant pieces still hung in one of the rooms—might explain, together with some other things, a noticeable trimness and comely whiteness about everything there—the curtains, the couches, the paint on the walls with which the light and shadow played so delicately, might explain also the tolerance of the great poplar in the garden, a tree most often despised by English people, but which French people love, having observed a certain fresh way its leaves have of dealing with the wind, making it sound in never so slight a stirring of the air, like running water.

The old-fashioned, low wainscoting went round the rooms and up the staircase with carved balusters and shadowy angles, landing half-way up at a broad window, with a swallow's nest below the sill, and the blossom of an old pear-tree showing across it in late April, against the blue, below which the perfumed juice of fallen fruit in autumn was so fresh. At the next turning came the closet which held on its deep shelves the best china. Little angel faces, and reedy flutings stood out round the fireplace of the children's room. And on the top of the house, above the large attic, where the white mice ran in the twilight—an infinite, unexplored wonderland of childish treasures, glass beads, empty scent-bottles still sweet, thrum of coloured silks, among its lumber—a flat space of roof, railed round, gave a view of the neighbouring steeples; for the house, as I said, stood near a great city, which sent up heavenwards, over the twisting weather-vanes, not seldom, its beds of rolling cloud and smoke, touched with storm or sunshine. But the child of whom I am writing did not hate the fog because of the crimson lights which fell from it sometimes upon the chimneys, and the whites which gleamed through its openings, on summer mornings, on turret or pavement. For it is false to suppose that a child's sense of beauty is dependent on any choiceness, or special fineness, in the objects which present themselves to it, though this indeed comes to be the rule with most of us in later life; earlier, in some degree, we see inwardly; and the child finds for itself, and with unstinted delight, a difference for the sense, in those whites and reds through the smoke on very homely buildings, and in the gold of the dandelions at the road-side, just beyond the houses, where not a handful of earth is virgin and untouched, in the lack of better ministries to its desire of beauty.

This house, then, stood not far beyond the gloom and rumours of the town, among high garden walls, bright all summertime with Golden-rod, and brown and golden Wall-flower,—*Flosparietis*, as the children's Latin-reading father taught them to call it, while he was with them. Tracing back the threads of his complex spiritual habit, as he was used in after years to do, Florian found that he owed to the place many tones of sentiment afterwards customary with him, certain inward lights under which things most naturally presented themselves to him. The coming and going of travellers to the town along the way, the shadow of the streets, the sudden breadth of the neighbouring gardens, the singular brightness of bright weather there, its singular darknesses which linked themselves in his mind to certain engraved illustrations in the old big Bible at home, the coolness of the dark, cavernous shops round the great church, with its giddy winding stair up to the pigeons and the bells—a citadel of peace in the heart of the trouble—all this acted on his childish fancy, so that ever afterwards the like aspects and incidents never failed to throw him into a well-recognised imaginative mood, seeming actually to have become a part of the texture of his mind. Also, Florian could trace home to this point a pervading preference in himself for a kind of comeliness and dignity, an *urbanity* literally, in modes of life, which he connected with the pale people of towns, and which made him susceptible to a kind of exquisite satisfaction in the trimness and well-considered grace of certain things and persons he afterwards met with, here and there, in his way through the world.

So the child of whom I am writing lived on there quietly; things without thus ministering to him, as he sat daily at the window with the birdcage hanging below it, and his mother taught him to read, wondering at the ease with which he learned, and at the quickness of his memory. The perfume of the little flowers of the lime-tree fell through the air upon them, like rain; while time seemed to move slowly to the murmur of the bees in it, till it almost stood still on June afternoons. How insignificant, at the moment, seem the influences of the sensible things which are tossed and fall and lie about us, so or so, in the environment of early childhood. How indelibly, as we afterward discover, they affect us; with what capricious attractions and associations they figure themselves on the white paper, the smooth wax of our ingenuous souls, as "with lead in the rock forever," giving form and feature, and as it were assigned house-room in our memory, to early experiences of feeling and thought, which abide with us ever afterwards, thus, and not otherwise. The realities and passions, the rumours of the greater world without, steal in upon us, each by its own special little passage-way, through the wall of custom about us; and never afterwards quite detach themselves from this or that accident, or trick, in the mode of their first entrance to us. Our susceptibilities, the discovery of our powers, manifold experiences—our various experiences of the coming and going of bodily pain, for instance—belong to this or the other well-remembered place in the material habitation—that little white room with the window across which the heavy blossoms could beat so peevishly in the wind, with just that particular catch or throb, such a sense of teasing in it, on gusty mornings: and the early habitation thus gradually becomes a sort of material shrine or sanctuary of sentiment; a system of visible symbolism interweaves itself through all our thoughts and passions; and, irresistibly, little shapes, voices, accidents—the angle at which the sun in the morning fell on the pillow—become parts of the great chain wherewith we are bound.

Thus far, for Florian, what all this had determined was a peculiarly strong sense of home—so forcible a motive with all of us—prompting to us our customary love of the earth, and the larger part of our fear of death, that revulsion we have from it as from something strange, untried, unfriendly; though life-long imprisonment, they tell you, and final banishment from home is a thing bitterer still; the looking forward to but a short space, a mere childish "goûter" and dessert of it, before the end, being so great a resource of effort to pilgrims and wayfarers, and the soldier in distant quarters, and lending, in lack of that, some power of solace to the thought of sleep in the home churchyard, at least—dead cheek by dead cheek, and with the rain soaking in upon one from above.

So powerful is this instinct, and yet accidents like those I have been speaking of so mechanically determine it; its essence being indeed the early familiar, as constituting our ideal, or typical conception, of rest and security. Out of so many possible conditions, just this for you, and that for me, brings ever the unmistakable realisation of the delightful *chez soi*; this for the Englishman, for me and you, with the closely-drawn white curtain and the shaded lamp; that, quite other, for the wandering Arab, who folds his tent every morning, and makes his sleeping-place among haunted ruins or in old tombs.

With Florian, then, the sense of home became singularly intense, his good fortune being that the special character of his home was in itself so essentially home-like. As, after many wanderings, I have come to fancy that some parts of Surrey and Kent are, for Englishmen, the true landscape, true home-counties, by right, partly, of a certain earthy warmth in the yellow of the sand below their gorse-bushes, and of a certain gray-blue mist after rain, in the hollows of the hills there, welcome to fatigued eyes, and never seen farther south; so, I think that the sort of house I have described, with precisely those proportions of red-brick and green, and with a just perceptible monotony in the subdued order of it, for its distinguishing note, is, for Englishmen at least, typically home-like. And so for Florian that general human instinct was reinforced by this special home-likeness in the place his wandering soul had happened to light on, as, in the second degree, its body and earthly tabernacle; the sense of harmony between his soul and its physical environment became, for a time at least, like perfectly played music, and the life led there singularly tranquil and filled with a curious sense of self-possession. The love of security, of an habitually undisputed standing-ground or sleeping-place, came to count for much in the generation and correcting of his thoughts, and afterwards as a salutary principle of restraint in all his wanderings of spirit. The wistful yearning towards home, in absence from it, as the shadows of evening deepened, and he followed in thought what was doing there from hour to hour, interpreted to him much of a yearning and regret he experienced afterwards, towards he knew not what, out of strange ways of feeling and thought in which, from time to time, his spirit found itself alone; and in the tears shed in such absences there seemed always to be some soul-subduing foretaste of what his last tears might be.

And the sense of security could hardly have been deeper, the quiet of the child's soul being one with the quiet of its home, a place "inclosed" and "sealed." But upon this assured place, upon the child's assured soul, which resembled it, there came floating in from the larger world without, as at windows left ajar unknowingly, or over the high garden walls, two streams of impressions, the sentiments of beauty and pain—recognitions of the visible, tangible, audible loveliness of things, as a very real and somewhat tyrannous element in them—and of the sorrow of the world, of grown people and children and animals, as a thing not to be put by in them. From this point he could trace two predominant processes of mental change in him—the growth of an almost diseased sensibility to the spectacle of suffering, and, parallel with this, the rapid growth of a certain capacity of fascination by bright colour and choice form—the sweet curvings, for instance, of the lips of those who seemed to him comely persons, modulated in such delicate unison to the things they said or sang,—marking early the activity in him of a more than customary sensuousness: the "lust of the eye," as the Preacher says, which might lead him, one day, how far! Could he have foreseen the weariness of the way! In music sometimes the two sorts of impressions came together, and he would weep, to the surprise of older people. Tears of joy, too, the child knew, also to older people's surprise; real tears, once, of relief from long-strung, childish expectation, when he found returned at evening, with new roses in her cheeks, the little sister who had been to a place where there was a wood, and brought back for him a treasure of fallen acorns, and black crow's feathers, and his peace at finding her again near him mingled all night with some intimate sense of the distant forest, the rumour of its breezes, with the glossy black-birds aslant and the branches lifted in them, and of the perfect nicety of the little cups that fell. So those two elementary apprehensions of the tenderness and of the colour in things grew apace in him, and were seen by him afterwards to send their roots back into the beginnings of life.

Let me note first some of the occasions of his recognition of the element of pain in things—incidents, now and again, which seemed suddenly to awake in him the whole force of that sentiment which Goethe has called the *Weltschmerz,* and in which the concentrated sorrow of the world seemed suddenly to lie heavy upon him. A book lay in an old bookcase, of which he cared to remember one picture—a woman sitting, with hands bound behind her, the dress, the cap, the hair, folded with a simplicity which touched him strangely, as if not by her own hands, but with some ambiguous care at the hands of others—Queen Marie Antoinette, on her way to execution—we all remember David's drawing, meant merely to make her ridiculous. The face that had been so high had learned to be mute and resistless; but out of its very resistlessness seemed now to call on men to have pity, and forbear; and he took note of that, as he closed the book, as a thing to look at again, if he should at any time find himself tempted to be cruel. Again, he would never quite forget the appeal in the small sister's face, in the garden under the lilacs, terrified at a spider lighted on her sleeve. He could trace back to the look then noted a certain mercy he conceived always for people in fear, even of little things, which seemed to make him, though but for a moment, capable of almost any sacrifice of himself. Impressible, susceptible persons, indeed, who had had their sorrows, lived about him; and this sensibility was due in part to the tacit influence of their presence, enforcing upon him habitually the fact that there are those who pass their days, as a matter of course, in a sort of "going quietly." Most poignantly of all he could recall, in unfading minutest circumstance, the cry on the stair, sounding bitterly through the house, and struck into his soul forever, of an aged woman, his father's sister, come now to announce his death in distant India; how it seemed to make the aged woman like a child again; and, he knew not why, but this fancy was full of pity to him. There were the little sorrows of the dumb animals too—

— 9 —

of the white angora, with a dark tail like an ermine's, and a face like a flower, who fell into a lingering sickness, and became quite delicately human in its valetudinarianism, and came to have a hundred different expressions of voice—how it grew worse and worse, till it began to feel the light too much for it, and at last, after one wild morning of pain, the little soul flickered away from the body, quite worn to death already, and now but feebly retaining it.

So he wanted another pet; and as there were starlings about the place, which could be taught to speak, one of them was caught, and he meant to treat it kindly; but in the night its young ones could be heard crying after it, and the responsive cry of the mother-bird towards them; and at last, with the first light, though not till after some debate with himself, he went down and opened the cage, and saw a sharp bound of the prisoner up to her nestlings; and therewith came the sense of remorse,—that he too was become an accomplice in moving, to the limit of his small power, the springs and handles of that great machine in things, constructed so ingeniously to play pain-fugues on the delicate nerve-work of living creatures.

I have remarked how, in the process of our brain-building, as the house of thought in which we live gets itself together like some airy bird's nest of floating thistle-down and chance straws, compact at last, little accidents have their consequence; and thus it happened that, as he walked one evening, a garden gate, usually closed, stood open; and lo! within, a great red hawthorn, in full flower, embossing heavily the bleached and twisted trunk and branches, so aged that there were but few green leaves thereon—a plumage of tender crimson fire out of the heart of the dry wood. The perfume of the tree had now and again reached him, in the currents of the wind, over the wall, and he had wondered what might be behind it, and was now allowed to fill his arms with the flowers—flowers enough for all the old blue-china pots along the chimney-piece, making fête in the children's room. Was it some periodic moment in the expansion of soul within him, or mere trick of heat in the heavily-laden summer air? But the beauty of the thing struck home to him feverishly, and in dreams, all night, he loitered along a magic roadway of crimson flowers, which seemed to open ruddily in thick, fresh masses about his feet, and fill softly all the little hollows in the banks on either side. Always afterwards, summer by summer, as the flowers came on, the blossom of the red hawthorn still seemed to him absolutely the reddest of all things; and the goodly crimson, still alive in the works of old Venetian masters, or old Flemish tapestries, called out always from afar, the recollection of the flame in those perishing little petals, as it pulsed gradually out of them, kept long in the drawers of an old cabinet. Also, then, for the first time, he seemed to experience a passionateness in his relation to fair outward objects, an inexplicable excitement in their presence, which disturbed him, and from which he half longed to be free. A touch of regret or desire mingled all night with the remembered presence of the red flowers, and their perfume in the darkness about him; and the longing for some undivined, entire possession of them was the beginning of a revelation to him, growing ever clearer, with the coming of the gracious summer guise of fields, and trees, and persons in each succeeding year, of a certain, at times seemingly exclusive, predominance in his interests, of beautiful physical things, a kind of tyranny of the senses over him.

In later years he came upon philosophies which occupied him much in the estimate of the proportion of the sensuous and the ideal elements in human knowledge, the relative parts they bear in it; and in his intellectual scheme, was led to assign very little to the abstract thought, and much to its sensible vehicle or occasion. Such metaphysical speculation did but reinforce what was instinctive in his way of receiving the world, and for him, everywhere, that sensible vehicle or occasion became, perhaps only too surely, the necessary concomitant of any perception of things, real enough to be of any weight or reckoning, in his house of thought. There were times when he could think of the necessity he was under of associating all thoughts to touch and sight, as a sympathetic link between himself and actual, feeling, living objects; a protest in favour of real men and women against mere gray, unreal abstractions; and he remembered gratefully how the Christian religion, hardly less than the religion of the ancient Greeks, translating so much of its spiritual verity into things that may be seen, condescends in part to sanction this infirmity, if so it be, of our human existence, wherein the world of sense is so much with us, and welcomed this thought as a kind of keeper and sentinel over his soul therein. But certainly he came, more and more, to be unable to care for, or think of soul but as in an actual body, or of any world but that wherein are water and trees, and where men and women look, so or so, and press actual hands. It was the trick even his pity learned, fastening those who suffered in anywise to his affections by a kind of sensible attachments. He would think of Julian, fallen into incurable sickness, as spoiled in the sweet blossom of his skin like pale amber, and his honey-like hair; of Cecil, early dead, as cut off from the lilies, from golden summer days, from women's voices; and then what comforted him a little was the thought of the turning of the child's flesh to violets in the turf above him. And thinking of the very poor, it was not the things which most men care most for that he yearned to give them; but fairer roses, perhaps, and power to taste quite as they will, at their ease and not talk-burdened, a certain desirable, clear light in the new morning, through which sometimes he had noticed them, quite unconscious of it, on their way to their early toil.

So he yielded himself to these things, to be played upon by them like a musical instrument, and began to note with deepening watchfulness, but always with some puzzled, unutterable longing in his enjoyment, the phases of the seasons and of the growing or waning day, down even to the shadowy changes wrought on bare wall or ceiling—the light cast up from the snow, bringing out their darkest angles; the brown light in the cloud, which meant rain; that almost too austere clearness, in the protracted light of the lengthening day, before warm weather began, as if it lingered but to make a severer workday, with the school-books opened earlier and later; that beam of June sunshine, at last, as he lay awake before the time, a way of gold-dust across the darkness; all the humming, the freshness, the perfume of the garden seemed to lie upon it—and coming in one afternoon in September, along the red gravel walk, to look for a basket of yellow crab-apples left in the cool, old parlour, he remembered it the more, and how the colours struck upon him, because a wasp on one bitten apple stung him, and he felt the passion of sudden, severe pain. For this too brought its curious reflexions; and, in relief from it, he would wonder over it—how it had then been with him—puzzled at the depth of the charm or spell over him, which lay, for a little while at least, in the mere absence of pain; once, especially, when an older boy taught him to make flowers of sealing-wax, and he had burnt his hand badly at the lighted taper, and been unable to sleep. He remembered that also afterwards, as a sort of typical thing—a white vision of heat about him, clinging closely, through the languid scent of the ointments put upon the place to make it well.

Also, as he felt this pressure upon him of the sensible world, then, as often afterwards, there would come another sort of curious questioning how the last impressions of eye and ear might happen to him, how they would find him—the scent of the last flower, the soft yellowness of the last morning, the last recognition of some object of affection, hand or voice; it could not be but that the latest look of the eyes, before their final closing, would be strangely vivid; one would go with the hot tears, the cry, the touch of the wistful bystander, impressed how deeply on one! or would it be, perhaps, a mere frail retiring of all things, great or little, away from one, into a level distance?

For with this desire of physical beauty mingleth itself early the fear of death—the fear of death intensified by the desire for beauty. Hitherto he had never gazed upon dead faces, as sometimes, afterwards, at the *Morgue* in Paris, or in that fair cemetery at Munich, where all the dead must go and lie in state before burial, behind glass windows, among the flowers and incense and holy candles—the aged clergy with their sacred ornaments, the young men in their dancing shoes and spotless white linen—after which visits, those waxen, resistless faces would always live with him for many days, making the broadest sunshine sickly. The child had heard indeed of the death of his father, and how, in the Indian station, a fever had taken him, so that though not in action he had yet died as a soldier; and hearing of the "resurrection of the just," he could think of him as still abroad in the world, somehow, for his protection—a grand, though perhaps rather terrible figure, in beautiful soldier's things, like the figure in the picture of Joshua's Vision in the Bible—and of that, round which the mourners moved so softly, and afterwards with such solemn singing, as but a worn-out garment left at a deserted lodging. So it was, until on a summer day he walked with his mother through a fair churchyard. In a bright dress he rambled among the graves, in the gay weather, and so came, in one corner, upon an open grave for a child—a dark space on the brilliant grass—the black mould lying heaped up round it, weighing down the little jewelled branches of the dwarf rose-bushes in flower. And therewith came, full-grown, never wholly to leave him, with the certainty that even children do sometimes die, the physical horror of death, with its wholly selfish recoil from the association of lower forms of life, and the suffocating weight above. No benign, grave figure in beautiful soldier's things any longer abroad in the world for his protection! only a few poor, piteous bones; and above them, possibly, a certain sort of figure he hoped not to see. For sitting one day in the garden below an open window, he heard people talking, and could not but listen, how, in a sleepless hour, a sick woman had seen one of the dead sitting beside her, come to call her hence; and from the broken talk, evolved with much clearness the notion that not all those dead people had really departed to the churchyard, nor were quite so motionless as they looked, but led a secret, half-fugitive life in their old homes, quite free by night, though sometimes visible in the day, dodging from room to room, with no great good-will towards those who shared the place with them. All night the figure sat beside him in the reveries of his broken sleep, and was not quite gone in the morning—an odd, irreconcilable new member of the household, making the sweet familiar chambers unfriendly and suspect by its uncertain presence. He could have hated the dead he had pitied so, for being thus. Afterwards he came to think of those poor home-returning ghosts, which all men have fancied to themselves—the *revenants*—pathetically, as crying, or beating with vain hands at the doors, as the wind came, their cries distinguishable in it as a wilder inner note. But, always making death more unfamiliar still, that old experience would ever, from time to time, return to him; even in the living he sometimes caught its likeness; at any time or place, in a moment, the faint atmosphere of the chamber of death would be breathed around him, and the image with the bound chin, the quaint smile, the straight, stiff feet, shed itself across the air upon the bright carpet, amid the gayest company, or happiest communing with himself.

To most children the sombre questionings to which impressions like these attach themselves, if they come at all, are actually suggested by religious books, which therefore they often regard with much secret distaste, and dismiss, as far as possible, from their habitual thoughts as a too depressing element in life. To Florian such impressions, these misgivings as to the ultimate tendency of the years, of the relationship between life and death, had been suggested spontaneously in the natural course of his mental growth by a strong innate sense for the soberer tones in things, further strengthened by actual circumstances; and religious sentiment, that system of biblical ideas in which he had been brought up, presented itself to him as a thing that might soften and dignify, and light up as with a "lively hope," a melancholy already deeply settled in him. So he yielded himself easily to religious impressions, and with a kind of mystical appetite for sacred things; the more as they came to him through a saintly person who loved him tenderly, and believed that this early preoccupation with them already marked the child out for a saint. He began to love, for their own sakes, church lights, holy days, all that belonged to the comely order of the sanctuary, the secrets of its white linen, and holy vessels, and fonts of pure water; and its hieratic purity and simplicity became the type of something he desired always to have about him in actual life. He pored over the pictures in religious books, and knew by heart the exact mode in which the wrestling angel grasped Jacob, how Jacob looked in his mysterious sleep, how the bells and pomegranates were attached to the hem of Aaron's vestment, sounding sweetly as he glided over the turf of the holy place. His way of conceiving religion came then to be in effect what it ever afterwards remained—a sacred history, indeed, but still more a sacred ideal, a transcendent version or representation, under intenser and more expressive light and shade, of human life and its familiar or exceptional incidents, birth, death, marriage, youth, age, tears, joy, rest, sleep, waking—a mirror, towards which men might turn away their eyes from vanity and dullness, and see themselves therein as angels, with their daily meat and drink, even, become a kind of sacred transaction—a complementary strain or burden, applied to our every-day existence, whereby the stray snatches of music in it re-set themselves, and fall into the scheme of some higher and more consistent harmony. A place adumbrated itself in his thoughts, wherein those sacred personalities, which are at once the reflex and pattern of our nobler phases of life, housed themselves; and this region in his intellectual scheme all subsequent experience did but tend still further to realise and define. Some ideal, hieratic persons he would always need to occupy it and keep a warmth there. And he could hardly understand those who felt no such need at all, finding themselves quite happy without such heavenly companionship, and sacred double of their life, beside them.

Thus a constant substitution of the typical for the actual took place in his thoughts. Angels might be met by the way, under English elm or beech-tree; mere messengers seemed like angels, bound on celestial errands; a deep mysticity brooded over real meetings and partings; marriages were made in heaven; and deaths also, with hands of angels thereupon, to bear soul and body quietly asunder, each to its appointed rest. All the acts and accidents of daily life borrowed a sacred colour and significance; the very colours of things became themselves weighty with meanings like the sacred stuffs of Moses' tabernacle, full of penitence or peace. Sentiment, congruous in the first instance only with those divine transactions, the deep, effusive unction of the house of Bethany, was assumed as the due attitude for the reception of our every-day existence; and for a time he walked through the world in a sustained, not unpleasurable awe, generated by the habitual recognition, beside every circumstance and event of life, of its celestial correspondent.

Sensibility—the desire of physical beauty—a strange biblical awe, which made any reference to the unseen act on him like solemn music—these qualities the child took away with him, when, at about the age of twelve years, he left the old house, and was taken to live in another place. He had never left home before, and, anticipating much from this change, had long dreamed over it, jealously counting the days till the time fixed for departure should come: had been a little careless about others, even, in his strong desire for it—when Lewis fell sick, for instance, and they must wait still two days longer. At last the morning came, very fine; and all things—the very pavement with its dust, at the road-side—seemed to have a white, pearl-like lustre in them. They were to travel by a favorite road on which he had often walked a certain distance, and on one of those two prisoner days, when Lewis was sick, had walked farther than ever before, in his great desire to reach the new place. They had started and gone a little way when a pet bird was found to have been left behind, and must even now—so it presented itself to him—have already all the appealing fierceness and wild self-pity at heart of one left by others to perish of hunger in a closed house; and he returned to fetch it, himself in hardly less stormy distress. But as he passed in search of it from room to room, lying so pale, with a look of meekness in their denudation, and at last through that little, stripped white room, the aspect of the place touched him like the face of one dead; and a clinging back towards it came over him, so intense that he knew it would last long, and spoiling all his pleasure in the realisation of a thing so eagerly anticipated. And so, with the bird found, but himself in an agony of home-sickness, thus capriciously sprung up within him, he was driven quickly away, far into the rural distance, so fondly speculated on, of that favorite country-road.

IMAGINARY PORTRAITS

I

A Prince of Court Painters

Extracts from an Old French Journal

Valenciennes, *September 1701.*

They have been renovating my father's large workroom. That delight-ful, tumble-down old place has lost its moss-grown tiles and the green weather-stains we have known all our lives on the high whitewashed wall, opposite which we sit, in the little sculptor's yard, for the coolness, in sum-mertime. Among old Watteau's work-people came his son, "the genius," my father's godson and namesake, a dark-haired youth, whose large, un-quiet eyes seemed perpetually wandering to the various drawings which lie exposed here. My father will have it that he is a genius indeed, and a painter born. We have had our September Fair in the *Grande Place*, a won-derful stir of sound and colour in the wide, open space beneath our win-dows. And just where the crowd was busiest young Antony was found, hoisted into one of those empty niches of the old *Hôtel de Ville*, sketching the scene to the life; but with a kind of grace (a marvellous tact of omis-sion, as my father pointed out to us, in dealing with the vulgar reality seen from one's own window) which has made trite old Harlequin, Clown, and Columbine, seem like people in some fairyland; or like infinitely clever tragic actors, who, for the humour of the thing, have put on motley for once, and are able to throw a world of serious innuendo into their burlesque looks, with a sort of comedy which shall be but tragedy seen from the other side.

He brought his sketch to our house to-day, and I was present when my father questioned him and commended his work. But the lad seemed not greatly pleased, and left untasted the glass of old Malaga which was offered to him. His father will hear nothing of educating him as a painter. Yet he is not ill-to-do, and has lately built himself a new stone house, big and gray and cold. Their old plastered house with the black timbers, in the *Rue des Cardinaux*, was prettier; dating from the time of the Spaniards, and one of the oldest in Valenciennes.

October 1701.

Chiefly through the solicitations of my father, old Watteau has consented to place Antony with a teacher of painting here. I meet him betimes on the way to his lessons, as I return from Mass; for he still works with the masons, but making the most of late and early hours, of every moment of liberty. And then he has the feast-days, of which there are so many in this old-fashioned place. Ah! such gifts as his, surely, may once in a way make much industry seem worth while. He makes a wonderful progress. And yet, far from being set-up, and too easily pleased with what, after all, comes to him so easily, he has, my father thinks, too little self-approval for ultimate success. He is apt, in truth, to fall out too hastily with himself and what he produces. Yet here also there is the "golden mean." Yes! I could fancy myself offended by a sort of irony which sometimes crosses the half-melancholy sweetness of manner habitual with him; only that, as I can see, he treats himself to the same quality.

October 1701.

Antony Watteau comes here often now. It is the instinct of a natural fineness in him, to escape when he can from that blank stone house, with so little to interest, and that homely old man and woman. The rudeness of his home has turned his feeling for even the simpler graces of life into a physical want, like hunger or thirst, which might come to greed; and methinks he perhaps over-values those things. Still, made as he is, his hard fate in that rude place must needs touch one. And then, he profits by the experience of my father, who has much knowledge in matters of art beyond his own art of sculpture; and Antony is not unwelcome to him. In these last rainy weeks especially, when he can't sketch out of doors, when the wind only half dries the pavement before another torrent comes, and people stay at home, and the only sound from without is the creaking of a restless shutter on its hinges, or the march across the *Place* of those weary soldiers, coming and going so interminably, one hardly knows whether to or from battle with the English and the Austrians, from victory or defeat—Well! he has become like one of our family. "He will go far!" my father declares. He would go far, in the literal sense, if he might—to Paris, to Rome. It must be admitted that our Valenciennes is a quiet—nay, a sleepy place; sleepier than ever since it became French, and ceased to be so near the frontier. The grass is growing deep on our old ramparts, and it is pleasant to walk there—to walk there and muse; pleasant for a tame, unambitious soul such as mine.

December 1702.

Antony Watteau left us for Paris this morning. It came upon us quite suddenly. They amuse themselves in Paris. A scene-painter we have here, well known in Flanders, has been engaged to work in one of the Parisian playhouses; and young Watteau, of whom he had some slight knowledge, has departed in his company. He doesn't know it was I who persuaded the scene-painter to take him—that he would find the lad useful. We offered him our little presents; fine thread-lace of our own making for his ruffles and the like; for one must make a figure in Paris; and he is slim and well-formed. For myself, I presented him with a silken purse I had long ago embroidered for another. Well! we shall follow his fortunes (of which I for one feel quite sure) at a distance. Old Watteau didn't know of his departure, and has been here in great anger.

December 1703.

Twelve months to-day since Antony went to Paris! The first struggle must be a sharp one for an unknown lad in that vast, over-crowded place, even if he be as clever as young Antony Watteau. We may think, however, that he is on the way to his chosen end, for he returns not home; though, in truth, he tells those poor old people very little of himself. The apprentices of the M. Métayer for whom he works, labour all day long, each at a single part only—*coiffure*, or robe, or hand—of the cheap pictures of religion or fantasy he exposes for sale at a low price along the footways of the *Pont Notre-Dame*. Antony is already the most skilful of them, and seems to have been promoted of late to work on church pictures. I like the thought of that. He receives three *livres* a week for his pains, and his soup daily.

May 1705.

Antony Watteau has parted from the dealer in pictures, *à bon marché*, and works now with a painter of furniture pieces (those headpieces for doors and the like, now in fashion) who is also *concierge* of the Palace of the Luxembourg. Antony is actually lodged somewhere in that grand place, which contains the king's collection of the Italian pictures he would so willingly copy. Its gardens also are magnificent, with something, as we understand from him, altogether of a novel kind in their disposition and embellishment. Ah! how I delight myself, in fancy at least, in those beautiful gardens, freer and trimmed less stiffly than those of other royal houses. Methinks I see him there, when his long summer-day's work is over, enjoying the cool shade of the stately, broad-foliaged trees, each of which is a great courtier, though it has its way almost as if it belonged to that open and unbuilt country beyond, over which the sun is sinking.

His thoughts, however, in the midst of all this, are not wholly away from home, if I may judge by the subject of a picture he hopes to sell for as much as sixty *livres*—*Un Départ de Troupes*—Soldiers Departing—one of those scenes of military life one can study so well here at Valenciennes.

June 1705.

Young Watteau has returned home—proof, with a character so independent as his, that things have gone well with him; and (it is agreed!) stays with us, instead of in the stone-mason's house. The old people suppose he comes to us for the sake of my father's instruction. French people as we have become, we are still old Flemish, if not at heart, yet on the surface. Even in *French* Flanders, at Douai and Saint Omer, as I understand, in the churches and in people's houses, as may be seen from the very streets, there is noticeable a minute and scrupulous air of care-taking and neatness. Antony Watteau remarks this more than ever on returning to Valenciennes, and savours greatly, after his lodging in Paris, our Flemish cleanliness, lover as he is of distinction and elegance. Those worldly graces he seemed as a young lad almost to hunger and thirst for, as if truly the mere adornments of life were its necessaries, he already takes as if he had been always used to them. And there is something noble—shall I say?—in his half-disdainful way of serving himself with what he still, as I think, secretly values overmuch. There is an air of seemly thought—*le bel sérieux*—about him, which makes me think of one of those grave old Dutch statesmen in their youth, such as that famous William the Silent; and yet the effect of this first success of his (of more importance than its mere money value, as insuring for the future the full play of his natural powers) I can trace like the bloom of a flower upon him; and he has, now and then, the gaieties which from time to time, surely, must refresh all true artists, however hard-working and "painful."

July 1705.

The charm of all this—his physiognomy and manner of being—has touched even my young brother, Jean-Baptiste. He is greatly taken with Antony, clings to him almost too attentively, and will be nothing but a painter, though my father would have trained him to follow his own profession. It may do the child good. He needs the expansion of some generous sympathy or sentiment in that close little soul of his, as I have thought, watching sometimes how his small face and hands are moved in sleep. A child of ten who cares only to save and possess, to hoard his tiny savings! Yet he is not otherwise selfish, and loves us all with a warm heart. Just now it is the moments of Antony's company he counts, like a little miser. Well! that may save him perhaps from developing a certain meanness of character I have sometimes feared for him.

August 1705.

We returned home late this summer evening—Antony Watteau, my father and sisters, young Jean-Baptiste, and myself—from an excursion to Saint-Amand, in celebration of Antony's last day with us. After visiting the great abbey-church and its range of chapels, with their costly encumbrance of carved shrines and golden reliquaries and funeral scutcheons in the coloured glass, half seen through a rich enclosure of marble and brasswork, we supped at the little inn in the forest. Antony, looking well in his new-fashioned, long-skirted coat, and taller than he really is, made us bring our cream and wild strawberries out of doors, ranging ourselves according to his judgment (for a hasty sketch in that big pocket-book he carries) on the soft slope of one of those fresh spaces in the wood, where the trees unclose a little, while Jean-Baptiste and my youngest sister danced a minuet on the grass, to the notes of some strolling lutanist who had found us out. He is visibly cheerful at the thought of his return to Paris, and became for a moment freer and more animated than I have ever yet seen him, as he discoursed to us about the paintings of Rubens in the church here. His words, as he spoke of them, seemed full of a kind of rich sunset with some moving glory within it. Yet I like far better than any of these pictures of Rubens a work of that old Dutch master, Peter Porbus, which hangs, though almost out of sight indeed, in our church at home. The patron saints, simple, and standing firmly on either side, present two homely old people to Our Lady enthroned in the midst, with the look and attitude of one for whom, amid her "glories" (depicted in dim little circular pictures, set in the openings of a chaplet of pale flowers around her) all feelings are over, except a great pitifulness; and her robe of shadowy blue suits my eyes better far than the hot flesh-tints of the Medicean ladies of the great Peter Paul, in spite of that amplitude and royal ease of action under their stiff court costumes, at which Antony Watteau declares himself in dismay.

August 1705.

I have just returned from early Mass. I lingered long after the office was over, watching, and pondering how in the world one could help a small bird which had flown into the church but could find no way out again. I suspect it will remain there, fluttering round and round distractedly, far up under the arched roof, till it dies exhausted. I seem to have heard of some one who likened man's life to a bird, passing just once only, on some winter night, from window to window, across a cheerfully-lighted hall. The bird, taken captive by the ill-luck of a moment, repeating its issueless circle till it expires within the close vaulting of that great stone church:—human life may be like that bird too!

Antony Watteau returned to Paris yesterday. Yes!—Certainly great heights of achievement would seem to lie before him,—access to regions where one may find it increasingly hard to follow him even in imagination, and figure to one's self after what manner his life moves therein.

January 1709.

Antony Watteau has competed for what is called the *Prix de Rome*, desiring greatly to profit by the grand establishment founded at Rome by King Lewis the Fourteenth, for the encouragement of French artists. He obtained only the second place, but does not renounce his desire to make the journey to Italy. Could I save enough by careful economies for that purpose? It might be conveyed to him in some indirect way that would not offend.

February 1712.

We read, with much pleasure for all of us, in the *Gazette* to-day, among other events of the great world, that Antony Watteau had been elected to the Academy of Painting under the new title of *Peintre des Fêtes Galantes*, and had been named also *Peintre du Roi*. My brother, Jean-Baptiste, ran to tell the news to old Jean-Philippe and Michelle Watteau.

A new manner of painting! The old furniture of people's rooms must needs be changed throughout, it would seem, to accord with this painting; or rather, the painting is designed exclusively to suit one particular kind of apartment. A manner of painting greatly prized, as we understand, by those Parisian judges who have had the best opportunity of acquainting themselves with whatever is most enjoyable in the arts:—such is the achievement of the young Watteau! He looks to receive more orders for his work than he will be able to execute. He will certainly relish—he, so elegant, so hungry for the colours of life—a free intercourse with those wealthy lovers of the arts, M. de Crozat, M. de Julienne, the Abbé de la Roque, the Count de Caylus, and M. Gersaint, the famous dealer in pictures, who are so anxious to lodge him in their fine *hôtels*, and to have him of their company at their country houses. Paris, we hear, has never been wealthier and more luxurious than now: and the great ladies outbid each other to have his work upon their very fans. Those vast fortunes, however, seem to change hands very rapidly. And Antony's new manner? I am unable even to divine it—to conceive the trick and effect of it—at all. Only, something of lightness and coquetry I discern there, at variance, methinks, with his own singular gravity, and even sadness, of mien and mind, more answerable to the stately apparelling of the age of Henry the Fourth, or of Lewis the Thirteenth, in these old, sombre Spanish houses of ours.

March 1713.

We have all been very happy,—Jean-Baptiste, as if in a delightful dream. Antony Watteau, being consulted with regard to the lad's training as a painter, has most generously offered to receive him for his own pupil. My father, for some reason unknown to me, seemed to hesitate at the first; but Jean-Baptiste, whose enthusiasm for Antony visibly refines and beautifies his whole nature, has won the necessary permission, and this dear young brother will leave us to-morrow. Our regrets and his, at his parting from us for the first time, overtook our joy at his good fortune by surprise, at the last moment, just as we were about to bid each other good-night. For a while there had seemed to be an uneasiness under our cheerful talk, as if each one present were concealing something with an effort; and it was Jean-Baptiste himself who gave way at last. And then we sat down again, still together, and allowed free play to what was in our hearts, almost till morning, my sisters weeping much. I know better how to control myself. In a few days that delightful new life will have begun for him: and I have made him promise to write often to us. With how small a part of my whole life shall I be really living at Valenciennes!

January 1714.

Jean-Philippe Watteau has received a letter from his son to-day. Old Michelle Watteau, whose sight is failing, though she still works (half by touch, indeed) at her pillow-lace, was glad to hear me read the letter aloud more than once. It recounts—how modestly, and almost as a matter of course!— his late successes. And yet!—does he, in writing to these old people, purposely underrate his great good fortune and present happiness, not to shock them too much by the contrast between the delicate enjoyments of the life he now leads among the wealthy and refined, and that bald existence of theirs in his old home? A life, agitated, exigent, unsatisfying! That is what this letter discloses, below so attractive a surface. As his gift expands so does that incurable restlessness, one supposed but a humour natural to a promising youth who had still everything to do. And now, the one realised enjoyment he has of all this, might seem to be the thought of the independence it has purchased him, so that he can escape from one lodging-place to another, just as it may please him. He has already deserted, somewhat incontinently, more than one of those fine houses, the liberal air of which he used so greatly to affect, and which have so readily received him. Has he failed really to grasp the fact of his great success and the rewards that lie before him? At all events, he seems, after all, not greatly to value that fine world he is now privileged to enter, and has certainly but little relish for his own works—those works which I for one so thirst to see!

March 1714.

We were all—Jean-Philippe, Michelle Watteau, and ourselves—half in expectation of a visit from Antony; and to-day, quite suddenly, he is with us. I was lingering after early Mass this morning in the church of Saint Vaast. It is good for me to be there. Our people lie under one of the great marble slabs before the *jubé*, some of the memorial brass ballusters of which are engraved with their names and the dates of their decease. The settle of carved oak which runs all round the wide nave is my father's own work. The quiet spaciousness of the place is itself like a meditation, an "act of recollection," and clears away the confusions of the heart. I suppose the heavy droning of the *carillon* had smothered the sound of his footsteps, for on my turning round, when I supposed myself alone, Antony Watteau was standing near me. Constant observer as he is of the lights and shadows of things, he visits places of this kind at odd times. He has left Jean-Baptiste at work in Paris, and will stay this time with the old people, not at our house: though he has spent the better part of to-day in my father's workroom. He hasn't yet put off, in spite of all his late intercourse with the great world, his distant and preoccupied manner—a manner, it is true, the same to every one. It is certainly not through pride in his success, as some might fancy, for he was thus always. It is rather as if, with all that success, life and its daily social routine were somewhat of a burden to him.

April 1714.

At last we shall understand something of that new style of his—the *Watteau style*—so much relished by the great world at Paris. He has taken it into his kind head to paint and decorate our chief *salon*—the room with the three long windows, which occupies the first floor of the house.

The room was a landmark, as we used to think, an inviolable mile-stone and landmark, of old Valenciennes fashion—that sombre style, in-dulging much in contrasts of black or deep brown with white, which the Spaniards left behind them here. Doubtless their eyes had found its shad-ows cool and pleasant, when they shut themselves in from the cutting sun-shine of their own country. But in our country, where we must needs economise not the shade but the sun, its grandiosity weighs a little on one's spirits. Well! the rough plaster we used to cover as well as might be with morsels of old figured arras-work, is replaced by dainty panelling of wood, with mimic columns, and a quite aerial scrollwork, around sunken spaces of a pale-rose stuff, and certain oval openings—two over the doors, open-ing on each side of the great couch which faces the windows, one over the chimney-piece, and one above the buffet which forms its *vis-à-vis*—four spaces in all, to be filled by and by with "fantasies" of the Four Seasons, painted by his own hand. He will send us from Paris arm-chairs of a new pattern he has devised, suitably covered, and a painted *clavecin*. Our old silver candlesticks look well on the chimney-piece. Odd, faint-coloured flowers fill coquettishly the little empty spaces here and there, like ghosts of nosegays left by visitors long ago, which paled thus, sympathetically, at the decease of their old owners,—for, in spite of its new-fashionedness, all this array is really less like a new thing than the last surviving result of all the more lightsome adornments of past times. Only, the very walls seem to cry out—No! to make delicate insinuation, for a music, a conversation, nim-bler than any we have known, or are likely to find here. For himself, he converses well, but very sparingly. He assures us, indeed, that this new style is in truth a thing of old days, of his own old days here in Valenciennes, when, working long hours as a mason's boy, he in fancy reclothed the walls of this or that house he was employed in, with this fairy arrangement— itself like a piece of "chamber-music," methinks, part answering to part; while no too trenchant note is allowed to break through the delicate har-

mony of white and pale red and little golden touches. Yet it is all very comfortable also, it must be confessed; with an elegant open place for the fire,
instead of the big old stove of brown tiles. The ancient, heavy furniture of
our grandparents goes up, with difficulty, into the garrets, much against
my father's inclination. To reconcile him to the change, Antony is painting
his portrait in a vast *perruque*, and with more vigorous massing of light
and shadow than he is wont to permit himself.

June 1714.

He has completed the ovals—The Four Seasons. Oh! the summerlike grace,
the freedom and softness of the "Summer"—a hayfield such as we visited
to-day, but boundless, and with touches of level Italian architecture in
the hot, white, elusive distance, and wreaths of flowers, fairy hayrakes and
the like, suspended from tree to tree, with that wonderful lightness which
is one of the charms of his work. I can understand through this, at last,
what it is he enjoys, what he selects by preference from all that various
world we pass our lives in. I am struck by the purity of the room he has
refashioned for us—a sort of *moral* purity; yet, in the *forms* and *colours* of
things. Is the actual life of Paris, to which he will soon return, equally
pure, that it relishes this kind of thing so strongly? Only, methinks 'tis a
pity to incorporate so much of his work, of himself, with objects of use,
which must perish by use, or disappear, like our own old furniture, with
mere change of fashion.

July 1714.

On the last day of Antony Watteau's visit we made a party to Cambrai. We
entered the cathedral church; it was the hour of Vespers, and it happened
that Monseigneur le Prince de Cambrai, the author of *Télémaque*, was in
his place in the choir. He appears of great age, assists but rarely at the
offices of religion, and is never to be seen in Paris; and Antony had much
desired to behold him. Certainly it was worth while to have come so far
only to see him, and hear him give his pontifical blessing, in a voice feeble
but of infinite sweetness, and with an inexpressibly graceful movement of
the hands. A veritable *grand seigneur!* His refined old age, the impress of
genius and honours, even his disappointments, concur with natural graces

to make him seem too distinguished (a fitter word fails me) for this world. *Omnia Vanitas!* he seems to say, yet with a profound resignation, which makes the things we are most of us so fondly occupied with seem petty enough. *Omnia Vanitas!* Is that indeed the proper comment on our lives, coming, as it does in this case, from one who might have made his own all that life has to bestow? Yet he was never to be seen at court, and has lived here almost as an exile. Was our "Great King Lewis" jealous of a true *grand seigneur* or *grand monarque* by natural gift and the favour of heaven, that he could not endure his presence?

July 1714.

My own portrait remains unfinished at his sudden departure. I sat for it in a walking-dress, made under his direction—a gown of a peculiar silken stuff, falling into an abundance of small folds, giving me "a certain air of piquancy" which pleases him, but is far enough from my true self. My old Flemish *faille*, which I shall always wear, suits me better.

I notice that our good-hearted but sometimes difficult friend said little of our brother Jean-Baptiste, though he knows us so anxious on his account—spoke only of his constant industry, cautiously, and not altogether with satisfaction, as if the sight of it wearied him.

September 1714.

Will Antony ever accomplish that long-pondered journey to Italy? For his own sake, I should be glad he might. Yet it seems desolately far, across those great hills and plains. I remember how I formed a plan for providing him with a sum sufficient for the purpose. But that he no longer needs.

With myself, how to pass time becomes sometimes the question,— unavoidably; though it strikes me as a thing unspeakably sad in a life so short as ours. The sullenness of a long wet day is yielding just now to an outburst of watery sunset, which strikes from the far horizon of this quiet world of ours, over fields and willow-woods, upon the shifty weather-vanes, and long-pointed windows of the tower on the square—from which the *Angelus* is sounding—with a momentary promise of a fine night. I prefer the *Salut* at Saint Vaast. The walk thither is a longer one; and I have a fancy always that I may meet Antony Watteau there again, any time; just as, when a child, having found one day a tiny box in the shape of a silver coin, for long afterwards I used to try every piece of money that came into my hands, expecting it to open.

September 1714.

We were sitting in the Watteau chamber for the coolness, this sultry evening. A sudden gust of wind ruffled the lights in the sconces on the walls; the distant rumblings, which had continued all the afternoon, broke out at last: and through the driving rain, a coach, rattling across the *Place*, stops at our door; and in a moment Jean-Baptiste is with us once again; but with bitter tears in his eyes;—dismissed!

October 1714.

Jean-Baptiste! he too, rejected by Antony! It makes our friendship and fraternal sympathy closer. And still as he works, not less sedulously than of old, and still so full of loyalty to his old master, in that Watteau chamber, I seem to see Antony himself, of whom Jean-Baptiste dares not yet speak,— to come very near his work, and understand his great parts. And Jean-Baptiste's work may stand, for the future, as the central interest of my life. I bury myself in that.

February 1715.

If I understand anything of these matters, Antony Watteau paints that delicate life of Paris so excellently, with so much spirit, partly because, after all, he looks down upon it or despises it. To persuade myself of that, is my womanly satisfaction for his preference—his apparent preference— for a world so different from mine. Those coquetries, those vain and perishable graces, can be rendered so perfectly, only through an intimate understanding of them. For him, to understand must be to despise them; while (I think I know why) he yet undergoes their fascination. Hence that discontent with himself, which keeps pace with his fame. It would have been better for him—he would have enjoyed a purer and more real happiness—had he remained here, obscure; as it might have been better for me!

It is altogether different with Jean-Baptiste. He approaches that life, and all its pretty nothingness, from a level no higher than its own; and beginning just where Antony Watteau leaves off in disdain, produces a solid and veritable likeness of it and of its ways.

March 1715.

There are points in his painting (I apprehend this through his own persistently modest observations) at which he works out his purpose more excellently than Watteau; of whom he has trusted himself to speak at last, with a wonderful self-effacement, pointing out in each of those pictures, for the rest so just and true, how Antony would have managed this or that; and, with what an easy superiority, have done the thing better—done the impossible.

February 1716.

There are good things, attractive things, in life, meant for one and not for another—not meant perhaps for me; as there are pretty clothes which are not suitable for every one. I find a certain immobility of disposition in me, to quicken or interfere with which is like physical pain. He, so brilliant, petulant, mobile! I am better far beside Jean-Baptiste—in contact with his quiet, even labour, and manner of being. At first he did the work to which he had set himself, sullenly; but the mechanical labour of it has cleared his mind and temper at last, as a sullen day turns quite clear and fine by imperceptible change. With the earliest dawn he enters his workroom, the Watteau chamber, where he remains at work all day. The dark evenings he spends in industrious preparation with the *crayon* for the pictures he is to finish during the hours of daylight. His toil is also his amusement; he goes but rarely into the society whose manners he has to reproduce. His animals, pet animals, are mere toys: he knows it. But he finishes a large number of works, door-heads, *clavecin* cases, and the like. His happiest, most genial moments, he puts, like savings of fine gold, into one particular picture, (true *opus magnum*, as he hopes,) *The Swing.* He has the secret of surprising effects with a certain pearl-gray silken stuff of his predilection; and it must be confessed that he paints hands—which a draughtsman, of course, should understand at least twice as well as all other people—with surpassing expression.

March 1716.

Is it the depressing result of this labour, of a too-exacting labour? I know not. But at times (it is his one melancholy) he expresses a strange apprehension of poverty, of penury, and mean surroundings in old age; reminding me of that childish disposition to hoard, which I noticed in him of old. And then—inglorious Watteau, as he is!—at times that steadiness, in which he is so great a contrast to Antony, as it were accumulates, changes, into a ray of genius, a grace, an inexplicable touch of truth, in which all his heaviness leaves him for a while, and he actually goes beyond the master; as himself protests to me, yet modestly. And still, it is precisely at those moments that he feels most the difference between himself and Antony Watteau. In *that* country, *all* the pebbles are golden nuggets, he says; with perfect good humour.

June 1716.

'Tis truly in a delightful abode that Antony Watteau is just now lodged—the *hôtel*, or town-house of M. de Crozat, which is not only a comfortable dwelling-place, but also a precious museum lucky people go far to see. Jean-Baptiste, too, has seen the place, and describes it. The antiquities, beautiful curiosities of all sorts—above all, the original drawings of those old masters Antony so greatly admires—are arranged all around one there, that the influence, the genius, of those things may imperceptibly play upon, and enter into one, and form what one does. The house is situated near the *Rue Richelieu,* but has a large garden about it. M. de Crozat gives his musical parties there, and Antony Watteau has painted the walls of one of the apartments with the Four Seasons, after the manner of ours, but doubtless improved by second thoughts. This beautiful place is now Antony's home for a while. The house has but one story, with attics in the *mansard* roofs, like those of a farmhouse in the country. I fancy Antony fled thither for a few moments, from the visitors who weary him; breathing the freshness of that dewy garden in the very midst of Paris. As for me, I suffocate this summer afternoon in this pretty Watteau chamber of ours, where Jean-Baptiste is working so contentedly.

May 1717.

In spite of what happened, Jean-Baptiste has been looking forward to a visit to Valenciennes which Antony Watteau had proposed to make. He hopes always—has a patient hope—that Antony's former patronage of him may be revived. And now he is among us, actually at his work—restless and disquieting, meagre, like a woman with some nervous malady. Is it pity, then, pity only, one must feel for the brilliant one? He has been criticising the work of Jean-Baptiste, who takes his judgments generously, gratefully. Can it be that, after all, he despises, and is no true lover of his own art, and is but chilled by an enthusiasm for it in another, such as that of Jean-Baptiste?—as if Jean-Baptiste over-valued it, or as if some ignobleness or blunder, and a sign that he has really missed his aim, started out of his work at the sound of praise—as if such praise could hardly be altogether sincere.

June 1717.

And at last one has actual sight of his work—what it is. He has brought with him certain long-cherished designs to finish here in quiet, as he protests he has never finished before. That charming *Noblesse*—can it be really so distinguished to the minutest point, so naturally aristocratic? Half in masquerade, playing the drawing-room or garden comedy of life, these persons have upon them, not less than the landscape he composes, and among the accidents of which they group themselves with such a perfect fittingness, a certain light we should seek for in vain upon anything real. For their framework they have around them a veritable architecture—a tree-architecture—of which those moss-grown balusters, *termes*, statues, fountains, are really but accessories. Only, as I gaze upon those windless afternoons, I find myself always saying to myself involuntarily, "The evening will be a wet one." The storm is always brooding through the massy splendour of the trees, above those sun-dried glades or lawns, where delicate children may be trusted thinly clad: and the secular trees themselves will hardly outlast another generation.

July 1717.

There has been an exhibition of his pictures in the Hall of the Academy of Saint Luke; and all the world has been to see.

Yes! Besides that unreal, imaginary light upon these scenes and persons, which is pure gift of his, there was a light, a poetry, in those persons and things themselves, close at hand, *we* had not seen. He has enabled us to see it: we are so much the better-off thereby, and I, for one, the better. The world he sets before us so engagingly has its care for purity, its cleanly preferences, in what one is to *see*—in the outsides of things—and there is something, a sign, a memento, at the least, of what makes life really valuable, even in that. There, is my simple notion, wholly womanly perhaps, but which I may hold by, of the purpose of the arts.

August 1717.

And yet! (to read my mind, my experience, in somewhat different terms) methinks Antony Watteau reproduces that gallant world, those patched and powdered ladies and fine cavaliers, so much to its own satisfaction, partly because he despises it: if this be a possible condition of excellent artistic production. People talk of a new era now dawning upon the world, of fraternity, liberty, humanity, of a novel sort of social freedom in which men's natural goodness of heart will blossom at a thousand points hitherto repressed, of wars disappearing from the world in an infinite, benevolent ease of life—yes! perhaps of infinite littleness also. And it is the outward manner of that, which, partly by anticipation, and through pure intellectual power, Antony Watteau has caught, together with a flattering something of his own, added thereto. Himself really of the old time—that serious old time which is passing away, the impress of which he carries on his physiognomy—he dignifies, by what in him is neither more nor less than a profound melancholy, the essential insignificance of what he *wills* to touch in all that; transforming its mere pettiness into grace. It looks certainly very graceful, fresh, animated, "piquant," as they love to say—yes! and withal, I repeat, perfectly pure; and may well congratulate itself on the loan of a fallacious grace, not its own. For in truth Antony Watteau is still the mason's boy, and deals with that world under a fascination, of the nature of which he is half-conscious methinks, puzzled at "the queer trick he possesses," to use his own phrase. You see him growing ever more and more meagre, as he goes through the world and its applause. Yet he reaches with wonderful sagacity the secret of an adjustment of colours, a *coiffure*, a toilette, setting I know not what air of real superiority on such things. He will never overcome his early training; and these light things will possess for him always a kind of worth, as characterising that impossible or forbidden world which the mason's boy saw through the closed gateways of the enchanted garden. Those trifling and petty graces, the *insignia* to him of that nobler world of aspiration and idea, even now that he is aware, as I conceive, of their true littleness, bring back to him, by the power of association, all the old magical exhilaration of his dream—his dream of a better world than the real one. There, is the formula, as I apprehend, of his success—of his extraordinary hold on things so alien from himself. And I think there is more real hilarity in my brother's *fêtes champêtres*—more truth to life, and therefore less distinction. Yes! the world profits by such reflection of its poor, coarse self, in one who renders all its caprices from the height of a Corneille. That is my way of making up to myself for the fact that I think *his* days, too, would have been really happier, had he remained obscure at Valenciennes.

September 1717.

My own poor likeness, begun so long ago, still remains unfinished on the easel, at his departure from Valenciennes—perhaps for ever; since the old people departed this life in the hard winter of last year, at no distant time from each other. It is pleasanter to him to sketch and plan than to paint and finish: and he is often out of humour with himself because he cannot project into a picture the life and spirit of his first thought with the *crayon*. He would fain begin where that famous master, Gerard Dow, left off, and snatch, as it were, with a single stroke, what in him was the result of infinite patience. It is the sign of this sort of promptitude that he values solely in the work of another. To my thinking there is a kind of greed or grasping in that humour; as if things were not to last very long, and one must snatch opportunity. And often he succeeds. The old Dutch painter cherished with a kind of piety his colours and pencils. Antony Watteau, on the contrary, will hardly make any preparations for his work at all, or even clean his

palette, in the dead-set he makes at improvisation. 'Tis the contrast perhaps between the staid Dutch genius and the petulant, sparkling French
temper of this new era, into which he has thrown himself. Alas! it is already apparent that the result also loses something of longevity, of dura-
bility—the colours fading or changing, from the first, somewhat rapidly,
as Jean-Baptiste notes. 'Tis true, a mere trifle alters or produces the expression. But then, on the other hand, in pictures the whole effect of which
lies in a kind of harmony, the treachery of a single colour must needs involve the failure of the whole to outlast the fleeting grace of those social
conjunctions it is meant to perpetuate. This is what has happened, in part,
to that portrait on the easel. Meantime, he has commanded Jean-Baptiste
to finish it; and so it must be.

October 1717.

Antony Watteau is an excellent judge of literature, and I have been reading (with infinite surprise!) in my afternoon walks in the little wood here,
a new book he left behind him—a great favourite of his; as it has been a
favourite with large numbers in Paris. Those pathetic shocks of fortune,
those sudden alternations of pleasure and remorse, which must always lie
among the very conditions of an irregular and guilty love, as in sinful games
of chance:—they have begun to talk of these things in Paris, to amuse themselves with the spectacle of them, set forth here, in the story, of poor Manon
Lescaut—for whom fidelity is impossible, so vulgarly eager for the money
which can buy pleasures such as hers—with an art like Watteau's own, for
lightness and grace. Incapacity of truth, yet with such tenderness, such a
gift of tears, on the one side: on the other, a faith so absolute as to give to
an illicit love almost the regularity of marriage! And this is the book those
fine ladies in Watteau's "conversations," who look so exquisitely pure, lay
down on the cushion when the children run up to have their laces righted.
Yet the pity of it! What floods of tears! There is a tone about it all, which
strikes me as going well with the grace of these leafless birch-trees against
the sky, the silver of their bark, and a certain delicate odour of decay which
rises from the soil. It is all one half-light; and the heroine (nay! the hero
himself also, that dainty Chevalier des Grieux, with all his fervour) have, I
think, but a half-life in them truly, from the first. And I could fancy myself

half of their condition sitting here alone, this evening, while a premature touch of winter makes the world seem so inhospitable a place of entertainment for one's spirit. With so little genial warmth to hold it there, one feels that the merest accident might detach that flighty guest altogether: so chilled at heart it seems to me, as I gaze on that glacial point in the motionless sky, like some mortal spot whence death begins to creep over the body.

And yet, in the midst of this, by mere force of contrast, comes back to me, very vividly, the true colour, ruddy with flower and fruit, of the past summer, among the streets and gardens of some of our old towns we visited; when the thought of cold was a luxury, and the earth dry enough to sleep upon. The summer was indeed a fine one; and the whole country seemed bewitched. A kind of infectious sentiment passed upon one, like an efflux from its flowers and flower-like architecture—flower-like to me at least, but of which I never felt the beauty before.

And as I think of that, certainly I have to confess that there is a wonderful reality about this lover's story; an accordance between themselves and the conditions of things around them, so deep as to make it seem that the course of their lives could hardly have been other than it was. That comes, perhaps, wholly of the writer's skill; but at all events, I must read the book no more.

June 1718.

And he has allowed that Mademoiselle Rosalba—*"ce bel esprit"*—who can discourse upon the arts like a master, to paint his portrait—has painted hers in return! She holds a lapful of white roses with her two hands. *Rosa Alba!* himself has inscribed it! It will be engraved, to circulate and perpetuate it the better.

One's journal, here in one's solitude, is of service at least in this, that it affords an escape for vain regrets, angers, impatience. One puts this and that angry spasm into it, and is delivered from it so.

And then, it was at the desire of M. de Crozat that the thing was done. One must oblige one's patrons. The lady also, they tell me, is consumptive, like Antony himself, and like to die. And he who has always lacked either the money or the spirits to make that long-pondered, much-desired journey to Italy, has found in her work the veritable accent and colour of those old Venetian masters he would so willingly have studied under the sunshine of their own land. Alas! How little peace have his great successes given him,—how little of that quietude of mind, without which, methinks, one fails in true dignity of character.

November 1718.

His thirst for change of place has actually driven him to England, that veritable home of the consumptive. Ah me! I feel it may be the finishing stroke. To have run into the native country of consumption! Strange caprice of that desire to travel, which he has really indulged so little in his life—of the restlessness which, they tell me, is itself a symptom of this terrible disease!

January 1720.

As once before, after long silence, a token has reached us—a slight token that he remembers—an etched plate, one of very few he has executed, with that old subject—Soldiers on the March. And the weary soldier himself is returning once more to Valenciennes, on his way from England to Paris.

February 1720.

Those sharply-arched brows, those restless eyes which seem larger than ever—something that seizes on one, and is almost terrible, in his expression—speak clearly, and irresistibly set one on the thought of a summing-up of his life. I am reminded of the day when, already with that air of seemly thought, *le bel sérieux*, he was found sketching, with so much truth to the inmost mind in them, those picturesque mountebanks at the Fair in the *Grande Place*; and I find, throughout his course of life, something of the essential melancholy of the comedian. He, so fastidious and cold, and who has never "ventured the representation of passion," does but amuse the gay world; and is aware of that, though certainly unamused himself all the while. Just now, however, he is finishing a very different picture—that too, full of humour—an English family-group, with a little girl riding a wooden horse; the father, and the mother, holding his tobacco-pipe, stand in the centre.

March 1720.

To-morrow he will depart finally. And this evening the Syndics of the Academy of Saint Luke came with their scarves and banners to conduct their illustrious fellow-citizen, by torch-light, to supper in their Guildhall, where all their beautiful old corporation plate will be displayed. The Watteau *salon* was lighted up to receive them. There is something in the payment of great honours to the living which fills one with apprehension, especially when the recipient of them looks so like a dying man. God have mercy on him!

April 1721.

We were on the point of retiring to rest last evening when a messenger arrived post-haste with a letter on behalf of Antony Watteau, desiring Jean-Baptiste's presence at Paris. We did not go to bed that night; and my brother was on his way before daylight, his heart full of a strange conflict of joy and apprehension.

May 1721.

A letter at last! from Jean-Baptiste, occupied with cares of all sorts at the bedside of the sufferer. Antony fancying that the air of the country might do him good, the Abbé Haranger, one of the canons of the Church of Saint Germain l'Auxerrois, where he was in the habit of hearing Mass, has lent him a house at Nogent-sur-Marne. There he receives a few visitors. But in truth the places he once liked best, the people, nay! the very friends, have become to him nothing less than insupportable. Though he still dreams of change, and would fain try his native air once more, he is at work constantly upon his art; but solely by way of a teacher, instructing (with a kind of remorseful diligence, it would seem) Jean-Baptiste, who will be heir to his unfinished work, and take up many of his pictures where he has left them. He seems now anxious for one thing only, to give his old "dismissed" disciple what remains of himself, and the last secrets of his genius. His property—9000 *livres* only—goes to his relations. Jean-Baptiste has found these last weeks immeasurably useful.

For the rest, bodily exhaustion, perhaps, and this new interest in an old friend, have brought him tranquillity at last, a tranquillity in which he is much occupied with matters of religion. Ah! it was ever so with me. And one *lives* also most reasonably so.—With women, at least, it is so, quite certainly. Yet I know not what there is of a pity which strikes deep, at the thought of a man, a while since so strong, turning his face to the wall from the things which most occupy men's lives. 'Tis that homely, but honest *curé* of Nogent he has caricatured so often, who attends him.

July 1721.

Our incomparable Watteau is no more! Jean-Baptiste returned unexpectedly. I heard his hasty footstep on the stairs. We turned together into that room; and he told his story there. Antony Watteau departed suddenly, in the arms of M. Gersaint, on one of the late hot days of July. At the last moment he had been at work upon a crucifix for the good *curé* of Nogent, liking little the very rude one he possessed. He died with all the sentiments of religion.

He has been a sick man all his life. He was always a seeker after something in the world, that is there in no satisfying measure, or not at all.

II

DENYS L'AUXERROIS

ALMOST EVERY PEOPLE, AS WE KNOW, HAS HAD ITS LEGEND OF A "GOLDEN AGE" and of its return—legends which will hardly be forgotten, however prosaic the world may become, while man himself remains the aspiring, never quite contented being he is. And yet in truth, since we are no longer children, we might well question the advantage of the return to us of a condition of life in which, by the nature of the case, the values of things would, so to speak, lie wholly on their surfaces, unless we could regain also the childish consciousness, or rather unconsciousness, in ourselves, to take all that adroitly and with the appropriate lightness of heart. The dream, however, has been left for the most part in the usual vagueness of dreams: in their waking hours people have been too busy to furnish it forth with details. What follows is a quaint legend, with detail enough, of such a return of a golden or poetically-gilded age (a denizen of old Greece itself actually finding his way back again among men) as it happened in an ancient town of medieval France.

Of the French town, properly so called, in which the products of successive ages, not without lively touches of the present, are blended together harmoniously, with a beauty *specific*—a beauty cisalpine and northern, yet at the same time quite distinct from the massive German picturesque of Ulm, or Freiburg, or Augsburg, and of which Turner has found the ideal in certain of his studies of the rivers of France, a perfectly happy conjunction of river and town being of the essence of its physiognomy—the town of Auxerre is perhaps the most complete realisation to be found by the actual wanderer. Certainly, for picturesque expression it is the most memorable of a distinguished group of three in these parts,—Auxerre, Sens, Troyes,—each gathered, as if with deliberate aim at such effect, about the central mass of a huge gray cathedral.

Around Troyes the natural picturesque is to be sought only in the rich, almost coarse, summer colouring of the Champagne country, of which the very tiles, the plaster and brickwork of its tiny villages and great, straggling, village-like farms have caught the warmth. The cathedral, visible far and wide over the fields seemingly of loose wild-flowers, itself a rich mixture of all the varieties of the Pointed style down to the latest *Flamboyant*, may be noticed among the greater French churches for breadth of proportions internally, and is famous for its almost unrivalled treasure of stained glass, chiefly of a florid, elaborate, later type, with much highly conscious artistic contrivance in design as well as in colour. In one of the richest of its windows, for instance, certain lines of pearly white run hither and thither, with delightful distant effect, upon ruby and dark blue. Approaching nearer you find it to be a Travellers' window, and those odd lines of white the long walking-staves in the hands of Abraham, Raphael, the Magi, and the other saintly patrons of journeys. The appropriate provincial character of the *bourgeoisie* of Champagne is still to be seen, it would appear, among the citizens of Troyes. Its streets, for the most part in timber and pargeting, present more than one unaltered specimen of the ancient *hôtel* or town-house, with forecourt and garden in the rear; and its more devout citizens would seem even in their church-building to have sought chiefly to please the eyes of those occupied with mundane affairs and out of doors, for they have finished, with abundant outlay, only the vast, useless portals of their parish churches, of surprising height and lightness, in a kind of wildly elegant Gothic-on-stilts, giving to the streets of Troyes a peculiar air of the grotesque, as if in some quaint nightmare of the Middle Age.

At Sens, thirty miles away to the west, a place of far graver aspect, the name of Jean Cousin denotes a more chastened temper, even in these sumptuous decorations. Here all is cool and composed, with an almost English austerity. The first growth of the Pointed style in England—the hard "early English" of Canterbury—is indeed the creation of William, a master reared in the architectural school of Sens; and the severity of his taste might seem to have acted as a restraining power on all the subsequent changes of manner in this place—changes in themselves for the most part towards luxuriance. In harmony with the atmosphere of its great church is the cleanly quiet of the town, kept fresh by little channels of clear water circulating through its streets, derivatives of the rapid Vanne which falls just below into the Yonne. The Yonne, bending gracefully, link after link, through a never-ending rustle of poplar trees, beneath lowly vine-clad hills, with relics of delicate woodland here and there, sometimes close at hand, sometimes leaving an interval of broad meadow, has all the lightsome characteristics of French river-side scenery on a smaller scale than usual, and might pass for the child's fancy of a river, like the rivers of the old miniature-painters, blue, and full to a fair green margin. One notices along its course a greater proportion than elsewhere of still untouched old seignorial residences, larger or smaller. The range of old gibbous towns along its banks, expanding their gay quays upon the water-side, have a common character—Joigny, Villeneuve, Saint Julien-du-Sault—yet tempt us to tarry at each and examine its relics, old glass and the like, of the Renaissance or the Middle Age, for the acquisition of real though minor lessons on the various arts which have left themselves a central monument at Auxerre.—Auxerre! A slight ascent in the winding road! and you have before you the prettiest town in France—the broad framework of vineyard sloping upwards gently to the horizon, with distant white cottages inviting one to walk: the quiet curve of river below, with all the riverside details: the three great purple-tiled masses of Saint Germain, Saint Pierre, and the cathedral of Saint Étienne, rising out of the crowded houses with more than the usual abruptness and irregularity of French building. Here, that rare artist, the susceptible painter of architecture, if he understands the value alike of line and mass, of broad masses and delicate lines, has "a subject made to his hand."

A veritable country of the vine, it presents nevertheless an expression peaceful rather than radiant. Perfect type of that happy mean be-

tween northern earnestness and the luxury of the south, for which we
prize midland France, its physiognomy is not quite happy—attractive in
part for its melancholy. Its most characteristic atmosphere is to be seen
when the tide of light and distant cloud is travelling quickly over it, when
rain is not far off, and every touch of art or of time on its old building is
defined in clear gray. A fine summer ripens its grapes into a valuable wine;
but in spite of that it seems always longing for a larger and more continuous allowance of the sunshine that is so much to its taste. You might fancy
something querulous or plaintive in that rustling movement of the vine-
leaves, as blue-frocked Jacques Bonhomme finishes his day's labour among
them.

To beguile one such afternoon when the rain set in early and walk-
ing was impossible, I found my way to the shop of an old dealer in *bric-à-
brac*. It was not a monotonous display, after the manner of the Parisian
dealer, of a stock-in-trade the like of which one has seen many times over,
but a discriminate collection of real curiosities. One seemed to recognise
a provincial school of taste in various relics of the housekeeping of the
last century, with many a gem of earlier times from the old churches and
religious houses of the neighbourhood. Among them was a large and brilliant fragment of stained glass which might have come from the cathedral itself. Of the very finest quality in colour and design, it presented a
figure not exactly conformable to any recognised ecclesiastical type; and
it was clearly part of a series. On my eager inquiry for the remainder, the
old man replied that no more of it was known, but added that the priest
of a neighbouring village was the possessor of an entire set of tapestries,
apparently intended for suspension in church, and designed to portray
the whole subject of which the figure in the stained glass was a portion.

Next afternoon accordingly I repaired to the priest's house, in reality a little Gothic building, part perhaps of an ancient manor-house, close
to the village church. In the front garden, flower-garden and *potager* in
one, the bees were busy among the autumn growths—many-coloured as-
ters, bignonias, scarlet-beans, and the old-fashioned parsonage flowers.
The courteous owner readily showed me his tapestries, some of which hung
on the walls of his parlour and staircase by way of a background for the
display of the other curiosities of which he was a collector. Certainly, those

tapestries and the stained glass dealt with the same theme. In both were the same musical instruments—pipes, cymbals, long reed-like trumpets. The story, indeed, included the building of an organ, just such an instrument, only on a larger scale, as was standing in the old priest's library, though almost soundless now; whereas in certain of the woven pictures the hearers appear as if transported, some of them shouting rapturously to the organ music. A sort of mad vehemence prevails, indeed, throughout the delicate bewilderments of the whole series—giddy dances, wild animals leaping, above all perpetual wreathings of the vine, connecting, like some mazy arabesque, the various presentations of one oft-repeated figure, translated here out of the clear-coloured glass into the sadder, somewhat opaque and earthen hues of the silken threads. The figure was that of the organ-builder himself, a flaxen and flowery creature, sometimes well-nigh naked among the vine-leaves, sometimes muffled in skins against the cold, sometimes in the dress of a monk, but always with a strong impress of real character and incident from the veritable streets of Auxerre. What is it? Certainly, notwithstanding its grace, and wealth of graceful accessories, a suffering, tortured figure. With all the regular beauty of a pagan god, he has suffered after a manner of which we must suppose pagan gods incapable. It was as if one of those fair, triumphant beings had cast in his lot with the creatures of an age later than his own, people of larger spiritual capacity and assuredly of a larger capacity for melancholy. With this fancy in my mind, by the help of certain notes which lay in the priest's curious library upon the history of the works at the cathedral during the period of its finishing, and in repeated examination of the old tapestried designs, the story shaped itself at last.

Towards the middle of the thirteenth century the cathedral of Saint Étienne was complete in its main outlines: what remained was the building of the great tower, and all that various labour of final decoration which it would take more than one generation to accomplish. Certain circumstances however, not wholly explained, led to a somewhat rapid finishing, as it were out of hand, yet with a marvellous fulness at once and grace. Of the result much has perished, or been transferred elsewhere; a portion is still visible in sumptuous relics of stained windows, and, above all, in the reliefs which adorn the western portals, very delicately carved in a fine, firm stone from Tonnerre, of which time has only browned the surface, and which, for early mastery in art, may be compared to the contemporary work of Italy. They come nearer than the art of that age was used to do to the expression of life; with a feeling for reality, in no ignoble form, caught, it might seem, from the ardent and full-veined existence then current in these actual streets and houses. Just then Auxerre had its turn in that political movement which broke out sympathetically, first in one, then in another of the towns of France, turning their narrow, feudal institutions into a free, communistic life—a movement of which those great centres of popular devotion, the French cathedrals, are in many instances the monument. Closely connected always with the assertion of individual freedom, alike in mind and manners, at Auxerre this political stir was associated also, as cause or effect, with the figure and character of a particular personage, long remembered. He was the very genius, it would appear, of that new, free, generous manner in art, active and potent as a living creature.

As the most skilful of the band of carvers worked there one day, with a labour he could never quite make equal to the vision within him, a finely-sculptured Greek coffin of stone, which had been made to serve for some later Roman funeral, was unearthed by the masons, with the thing done, and art achieved, as far as regards those final graces and harmonies of execution, which were precisely what lay beyond the hand of the medieval workman, who for his part had largely at command a seriousness of conception lacking in the old Greek. Within the coffin lay an object of a fresh and brilliant clearness among the ashes of the dead—a flask of lively green glass, like a great emerald. It might have been "the wondrous vessel of the Grail." Only this object seemed to bring back no ineffable purity, but rather the riotous and earthy heat of old paganism itself. Coated within, and, as some were persuaded, still redolent with the tawny sediment of the Roman wine it had held so long ago, it was set aside for use at the supper which was shortly to celebrate the completion of the masons' work. Amid much talk of the great age of gold, and some random expressions of hope that it might return again, fine old wine of Auxerre was sipped in small glasses from the precious flask as supper ended. And, whether or not the opening of the buried vessel had anything to do with it, from that time a sort of golden age seemed indeed to be reigning there for a while, and the triumphant completion of the great church was contemporary with a series of remarkable wine seasons. The vintage of those years was long remembered. Fine and abundant wine was to be found stored up even in poor men's cottages; while a new beauty, a gaiety, was abroad, as all the conjoint arts branched out exuberantly in a reign of quiet, delighted labour, at the prompting, as it seemed, of the singular being who came suddenly and oddly to Auxerre to be the centre of so pleasant a period, though in truth he made but a sad ending.

A singular usage long perpetuated itself at Auxerre. On Easter Day the canons, in the very centre of the great church, played solemnly at ball. Vespers being sung, instead of conducting the bishop to his palace, they proceeded in order into the nave, the people standing in two long rows to watch. Girding up their skirts a little way, the whole body of clerics awaited their turn in silence, while the captain of the singing-boys cast the ball into the air, as high as he might, along the vaulted roof of the central aisle to be caught by any boy who could, and tossed again with hand or foot till it passed on to the portly chanters, the chaplains, the canons themselves, who finally played out the game with all the decorum of an ecclesiastical ceremony. It was just then, just as the canons took the ball to themselves so gravely, that Denys—Denys l'Auxerrois, as he was afterwards called— appeared for the first time. Leaping in among the timid children, he made the thing really a game. The boys played like boys, the men almost like madmen, and all with a delightful glee which became contagious, first in the clerical body, and then among the spectators. The aged Dean of the Chapter, Protonotary of his Holiness, held up his purple skirt a little higher, and stepping from the ranks with an amazing levity, as if suddenly re-lieved of his burden of eighty years, tossed the ball with his foot to the venerable capitular Homilist, equal to the occasion. And then, unable to stand inactive any longer, the laity carried on the game among themselves, with shouts of not too boisterous amusement; the sport continuing till the flight of the ball could no longer be traced along the dusky aisles.

Though the home of his childhood was but a humble one—one of those little cliff-houses cut out in the low chalky hillside, such as are still to be found with inhabitants in certain districts of France—there were some who connected his birth with the story of a beautiful country girl, who, about eighteen years before, had been taken from her own people, not unwillingly, for the pleasure of the Count of Auxerre. She had wished indeed to see the great lord, who had sought her privately, in the glory of his own house; but, terrified by the strange splendours of her new abode and manner of life, and the anger of the true wife, she had fled suddenly from the place during the confusion of a violent storm, and in her flight given birth prematurely to a child. The child, a singularly fair one, was found alive, but the mother dead, by lightning-stroke as it seemed, not far from her lord's chamber-door, under the shelter of a ruined ivy-clad tower. Denys himself certainly was a joyous lad enough. At the cliff-side cottage, nestling actually beneath the vineyards, he grew to be an unrivalled gardener, and, grown to manhood, brought his produce to market, keeping a stall in the great cathedral square for the sale of melons and pomegranates, all manner of seeds and flowers, (*omnia speciosa camporum,*) honey also, wax tapers, sweetmeats hot from the frying-pan, rough home-made pots and pans from the little pottery in the wood, loaves baked by the aged woman in whose house he lived. On that Easter Day he had entered the great church for the first time, for the purpose of seeing the game.

And from the very first, the women who saw him at his business, or watering his plants in the cool of the evening, idled for him. The men who noticed the crowd of women at his stall, and how even fresh young girls from the country, seeing him for the first time, always loitered there, suspected—who could tell what kind of powers? hidden under the white veil of that youthful form; and pausing to ponder the matter, found themselves also fallen into the snare. The sight of him made old people feel young again. Even the sage monk Hermes, devoted to study and experiment, was unable to keep the fruit-seller out of his mind, and would fain have discovered the secret of his charm, partly for the friendly purpose of explaining to the lad himself his perhaps more than natural gifts with a view to their profitable cultivation.

It was a period, as older men took note, of young men and their influence. They took fire, no one could quite explain how, as if at his presence, and asserted a wonderful amount of volition, of insolence, yet as if with the consent of their elders, who would themselves sometimes lose

their balance, a little comically. That revolution in the temper and manner of individuals concurred with the movement then on foot at Auxerre,
as in other French towns, for the liberation of the *commune* from its old
feudal superiors. Denys they called *Frank*, among many other nicknames.
Young lords prided themselves on saying that labour should have its ease,
and were almost prepared to take freedom, plebeian freedom (of course
duly decorated, at least with wild-flowers) for a bride. For in truth Denys
at his stall was turning the grave, slow movement of politic heads into a
wild social license, which for a while made life like a stage-play. He first
led those long processions, through which by and by "the little people,"
the discontented, the despairing, would utter their minds. One man engaged with another in talk in the market-place; a new influence came forth
at the contact; another and then another adhered; at last a new spirit was
abroad everywhere. The hot nights were noisy with swarming troops of
dishevelled women and youths with red-stained limbs and faces, carrying their lighted torches over the vine-clad hills), or rushing down the
streets, to the horror of timid watchers, towards the cool spaces by the
river. A shrill music, a laughter at all things, was everywhere. And the new
spirit repaired even to church to take part in the novel offices of the Feast
of Fools. Heads flung back in ecstasy—the morning sleep among the vines,
when the fatigue of the night was over—dew-drenched garments—the serf
lying at his ease at last:—the artists, then so numerous at the place, caught
what they could, something, at least, of the richness, the flexibility of the
visible aspects of life, from all this. With them the life of seeming idleness, to which Denys was conducting the youth of Auxerre so pleasantly,
counted but as the cultivation, for their due service to man, of delightful
natural things. And the powers of nature concurred. It seemed there would
be winter no more. The planet Mars drew nearer to the earth than usual,
hanging in the low sky like a fiery red lamp. A massive but well-nigh life-
less vine on the wall of the cloister, allowed to remain there only as a curiosity on account of its immense age, in that *great* season, as it was long
after called, clothed itself with fruit once more. The culture of the grape
greatly increased. The sunlight fell for the first time on many a spot of
deep woodland cleared for vine-growing; though Denys, a lover of trees,
was careful to leave a stately specimen of forest growth here and there.

When his troubles came, one characteristic that had seemed most amiable in his prosperity was turned against him,—a fondness for oddly grown or even misshapen, yet potentially happy, children; for odd animals also; he sympathised with them all, was skilful in healing their maladies, saved the hare in the chase, and sold his mantle to redeem a lamb from the butcher. He taught the people not to be afraid of the strange, ugly creatures which the light of the moving torches drew from their hiding-places, nor think it a bad omen that they approached. He tamed a veritable wolf to keep him company like a dog. It was the first of many ambiguous circumstances about him, from which, in the minds of an increasing number of people, a deep suspicion and hatred began to define itself. The rich *bestiary*; then compiling in the library of the great church, became, through his assistance, nothing less than a garden of Eden—the garden of Eden grown wild. The owl alone he abhorred. A little later, partly as if in revenge, alone of all animals it clung to him, haunting him persistently among the dusky stone towers; when grown gentler than ever he dared not kill it. He moved unhurt in the famous *ménagerie* of the castle, of which the common people were so much afraid, and let out the lions, themselves timid prisoners enough, through the streets during the fair. The incident suggested to the somewhat barren penmen of the day a "morality" adapted from the old pagan books,—a stage-play in which the God of Wine should return in triumph from the East. In the cathedral square the pageant was presented, amid an intolerable noise of every kind of pipe-music, with Denys in the chief part, upon a gaily-painted chariot, in soft silken raiment and, for headdress, a strange elephant scalp with gilded tusks.

And that unrivalled fairness and freshness of aspect—how did he alone preserve it untouched, through the wind and heat? In truth, it was not by magic, as some said, but by a natural simplicity in his living. When that dark season of his troubles arrived he was heard begging querulously one wintry night, "Give me wine, meat; dark wine and brown meat!"—come back to the rude door of his old home in the cliff-side. Till that time the great vine-dresser himself drank only water; he had lived on spring-water and fruit. A lover of fertility in all its forms, in what did but suggest it, he was curious and penetrative concerning the habits of water, and had the secret of the divining-rod. Long before it came he could detect the scent of rain from afar, and would climb with delight to the great scaffolding on the unfinished tower to watch its coming over the thirsty vineland, till it rattled on the great tiled roof of the church below; and then, throwing off his mantle, allow it to bathe his limbs freely, clinging firmly against the tempestuous wind among the carved imageries of dark stone.

It was on his sudden return after a long journey, (one of many inexplicable disappearances,) coming back changed somewhat, that he ate flesh for the first time, tearing the hot, red morsels with his delicate fingers in a kind of wild greed. He had fled to the south from the first forbidding days of a hard winter which came at last. At the great seaport of Marseilles he had trafficked with sailors from all parts of the world, from Arabia and India, and bought their wares, exposed now for sale, to the wonder of all, at the Easter fair—richer wines and incense than had been known in Auxerre, seeds of marvellous new flowers, creatures wild and tame, new pottery painted in raw gaudy tints, the skins of animals, meats fried with unheard-of condiments. His stall formed a strange, unwonted patch of colour, found suddenly displayed in the hot morning.

The artists were more delighted than ever, and frequented his company in the little manorial habitation, deserted long since by its owners and haunted, so that the eyes of many looked evil upon it, where he had taken up his abode, attracted, in the first instance, by its rich though neglected garden, a tangle of every kind of creeping, vine-like plant. Here, surrounded in abundance by the pleasant materials of his trade, the vinedresser as it were turned pedant and kept school for the various artists, who learned here an art supplementary to their own,—that gay magic, namely, (art or trick,) of his existence, till they found themselves grown into a kind of aristocracy, like veritable *gens fleur-de-lisés*, as they worked together for the decoration of the great church and a hundred other places beside. And yet a darkness had grown upon him. The kind creature had lost something of his gentleness. Strange motiveless misdeeds had happened; and, at a loss for other causes, not the envious only would fain have traced the blame to Denys. He was making the younger world mad. Would he make himself Count of Auxerre? The lady Ariane, deserted by her former lover, had looked kindly upon him; was ready to make him son-in-law to the old count her father, old and not long for this world.

The wise monk Hermes bethought him of certain old readings in which the Wine-god, whose part Denys had played so well, had his contrast, his dark or antipathetic side; was like a double creature of two natures, difficult or impossible to harmonise. And in truth the much-prized wine of Auxerre has itself but a fugitive charm, being apt to sicken and turn gross long before the bottle is empty, however carefully sealed; as it goes indeed, at its best, by hard names, among those who grow it, such as Chainette and Migraine.

A kind of degeneration, of coarseness—the coarseness of satiety and shapeless, battered-out appetite—with an almost savage taste for carnivorous diet, had come over the company. A rumour went abroad of certain women who had drowned, in mere wantonness, their newborn babes. A girl with child was found hanged by her own act in a dark cellar. Ah! if Denys also had not felt himself mad! But when the guilt of a murder, committed with a great vine-axe far out among the vineyards, was attributed vaguely to him, he could but wonder whether it had been indeed thus, and the shadow of a fancied crime abode with him. People turned against their favourite, whose former charms must now be counted only as the fascinations of witchcraft. It was as if the wine poured out for them had soured in the cup. The golden age had indeed come back for a while:— golden was it, or gilded only, after all? and they were too sick, or at least too serious, to carry through their parts in it. The monk Hermes was whimsically reminded of that *after-thought* in pagan poetry, of a Wine-god who had been in hell. Denys certainly, with all his flaxen fairness about him, was manifestly a sufferer. At first he thought of departing secretly to some other place. Alas! his wits were too far gone for certainty of success in the attempt. He feared to be brought back prisoner. Those fat years were over. It was time of scarcity. The working people might not eat and drink of the good things they had helped to store away. Tears rose in the eyes of needy children, of old or weak people like children, as they woke up again and again to sunless, frost-bound, ruinous mornings; and the little hungry creatures went prowling after scattered hedge-nuts or dried vine-tendrils. Mysterious, dark rains prevailed throughout the summer. The great offices of Saint John were fumbled through in a sudden darkness of unseasonable storm, which greatly damaged the carved ornaments of the church, the bishop reading his midday Mass by the light of the little candle at his book. And then, one night, the night which seemed literally to have swallowed up the shortest day in the year, a plot was contrived by certain persons to take Denys as he went and kill him privately for a sorcerer. He could hardly tell how he escaped, and found himself safe in his earliest home, the cottage in the cliff-side, with such a big fire as he delighted in burning upon the hearth. They made a little feast as well as they could for the beautiful hunted creature, with abundance of waxlights.

And at last the clergy bethought themselves of a remedy for this evil time. The body of one of the patron saints had lain neglected somewhere under the flagstones of the sanctuary. This must be piously exhumed, and provided with a shrine worthy of it. The goldsmiths, the jewellers and lapidaries, set diligently to work, and no long time after, the shrine, like a little cathedral with portals and tower complete, stood ready, its chiselled gold framing panels of rock crystal, on the great altar. Many bishops arrived with King Lewis the Saint himself, accompanied by his mother, to assist at the search for and disinterment of the sacred relics. In their presence, the Bishop of Auxerre, in vestments of deep red in honour of the relics, blessed the new shrine, according to the office *De benedictione capsarum pro reliquiis*. The pavement of the choir, removed amid a surging sea of lugubrious chants, all persons fasting, discovered as if it had been a battlefield of mouldering human remains. Their odour rose plainly above the plentiful clouds of incense, such as was used in the king's private chapel. The search for the Saint himself continued in vain all day and far into the night. At last from a little narrow chest, into which the remains had been almost crushed together, the bishop's red-gloved hands drew the dwindled body, shrunken inconceivably, but still with every feature of the face traceable in a sudden oblique ray of ghastly dawn.

That shocking sight, after a sharp fit as if a demon were going out of him, as he rolled on the turf of the cloister, to which he had fled alone from the suffocating church where the crowd still awaited the Procession of the relics and the Mass *De reliquiis quæ continentur in Ecclesiis*, seemed indeed to have cured the madness of Denys, but certainly did not restore his gaiety. He was left a subdued, silent, melancholy creature. Turning now, with an odd revulsion of feeling, to gloomy objects, he picked out a ghastly shred from the common bones on the pavement to wear about his neck, and in a little while found his way to the monks of Saint Germain, who gladly received him into their workshop, though secretly, in fear of his foes.

The busy tribe of variously gifted artists, labouring rapidly at the many works on hand for the final embellishment of the cathedral of St. Étienne, made those conventual buildings just then cheerful enough to lighten a melancholy, heavy even as that of our friend Denys. He took his place among the workmen, a conventual novice; a novice also as to whatever concerns any actual handicraft. He could but compound sweet incense for the sanctuary. And yet, again by merely visible presence, he made himself felt in all the varied exercise around him of those arts which address themselves first of all to sight. He defined unconsciously a manner, alike of feeling and expression, to those skilful hands at work day by day with the chisel, the pencil, or the needle, in many an enduring form of exquisite fancy. In three successive phases or fashions might be traced, especially in the carved work, the humours he had determined. There was first wild gaiety, exuberant in a wreathing of lifelike imageries, from which nothing really present in nature was excluded. That, as the soul of Denys darkened, had passed into obscure regions of the satiric, the grotesque and coarse. But from this time there was manifest, with no loss of power or effect, a well-assured seriousness, somewhat jealous and exclusive, not so much in the selection of the material on which the arts were to work, as in the precise sort of expression that should be induced upon it. It was as if the gay old pagan world had been *blessed* in some way; with effects to be seen most clearly in the rich miniature work of the manuscripts of the capitular library,—a marvellous Ovid especially, upon the pages of which those old loves and sorrows seemed to come to life again in medieval costume, as Denys, in cowl now and with tonsured head, leaned over the painter, and by a kind of visible sympathy, often unspoken, led his work, rather than by any formal comment.

Above all, there was a desire abroad to attain the instruments of a freer and more various sacred music than had been in use hitherto—a music that might express the whole compass of souls now grown to manhood. Auxerre, indeed, then as afterwards, was famous for its liturgical music. It was Denys, at last, to whom the thought occurred of combining in a fuller tide of music all the instruments then in use. Like the Wine-god of old, he had been a lover and patron especially of the music of the pipe, in all its varieties. Here, too, there had been evident those three fashions or "modes":—first, the simple and pastoral, the homely note of the pipe, like the piping of the wind itself from off the distant fields; then, the wild, savage din, that had cost so much to quiet people, and driven excitable people mad. Now he would compose all this to sweeter purposes; and the building of the first organ became like the book of his life; it expanded to the full compass of his nature, in its sorrow and delight. In long, enjoyable days of wind and sun by the river-side, the seemingly half-witted "brother" sought and found the needful varieties of reed. The carpenters, under his instruction, set up the great wooden passages for the thunder; while the little pipes of pasteboard simulated the sound of the human voice singing to the victorious notes of the long metal trumpets. At times this also, as people heard night after night those wandering sounds, seemed like the work of a madman, though they awoke sometimes in wonder at snatches of a new, an unmistakable new music. It was the triumph of all the various modes of the power of the pipe, tamed, ruled, united. Only, on the painted shutters of the organ-case Apollo with his lyre in his hand, as lord of the strings, seemed to look askance on the music of the reed, in all the jealousy with which he put Marsyas to death so cruelly.

Meantime, the people, even his enemies, seemed to have forgotten him. Enemies, in truth, they still were, ready to take his life should the opportunity come; as he perceived when at last he ventured forth on a day of public ceremony. The bishop was to pronounce a blessing upon the foundations of a new bridge, designed to take the place of the ancient Roman bridge which, repaired in a thousand places, had hitherto served for the chief passage of the Yonne. It was as if the disturbing of that time-worn masonry let out the dark spectres of departed times. Deep down, at the core of the central pile, a painful object was exposed—the skeleton of a child, placed there alive, it was rightly surmised, in the superstitious belief that, by way of vicarious substitution, its death would secure the safety of all who should pass over. There were some who found themselves, with a little surprise, looking round as if for a similar pledge of security in their new undertaking. It was just then that Denys was seen plainly, standing, in all essential features precisely as of old, upon one of the great stones prepared for the foundation of the new building. For a moment he felt the eyes of the people upon him full of this strange humour, and with characteristic alertness, after a rapid gaze over the gray city in its broad green frame of vineyards, best seen from this spot, flung himself down into the water and disappeared from view where the stream flowed most swiftly below a row of flour-mills. Some indeed fancied they had seen him emerge again safely on the deck of one of the great boats, loaded with grapes and wreathed triumphantly with flowers like a floating garden, which were then bringing down the vintage from the country; but generally the people believed their strange enemy now at last departed for ever. Denys in truth was at work again in peace at the cloister, upon his house of reeds and pipes. At times his fits came upon him again; and when they came, for his cure he would dig eagerly, turned sexton now, digging, by choice, graves for the dead in the various churchyards of the town. There were those who had seen him thus employed (that form seeming still to carry the sunlight upon it) peering into the darkness, while his tears fell sometimes among the grim relics his mattock had disturbed.

In fact, from the day of the exhumation of the body of the Saint in the great church, he had had a wonderful curiosity for such objects, and one wintry day bethought him of removing the body of his mother from the unconsecrated ground in which it lay, that he might bury it in the cloister near the spot where he now worked. At twilight he came over the frozen snow. As he passed through the stony barriers of the place the world around seemed curdled to the centre—all but himself, fighting his way across it, turning now and then right-about from the persistent wind, which dealt so roughly with his blond hair and the purple mantle whirled about him. The bones, hastily gathered, he placed, awfully but without ceremony, in a hollow space prepared secretly within the grave of another.

Meantime the winds of his organ were ready to blow; and with difficulty he obtained grace from the Chapter for a trial of its powers on a notable public occasion, as follows. A singular guest was expected at Auxerre. In recompense for some service rendered to the Chapter in times gone by, the Sire de Chastellux had the hereditary dignity of a canon of the church. On the day of his reception he presented himself at the entrance of the choir in surplice and amice, worn over the military habit. The old count of Chastellux was lately dead, and the heir had announced his coming, according to custom, to claim his ecclesiastical privilege. There had been long feud between the houses of Chastellux and Auxerre; but on this happy occasion an offer of peace came with a proposal for the hand of the Lady Ariane.

The goodly young man arrived, and, duly arrayed, was received into his stall at vespers, the bishop assisting. It was then that the people heard the music of the organ, rolling over them for the first time, with various feelings of delight. But the performer on and author of the instrument was forgotten in his work, and there was no reinstatement of the former favourite. The religious ceremony was followed by a civic festival, in which Auxerre welcomed its future lord. The festival would end at nightfall with a somewhat rude, popular pageant, in which the person of Winter would be hunted blindfold through the streets. It was the sequel to that old stage-play of the *Return from the East* in which Denys had been the central figure. The old forgotten player saw his part before him, and, as if mechanically, fell again into the chief place, monk's dress and all. It might restore his popularity: who could tell? Hastily he donned the ashen-gray mantle, the rough haircloth about the throat, and went through the preliminary play. And it happened that a point of the haircloth scratched his lip deeply, with a long trickling of blood upon the chin. It was as if the sight of blood transported the spectators with a kind of mad rage, and suddenly revealed to them the truth. The pretended hunting of the unholy creature became a real one, which brought out, in rapid increase, men's evil passions. The soul of Denys was already at rest, as his body, now borne along in front of the crowd, was tossed hither and thither, torn at last limb from limb. The men stuck little shreds of his flesh, or, failing that, of his torn raiment into their caps; the women lending their long hairpins for the purpose. The monk Hermes sought in vain next day for any remains of the body of his friend. Only, at nightfall, the heart of Denys was brought to him by a stranger, still entire. It must long since have mouldered into dust under the stone, marked with a cross, where he buried it in a dark corner of the cathedral aisle.

So the figure in the stained glass explained itself. To me, Denys seemed to have been a real resident at Auxerre. On days of a certain atmosphere, when the trace of the Middle Age comes out, like old marks in the stones in rainy weather, I seemed actually to have seen the tortured figure there—to have met Denys l'Auxerrois in the streets.

III

Sebastian van Storck

It was a winter-scene, by Adrian van de Velde, or by Isaac van Ostade. All the delicate poetry together with all the delicate comfort of the frosty season was in the leafless branches turned to silver, the furred dresses of the skaters, the warmth of the red-brick house-fronts under the gauze of white fog, the gleams of pale sunlight on the cuirasses of the mounted soldiers as they receded into the distance. Sebastian van Storck, confessedly the most graceful performer in all that skating multitude, moving in endless maze over the vast surface of the frozen water-meadow, liked best this season of the year for its expression of a perfect impassivity, or at least of a perfect repose. The earth was, or seemed to be, at rest, with a breathlessness of slumber which suited the young man's peculiar temper. The heavy summer, as it dried up the meadows now lying dead below the ice, set free a crowded and competing world of life, which, while it gleamed very pleasantly russet and yellow for the painter Albert Cuyp, seemed well-nigh to suffocate Sebastian van Storck. Yet with all his appreciation of the national winter, Sebastian was not altogether a Hollander. His mother, of Spanish descent and Catholic, had given a richness of tone and form to the healthy freshness of the Dutch physiognomy, apt to preserve its youthfulness of aspect far beyond the period of life usual with other peoples. This mixed expression charmed the eye of Isaac van Ostade, who had painted his portrait from a sketch taken at one of those skating parties, with his plume of squirrel's tail and fur muff, in all the modest pleasantness of boyhood. When he returned home lately from his studies at a place far inland, at the proposal of his tutor, to recover, as the tutor suggested, a certain loss of robustness, something more than that cheerful indifference of early youth had passed away. The learned man, who held, as was alleged, the tenets of a surprising new philosophy, reluctant to disturb too early the fine intelligence of the pupil entrusted to him, had found it, perhaps, a matter of honesty to send back to his parents one likely enough to catch from others any sort of theoretic light; for the letter he wrote dwelt much on the lad's intellectual fearlessness. "At present," he had written, "he is influenced more by curiosity than by a care for truth, according to the character of youth. Certainly, he is strikingly different from his equals in age, in his passion for a vigorous intellectual gymnastic, such as their supineness of mind causes to be distasteful to most young men, but in which he shows a fearlessness that at times makes me fancy that his ultimate destination may be the military life; for indeed the rigidly logical character of his mind always leads him out upon the practical. Don't misunderstand me! At present, he is strenuous only intellectually; and has given no definite sign of preference, as regards a vocation in life. But he seems to me to be one, practical in this sense, that his theorems will shape life for him, directly; that he will always seek, as a matter of course, the effective equivalent to—the line of being which shall be the proper continuation of—his line of thinking. This intellectual rectitude, or candour, which to my mind has a kind of beauty in it, has reacted upon myself, I confess, with a searching quality." That "searching quality," indeed, many others also, people far from being intellectual, had experienced—an agitation of mind in his neighbourhood, oddly at variance with the composure of the young man's manner and surrounding, so jealously preserved.

In the crowd of spectators at the skating, whose eyes followed, so well-satisfied, the movements of Sebastian van Storck, were the mothers of marriageable daughters, who presently became the suitors of this rich and distinguished youth, introduced to them, as now grown to man's estate, by his delighted parents. Dutch aristocracy had put forth all its graces to become the winter morn: and it was characteristic of the period that the artist tribe was there, on a grand footing—in waiting for the lights and shadows they liked best. The artists were, in truth, an important body just then, as the natural complement of the nation's hard-won prosperity; helping it to a full consciousness of the genial yet delicate homeliness it loved for which it had fought so bravely, and was ready at any moment to fight anew, against man or the sea. Thomas de Keyser, who understood better than any one else the kind of quaint new Atticism which had found its way into the world over those waste salt marshes, wondering whether quite its finest type as he understood it might ever actually be seen there, saw it at last, in lively motion, in the person of Sebastian van Storck, and desired to paint his portrait. A little to his surprise, the young man declined the offer; not graciously, as was thought.

Holland, just then, was reposing on its laurels after its long contest with Spain, in a short period of complete well-being, before troubles of another kind should set in. That a darker time might return again, was clearly enough felt by Sebastian the elder—a time like that of William the Silent, with its insane civil animosities, which might demand similarly energetic personalities, and offer them similar opportunities And then, it was part of his honest geniality of character to admire those who "get on" in the world. Himself had been, almost from boyhood, in contact with great affairs. A member of the States-General which had taken so hardly the kingly airs of Frederick Henry, he had assisted at the Congress of Munster, and figures conspicuously in Terburgh's picture of that assembly, which had finally established Holland as a first-rate power. The heroism by which the national well-being had been achieved was still of recent memory—the air full of its reverberation, and great movement. There was a tradition to be maintained; the sword by no means resting in its sheath. The age was still fitted to evoke a generous ambition; and this son, from whose natural gifts there was so much to hope for, might play his part, at least as a diplomatist, if the present quiet continued. Had not the learned man said that his natural disposition would lead him out always upon practice? And in truth, the memory of that Silent hero had its fascination for the youth. When, about this time, Peter de Keyser, Thomas's brother, unveiled at last his tomb of wrought bronze and marble in the *Nieuwe Kerk* at Delft, the young Sebastian was one of a small company present, and relished greatly the cold and abstract simplicity of the monument, so conformable to the great, abstract, and unuttered force of the hero who slept beneath.

In complete contrast to all that is abstract or cold, in art, the home of Sebastian, the family mansion of the Storcks—a house, the front of which still survives in one of those patient architectural pieces by Jan van der Heyden—was, in its minute and busy well-being, like an epitome of Holland itself, with all the good-fortune of its "thriving genius" reflected, quite spontaneously, in the national taste. The nation had learned to content itself with a religion which told little, or not at all, on the outsides of things. But we may fancy that something of the religious spirit had gone, according to the law of the transmutation of forces, into the scrupulous care for cleanliness, into the grave, old-world, conservative beauty of Dutch houses, which meant that the life people maintained in them was normally affectionate and pure.

The most curious florists of Holland were ambitious to supply the Burgomaster van Storck with the choicest products of their skill, for the garden spread below the windows on either side of the portico and the central avenue of hoary beeches which led to it. Naturally this house, within a mile of the city of Haarlem, became a resort of the artists, then mixing freely in great society, giving and receiving hints as to the domestic picturesque. Creatures of leisure—of leisure on both sides—they were the appropriate complement of Dutch prosperity, as it was understood just then. Sebastian the elder could almost have wished his son to be one of them: it was the next best thing to being an influential publicist or statesman. The Dutch had just begun to see what a picture their country was—its canals, and *boompjis*, and endless, broadly-lighted meadows, and thousands of miles of quaint water-side: and their painters, the first true masters of landscape for its own sake, were further informing them in the matter. They were bringing proof, for all who cared to see, of the wealth of colour there was all around them in this, supposably, sad land. Above all, they developed the old Low-country taste for interiors. Those innumerable *genre* pieces—conversation, music, play—were in truth the equivalent of novel-reading for that day; its own actual life, in its own proper circumstances, reflected in various degrees of idealisation, with no diminution of the sense of reality (that is to say) but with more and more purged and perfected delightfulness of interest. Themselves illustrating, as every student of their history knows, the good-fellowship of family life, it was the ideal of that life which these artists depicted; the ideal of home in a country where the preponderant interest of life, after all, could not well be out of doors. Of the earth earthy—genuine red earth of the old Adam—it was an ideal very different from that which the sacred Italian painters had evoked from the life of Italy, yet, in its best types, was not without a kind of natural religiousness. And in the achievement of a type of beauty so national and vernacular, the votaries of purely Dutch art might well feel that the Italianisers, like Berghem, Boll, and Jan Weenix, went so far afield in vain.

The fine organisation and acute intelligence of Sebastian would have made him an effective connoisseur of the arts, as he showed by the justice of his remarks in those assemblies of the artists which his father so much loved. But in truth the arts were a matter he could but just tolerate. Why add, by a forced and artificial production, to the monotonous tide of competing, fleeting existences? Only, finding so much fine art actually about him, he was compelled (so to speak) to adjust himself to it; to ascertain and accept that in it which should least collide with, or might even carry forward a little, his own characteristic tendencies. Obviously somewhat jealous of his intellectual interests, he loved inanimate nature, it might have been thought, better than man. He cared nothing, indeed, for the warm sandbanks of Wynants, nor for those eerie relics of ancient woodland which survive in Hobbema and Ruysdael, still less for the highly-coloured sceneries of the academic band at Rome, in spite of the escape they provide one into clear breadth of atmosphere. For though Sebastian van Storck refused to travel, he loved the distant—he enjoyed the sense of things seen from a distance, carrying us, as on wide wings of space itself, far out of one's actual surrounding. His preference in the matter of art was, therefore, for those prospects *à vol d'oiseau*—of the caged bird on the wing at last—of which Rubens had the secret, and still more Philip de Koninck, four of whose choicest works occupied the four walls of his chamber— visionary escapes, north, south, east, and west, into a wide-open though, it must be confessed, a somewhat sullen land. For the fourth of them he had exchanged with his mother a marvellously vivid Metsu, lately bequeathed to him, in which she herself was presented. They were the sole ornaments he permitted himself. From the midst of the busy and busy-looking house, crowded with the furniture and the pretty little toys of many generations, a long passage led the rare visitor up a winding staircase, and (again at the end of a long passage) he found himself as if shut off from the whole talkative Dutch world, and in the embrace of that wonderful quiet, which is also possible in Holland, at its height all around him. It was here that Sebastian could yield himself, with the only sort of love he had ever felt, to the supremacy of his difficult thoughts.—A kind of *empty* place! Here, you felt, all had been mentally put to rights by the working-out of a long equation, which had zero equals zero for its result Here one did, and perhaps felt, nothing; one only thought. Of living creatures only birds came there freely, the sea-birds especially, to attract and detain which there were all sorts of ingenious contrivances about the windows, such as one may see in the cottage sceneries of Jan Steen and others. There was something perhaps of his passion for distance in this welcoming of the creatures of the air. An extreme simplicity in their manner of life, indeed, was charac-teristic of many a distinguished Hollander—William the Silent, Baruch de Spinosa, the brothers de Witt. But the simplicity of Sebastian van Storck was something different from that, and certainly nothing democratic. His mother thought him like one disembarrassing himself carefully, and little by little, of all impediments, habituating himself gradually to make shift with as little as possible, in preparation for a long journey.

The Burgomaster van Storck entertained a party of friends, consist-ing chiefly of his favourite artists, one summer evening. The guests were seen arriving on foot in the fine weather, some of them accompanied by their wives and daughters, against the light of the low sun, falling red on the old trees of the avenue and the faces of those who advanced along it—Willem van Aelst, expecting to find hints for a flower-portrait in the exot-ics which would decorate the banqueting-room; Gerard Dow, to feed his eye, amid all that glittering luxury, on the combat between candle-light and the last rays of the departing sun; Thomas de Keyser, to catch by stealth the likeness of Sebastian the younger. Albert Cuyp was there, who, devel-oping the latent gold in Rembrandt, had brought into his native Dordrecht a heavy wealth of sunshine, as exotic as those flowers or the eastern carpets on the Burgomaster's tables, with Hooch, the in-door Cuyp, and Willem van de Velde, who painted those shore-pieces, with gay ships of war, such as he loved, for his patron's cabinet. Thomas de Keyser came, in company with his brother Peter, his niece, and young Mr. Nicholas Stone from England, pupil of that brother Peter, who afterwards married the niece. For the life of Dutch artists, too, was exemplary in matters of domestic relationship, its history telling many a cheering story of mutual faith in misfortune. Hardly less exemplary was the comradeship which they displayed among themselves, obscuring their best gifts sometimes, one in the mere accessories of another man's work, so that they came together to-night with no fear of falling out, and spoiling the musical interludes of Madame van Storck in the large back parlour. A little way behind the other guests, three of them together, son, grandson, and the grandfather, moving slowly, came the Hondecoeters—Giles, Gybrecht, and Melchior. They led the party before the house was entered, by fading light, to see the curious poultry of the Burgomaster go to roost; and it was almost night when the supper-room was reached at last. The occasion was an important one to Sebastian, and to others through him. For—was it the music of the duets? he asked himself next morning, with a certain distaste as he remembered it all, or the heady Spanish wines poured out so freely in those narrow but deep Venetian glasses?—on this evening he approached more nearly than he had ever yet done to Mademoiselle van Westrheene, as she sat there beside the *clavecin* looking very ruddy and fresh in her white satin, trimmed with glossy crimson swan's down.

So genially attempered, so warm, was life become, in the land of which Pliny had spoken as scarcely dry land at all. And, in truth, the sea which Sebastian so much loved, and with, so great a satisfaction and sense of well-being in every hint of its nearness, is never far distant in Holland. Invading all places, stealing under one's feet, insinuating itself everywhere along an endless network of canals (by no means such formal channels as we understand by the name, but picturesque rivers, with sedgy banks and haunted by innumerable birds) its incidents present themselves oddly even in one's park or woodland walks; the ship in full sail appearing suddenly among the great trees or above the garden wall, where we had no suspicion of the presence of water. In the very conditions of life in such a country there was a standing force of pathos. The country itself shared the uncertainty of the individual human life; and there was pathos also in the constantly renewed, heavily-taxed labour, necessary to keep the native soil, fought for so unselfishly, there at all; with a warfare that must still be maintained when that other struggle with the Spaniard was over. But though Sebastian liked to breathe, so nearly, the sea and its influences, those were considerations he scarcely entertained. In his passion for *Schwindsucht*— we haven't the word—he found it pleasant to think of the resistless element which left one hardly a foot-space amidst the yielding sand; of the old beds of lost rivers, surviving now only as deeper channels in the sea; of the remains of a certain ancient town, which within men's memory had lost its few remaining inhabitants, and, with its already empty tombs, dissolved and disappeared in the flood.

It happened, on occasion of an exceptionally low tide, that some remarkable relics were exposed to view on the coast of the island of Vleeland. A countryman's waggon overtaken by the tide, as he returned with merchandise from the shore! you might have supposed, but for a touch of grace in the construction of the thing—lightly-wrought timber-work, united and adorned by a multitude of brass fastenings, like the work of children for their simplicity, while the rude, stiff, chair, or throne, set upon it, seemed to distinguish it as a chariot of state. To some antiquarians it told the story of the overwhelming of one of the chiefs of the old primeval people of Holland, amid all his gala array, in a great storm. But it was another view which Sebastian preferred; that this object was sepulchral, namely, in its motive— the one surviving relic of a grand burial, in the ancient manner, of a king or hero, whose very tomb was dissolved away.—*Sunt metis metæ!* There came with it the odd fancy that he himself would like to have been dead and gone as long ago, with a kind of envy of those whose deceasing was so long since over.

On more peaceful days he would ponder Pliny's account of those primeval forefathers, but without Pliny's contempt for them. A cloyed Roman might despise their humble existence, fixed by necessity from age to age, and with no desire of change, as "the ocean poured in its flood twice a day, making it uncertain whether the country was a part of the continent or of the sea." But for his part Sebastian found something of poetry in all that, as he conceived what thoughts the old Hollander might have had at his fishing, with nets themselves woven of seaweed, waiting carefully for his drink on the heavy rains, and taking refuge, as the flood rose, on the sand-hills, in a little hut constructed but airily on tall stakes, conformable to the elevation of the highest tides, like a navigator, thought the learned writer, when the sea was risen, like a ship-wrecked mariner when it was retired. For the fancy of Sebastian he lived with great breadths of calm light above and around him, influenced by, and, in a sense, living upon them; and he felt that he might well complain to Pliny's so infinite surprise on being made a Roman citizen.

And certainly Sebastian van Storck did not felicitate his people on the luck which, in the words of another old writer, "hath disposed them to so thriving a genius." Their restless ingenuity in making and maintaining dry land where nature had willed the sea, was even more like the industry of animals than had been that life of their forefathers. Away! with that tetchy, feverish, unworthy agitation, with this and that all too importunate motive of interest! And then, "My son!" said his father, "be stimulated to action!" he, too, thinking of that heroic industry which had triumphed over nature precisely where the contest had been most difficult.

Yet, in truth, Sebastian was forcibly taken by the simplicity of a great affection, as set forth in an incident of real life of which he heard just then. The eminent Grotius being condemned to perpetual imprisonment, his wife determined to share his fate, alleviated only by the reading of books sent by friends. The books, finished, were returned in a great chest. In this chest the wife enclosed the husband, and was able to reply to the objections of the soldiers who carried it, complaining of its weight, with a self-control, which she maintained till the captive was in safety, herself remaining to face the consequences; and there was a kind of absoluteness of affection in that, which attracted Sebastian for a while to ponder on the practical forces which shape men's lives. Had he turned, indeed, to a practical career it would have been less in the direction of the military or political life than of another form of enterprise popular with his countrymen. In the eager, gallant life of that age, if the sword fell for a moment into its sheath, they were for starting off on perilous voyages to the regions of frost and snow in search after that "North-Western passage," for the discovery of which the States-General had offered large rewards. Sebastian, in effect, found a charm in the thought of that still, drowsy, spellbound world of perpetual ice, as in art and life he could always tolerate the sea. Admiral-general of Holland, as painted by Van der Helst, with a marine background by Backhuizen—at moments his father could fancy him so.

There was still another very different sort of character to which Sebastian would let his thoughts stray, without check, for a time. His mother, whom he much resembled outwardly, a Catholic from Brabant, had had saints in her family, and from time to time the mind of Sebastian had been occupied on the subject of monastic life, its quiet, its negation. The portrait of a certain Carthusian prior, which, like the famous statue of Saint Bruno, the first Carthusian, in the church of Santa Maria dei Angeli at Rome, could it have spoken, would have said, "Silence!" kept strange company with the painted visages of men of affairs. A great theological strife was then raging in Holland. Grave ministers of religion assembled sometimes, like the painted scene by Rembrandt, in the Burgomaster's house, and once, not however in their company, came a renowned young Jewish divine, Baruch de Spinosa, with whom, most unexpectedly, Sebastian found himself in sympathy, meeting the young Jew's far-reaching thoughts half-way, to the confirmation of his own; and he did not know that his visitor, very ready with the pencil, had taken his likeness as they talked on the fly-leaf of his notebook. Alive to that theological disturbance in the air all around him, he refused to be moved by it, as essentially a strife on small matters, anticipating a vagrant regret which may have visited many other minds since, the regret, namely, that the old, pensive, use-and-wont Catholicism, which had accompanied the nation's earlier struggle for existence, and consoled it therein, had been taken from it. And for himself, indeed, what impressed him in that old Catholicism was a kind of lull in it—a lulling power—like that of the monotonous organ-music, which Holland, Catholic or not, still so greatly loves. But what he could not away with in the Catholic religion was its unfailing drift towards the concrete—the positive imageries of a faith, so richly beset with persons, things, historical incidents.

Rigidly logical in the method of his inferences, he attained the poetic quality only by the audacity with which he conceived the whole sublime extension of his premises. The contrast was a strange one between the careful, the almost petty, fineness of his personal surrounding—all the elegant conventionalities of life, in that rising Dutch family—and the mortal coldness of a temperament, the intellectual tendencies of which seemed to necessitate straightforward flight from all that was positive. He seemed, if one may say so, in love with death; preferring winter to summer; finding only a tranquillising influence in the thought of the earth beneath our feet cooling down for ever from its old cosmic heat; watching pleasurably how their colours fled out of things, and the long sandbank in the sea, which had been the rampart of a town, was washing down in its turn. One of his acquaintance, a penurious young poet, who, having nothing in his pockets but the imaginative or otherwise barely potential gold of manuscript verses, would have grasped so eagerly, had they lain within his reach, at the elegant outsides of life, thought the fortunate Sebastian, possessed of every possible opportunity of that kind, yet bent only on dispensing with it, certainly a most puzzling and comfortless creature. A few only, half discerning what was in his mind, would fain have shared his intellectual clearness, and found a kind of attractive beauty in this youthful enthusiasm for an abstract theorem. Extremes meeting, his cold and dispassionate detachment from all that is most attractive to ordinary minds came to have the impressiveness of a great passion. And for the most part, people had loved him; feeling instinctively that somewhere there must be the justification of his difference from themselves. It was like being in love: or it was an intellectual malady, such as pleaded for forbearance, like bodily sickness, and gave at times a resigned and touching sweetness to what he did and said. Only once, at a moment of the wild popular excitement which at that period was easy to provoke in Holland, there was a certain group of persons who would have shut him up as no well-wisher to, and perhaps a plotter against, the common weal. A single traitor might cut the dykes in an hour, in the interest of the English or the French. Or, had he already committed some treasonable act, who was so anxious to expose no writing of his that he left his letters unsigned, and there were little stratagems to get specimens of his fair manuscript? For with all his breadth of mystic intention, he was anxious, as the hours crept on, to leave all the inevitable details of life at least in order, in equation. And all his singularities appeared to be summed up in his refusal to take his place in the life-sized family group, painted—*très distingué et très soigné*—remarks a modern critic of the work, about this time. His mother expostulated with him on the matter:—she must needs feel, a little icily, the emptiness of hope, and something more than the due measure of cold in things for a woman of her age, in the person of a son who desired but to fade out of the world like a breath—and she suggested filial duty. "Good mother," he answered, "there are duties towards the intellect also, which women can but rarely understand."

The artists and their wives were come to supper again, with the Burgomaster van Storck. Mademoiselle van Westrheene was also come, with her sister and mother. The girl was by this time fallen in love with Sebastian; and, she was one of the few who, in spite of his terrible coldness, really loved him for himself. But though of good birth she was poor, while Sebastian could not but perceive that he had many suitors of his wealth. In truth, Madame van Westrheene, her mother, did wish to marry this daughter into the great world, and plied many arts to that end, such as "daughterful" mothers use. Her healthy freshness of mien and mind, her ruddy beauty, some showy presents that had passed, were of a piece with the ruddy colouring of the very house these people lived in; and for a moment the cheerful warmth that may be felt in life seemed to come very close to him,— to come forth, and enfold him. Meantime the girl herself taking note of this, and that on a former occasion of their meeting he had seemed likely to respond to her inclination, and that his father would readily consent to such a marriage, surprised him on the sudden with those coquetries and importunities, all those little arts of love, which often succeed with men. Only, to Sebastian they seemed opposed to that absolute nature we suppose in love. And while, in the eyes of all around him to-night, this courtship seemed to promise him, thus early in life, a kind of quiet happiness, he was coming to an estimate of the situation, with regard to that ideal of a calm, intellectual indifference, of which he was the sworn chevalier. Set in the cold, hard light of that, this girl, with the pronounced personal views of her mother, and in the very effectiveness of arts prompted by a real affection, bringing the warm life they prefigured so close to him, seemed vulgar! And still he felt himself bound in honour; or judged from their manner that she and those about them thought him thus bound. He did not reflect on the inconsistency of the feeling of honour (living, as it does essentially, upon the concrete and minute detail of social relationship) for one who, on principle, set so slight a value on anything, whatever that is merely relative in its character.

The guests growing late and lively, were almost pledging the betrothed in the rich wine. Only Sebastian's mother knew; and at that advanced hour, while the company were thus intently occupied, drew away the Burgomaster to confide to him the misgiving she felt, grown to a great height just then. The young man had slipped from the assembly; but certainly not with Mademoiselle van Westrheene, who was suddenly withdrawn also. And she never appeared again in the world. Already, next day, with the rumour that Sebastian had left his home, it was known that the expected marriage would not take place. The girl, indeed, alleged something in the way of a cause on her part; but seemed to fade away continually afterwards, and in the eyes of all who saw her was like one perishing of wounded pride. But to make a clean breast of her poor girlish worldliness, before she became a *béguine*, she confessed to her mother the receipt of the letter—the cruel letter that had killed her. And in effect, the first copy of this letter, written with a very deliberate fineness, rejecting her—accusing her, so natural, and simply loyal! of a vulgar coarseness of character—was found, oddly tacked on, as their last word, to the studious record of the abstract thoughts which had been the real business of Sebastian's life, in the room whither his mother went to seek him next day, littered with the fragments of the one portrait of him in existence.

The neat and elaborate manuscript volume, of which this letter formed the final page (odd transition! by which a train of thought so abstract drew its conclusion in the sphere of action) afforded at length to the few who were interested in him a much-coveted insight into the curiosity of his existence; and I pause just here to indicate in outline the kind of reasoning through which, making the "Infinite" his beginning and his end, Sebastian had come to think all definite forms of being, the warm pressure of life, the cry of humanity itself, no more than a troublesome irritation of the surface of the one absolute mind, a passing vexatious thought or uneasy dream there, at its height of petulant importunity in the eager, human creature.

The volume was, indeed, a kind of treatise to be; a hard, systematic, well-concatenated train of thought, still implicated in the circumstances of a journal. Liberated from the accidents of that particular form with its unavoidable details of place and occasion, the theoretic strain would have been found mathematically continuous. The already so weary Sebastian might perhaps never have taken in hand, or succeeded in, this detachment of his thoughts; every one of which, beginning with himself, as the peculiar and intimate apprehension of this or that particular day and hour, seemed still to protest against such disturbance, as if reluctant to part from those accidental associations of the personal history which had prompted it, and become a purely intellectual abstraction.

The series began with Sebastian's boyish enthusiasm for a strange, fine saying of Doctor Baruch de Spinosa, concerning the Divine Love— That whoso loveth God truly must not expect to be loved by Him in return. In mere reaction against an actual surrounding of which every circumstance tended to make him a finished egotist, that bold assertion defined for him the ideal of an intellectual disinterestedness, of a domain of unimpassioned mind, with the desire to put one's subjective side out of the way, and let pure reason speak.

And what pure reason affirmed in the first place, as the "beginning of wisdom," was that the world is but a thought, or series of thoughts; that it exists, therefore, solely in mind. It showed him, as he fixed the mental eye with more and more of self-absorption on the facts of his intellectual existence, a picture or vision of the universe as actually the product, so far as he really knew it, of his own lonely thinking power—of himself, there, thinking: as being zero without him: and as possessing a perfectly homogeneous unity in that. "Things that have nothing in common with each other," said the axiomatic reason, "cannot be understood or explained by means of each other." But to pure reason things discovered themselves as being in their essence thought: all things, even the most opposite things, mere transmutations of a single power—the power of thought. All was but conscious mind. Therefore, all the more exclusively, he must minister to mind, to the intellectual power submitting himself to the sole direction of that, whithersoever it might lead him. Everything must be referred to, and, as it were, changed into the terms of that, if its essential value was to be ascertained. "Joy," he said, anticipating Spinosa—that, for the attainment

of which men are ready to surrender all beside—"is but the name of a passion, in which the mind passes to a greater perfection or power of thinking; as grief of the passion, in which it passes to a less."

Looking backward for the generative source of that creative power
of thought in him, from himself to the cause of his mysterious intellectual
being, he still reflected, as one can but do the enlarged pattern of himself,
into the vague region of hypothesis. In this way, some, at all events, would
have explained his mental process. To him it was nothing less than the
apprehension, the revelation, of the greatest and most real of ideas—the
true substance of all things. He, too, with his vividly-coloured existence,
with this picturesque and sensuous world of Dutch art and Dutch reality
all around, which would fain have made him the prisoner of its colours, its
genial warmth, its struggle for life, its selfish and crafty love, was but a
transient perturbation of the one absolute mind; of which, indeed, all finite
things whatever, time itself, the most durable achievements of nature and
man, and all that seems most like independent energy, are no more than
petty accidents or affections. Theorem and corollary! Thus they stood:

"*There can be only one substance:* (corollary): the greatest of errors
is to think that the non-existent, the world of finite things seen and felt,
really is: (theorem): *for, whatever is, is but in that:* (practical corollary): one's
wisdom, therefore, consists in hastening, so far as may be, the action of
those forces which tend to the restoration of equilibrium, to the calm surface of the absolute, untroubled mind, to *tabula rasa*, by the extinction in
one's self of all that is but correlative to the finite illusion—by the suppression of ourselves."

In the loneliness which was gathering round him, and oddly enough
as a somewhat surprising thing, he wondered whether there were, or had
been others, possessed of like thoughts, ready to welcome any such as his
veritable compatriots. And, in fact, he became aware just then, in readings difficult indeed, but which their absorbing interest caused to seem
almost like an illicit pleasure, a sense of kinship with certain older minds.
The study of many an earlier adventurous theorist satisfied his curiosity
as the record of daring physical adventure, for instance, might satisfy the
curiosity of the healthy. It was a tradition—a constant tradition—that daring
thought of his; an echo, or haunting, recurrent voice of the human soul

itself, and as such sealed with natural truth, which certain minds would not fail to heed; discerning also, if they were really loyal to themselves, its practical conclusion.—The one alone is: and all things beside are but its passing affections, which have no proper right to be.

As but its accidents or affections, indeed, there might have been found, within the circumference of that one infinite thinker, some scope for the joy and love of the creature. There have been dispositions in which that abstract theorem has only induced a renewed value for the finite interests around and within us. Centre of heat and light, truly nothing has seemed to lie beyond the touch of its perpetual summer. It has allied itself to the poetical or artistic sympathy, which feels challenged to acquaint itself with and explore the various forms of finite existence all the more intimately, just because of that sense of one lively spirit circulating through all things— a tiny particle of the one soul in the sunbeam, or the leaf. Sebastian van Storck, on the contrary, was determined, perhaps, by some inherited satiety and fatigue in his nature, to the opposite issue of the practical dilemma. For him, that one abstract being was as the pallid arctic sun, disclosing itself over the dead level of a glacial, a barren and absolutely lonely sea. The lively purpose of life had been frozen out of it. What he must admire, and love if he could, was "equilibrium," the void, the *tabula rasa*, into which, through all those apparent energies of man and nature which, in truth, are but forces of disintegration, the world was really settling. And, himself a mere circumstance in a fatalistic series, to which the clay of the potter was no adequate parallel, he could not expect to be "loved in return." At first, indeed, he had a kind of delight in his thoughts—in the eager pressure forward, to whatsoever conclusion, of a rigid intellectual gymnastic, which was like the making of Euclid. Only, little by little, under the freezing influence of the propositions themselves, the theoretic vitality itself, and with it his old eagerness for truth, the care to track it from proposition to proposition, was chilled out of him. And, in fact, the conclusion was there already, might be foreseen, in the premises. By a singular perversity, it seemed to him that every one of those passing affections—himself, alas! at times—was for ever trying to be—to assert itself; to maintain its isolated and petty self, by a kind of practical lie in things; although through every incident of its hypothetic existence it had protested that its proper function was to die. Surely! those transient affections marred the freedom, the truth, the beatific calm, of the absolute selfishness, which could not, if it would, pass beyond the circumference of itself; to which, at times, with a fantastic sense of well-being, he found himself capable of a kind of fanatical devotion. And those, as he conceived, were his moments of genuine theoretic insight, in which, under the abstract "light perpetual," he died to self; while yet the intellect, after all, had attained a freedom of its own, through the vigorous act which assured him that as nature was but a thought of his, so himself also was but the passing thought of God.

No! rather a puzzle only—an anomaly—upon that one, white, unruffled consciousness! His first principle once recognised, all the rest, the whole array of propositions down to the heartless practical conclusion, must follow of themselves. Detachment: to hasten hence: to fold up one's whole self, as a vesture put aside: to anticipate, by such individual force as he could find in him, the slow disintegration by which nature herself is levelling the eternal hills,—here would be the secret of peace, of such dignity and truth as there could be in a world which after all was essentially an illusion. For Sebastian, at least, the world and the individual alike had been divested of all effective purpose. The most vivid of finite objects, the dramatic episodes of Dutch history, the brilliant personalities which had found their parts to play in them, that golden art, surrounding one with an ideal world, beyond which the real world was discernible indeed, but etherealised by the medium through which it came to one; all this, for most men so powerful a link to existence, only set him on the thought of escape—means of escape—into a formless and nameless infinite world, evenly gray. The very emphasis of those objects, their importunity to the eye, the ear, the finite intelligence, was but the measure of their distance from what really is. One's personal presence, the presence, such as it is, of the most incisive things and persons around one, could only lessen by so much, that which really is. To restore *tabula rasa*, then, by a continual effort at self-efface-ment! Actually proud, at times, of his curious, well-reasoned nihilism, he could but regard what is called the business of life as no better than a trifling and wearisome delay. Bent on making sacrifice of the rich life possible for him (as he would readily have sacrificed that of other people) to the bare and formal logic of the reply to a query, not proposed at all by entirely healthy minds, regarding the remote conditions and tendencies of that life, he did not reflect that if others had inquired as curiously as himself the world could never have come so far at all—that the fact of its having come so far was itself a weighty exception to his hypothesis. His fantastic devotion, soaring into fanaticism, into a kind of religious mania, with what was really a vehement assertion of his individual will, he had formulated duty as the principle to hinder as little as possible what he called the restoration of equilibrium, of the primary consciousness to itself—its relief from that uneasy, tetchy, unworthy dream of a world, made so ill, or dreamt so weakly—to forget to be forgotten.

And at length this dark fanaticism, losing the support of his pride in the mere novelty of a reasoning so hard and dry, turned round upon him, as our fanaticism will, in black melancholy. The theoretic, or imaginative, desire to urge Time's creeping footsteps, was felt now as the physical fatigue which leaves the book or the letter unfinished, or finishes eagerly out of hand, for mere finishing's sake, unimportant business. Strange! that the presence to the mind of a metaphysical abstraction should have had this power over one so fortunately endowed for the reception of the sensible world. It could hardly have been so with him but for the concurrence of physical causes with the influences proper to a mere thought. The moralist, indeed, might have noted that a kind of pride, a morbid fear of vulgarity, lent secret strength to the intellectual prejudice, which realised duty as the renunciation of all finite objects, the fastidious refusal to be or do any limited thing. But beyond this, it was legible in his own admissions from time to time, that the body, following, as it does with powerful temperaments, the lead of mind and the will, the intellectual consumption (so to term it) had been concurrent with, strengthened and was strengthened by, a vein of physical *phthisis*—by a merely physical accident, after all, of his bodily constitution; which might have taken a different turn, had another accident fixed his home among the hills instead of on the shore. Is it only the result of disease? he would ask himself sometimes with a sudden suspicion of his intellectual cogency—this persuasion that myself, and all that surrounds me, are but a diminution of that which really is?—this unkindly melancholy?

The journal, with that "cruel" letter to Mademoiselle van Westrheene coming as the last step in the rigid process of theoretic deduction, circulated among the curious; and people made their judgments upon it. There were some who held that such opinions should be suppressed by law; that they were, or might become, dangerous to society. Perhaps it was the confessor of his mother who thought of the matter most justly. The aged man smiled, observing how, even for minds by no means superficial, the mere dress it wears alters the look of a familiar thought—with a happy sort of smile as he added (reflecting that the truth of Sebastian's apprehension was duly covered by the propositions of his own creed, and quoting Sebastian's favourite pagan wisdom from the lips of Saint Paul) "In Him, we live, and move, and have our being."

Next day, as Sebastian escaped to the sea under the long, monotonous line of wind-mills, in comparative calm of mind—reaction of that pleasant morning from the madness of the night before—he was making light, or trying to make light, with some success, of his late distress. He would fain have thought it a small matter, to be adequately set at rest for him by certain well-tested influences of external nature, in a long visit to the place he liked best: a desolate house, amid the sands of the Helder, one of the old lodgings of his family, property now, rather, of the sea-birds, and almost surrounded by the encroaching tide; though there were still relics enough of hardy, sweet things about it, to form what was to Sebastian the most perfect garden in Holland. Here he could make "equation" between himself and what was not himself, and set things in order, in preparation towards such deliberate and final change in his manner of living as circumstances so clearly necessitated.

As he stayed in this place, with one or two silent serving people, a sudden rising of the wind altered, as it might seem, in a few dark, tempestuous hours, the entire world around him. The strong wind changed not again for fourteen days; and its effect was a permanent one; so that people might have fancied that an enemy had indeed cut the dykes somewhere—a pin-hole enough to wreck the ship of Holland or at least this portion of it, which underwent an inundation of the sea the like of which had not occurred in that province for half a century. Only, when the body of Sebastian was found, apparently not long after death, a child lay asleep, swaddled warmly in his heavy furs, in an upper room of the old tower, to which the tide was almost risen; though the building still stood firmly, and still with the means of life in plenty. And it was in the saving of this child, with a great effort, as certain circumstances seemed to indicate, that Sebstian had lost his life.

His parents were come to seek him, believing him bent on self-destruction, and were almost glad to find him thus. A learned physician, moreover, endeavoured to comfort his mother by remarking that in any case he must certainly have died ere many years were passed, slowly, perhaps painfully, of a disease then coming into the world; disease begotten by the fogs of that country—waters, he observed, not in their place, "above the firmament"—on people grown somewhat over-delicate in their nature by the effects of modern luxury.

IV

DUKE CARL OF ROSENMOLD

ONE STORMY SEASON ABOUT THE BEGINNING OF THE PRESENT CENTURY, A GREAT
tree came down among certain moss-covered ridges of old masonry which
break the surface of the Rosenmold heath, exposing, together with its roots,
the remains of two persons. Whether the bodies (male and female, said
German bone-science) had been purposely buried there was questionable.
They seemed rather to have been hidden away by the accident, whatever it
was, which had caused death—crushed, perhaps, under what had been the
low wall of a garden—being much distorted, and lying, though neatly enough
discovered by the upheaval of the soil, in great confusion. People's attention was the more attracted to the incident because popular fancy had
long run upon a tradition of buried treasures, golden treasures, in or about
the antiquated ruin which the garden boundary enclosed; the roofless shell
of a small but solidly-built stone house, burnt or overthrown, perhaps in
the time of the wars at the beginning of the eighteenth century. Many persons went to visit the remains lying out on the dark, wild *plateau*, which
stretches away above the tallest roofs of the old grand-ducal town, very
distinctly outlined, on that day, in deep fluid gray against a sky still heavy
with coming rain. No treasure, indeed, was forthcoming among the masses
of fallen stone. But the tradition was so far verified, that the bones had
rich golden ornaments about them; and for the minds of some long-re-

membering people their discovery set at rest an old query. It had never been precisely known what was become of the young Duke Carl, who disappeared from the world just a century before, about the time when a great army passed over those parts, at a political crisis, one issue of which was the final absorption of his small territory in a neighbouring dominion. Restless, romantic, eccentric, had he passed on with the victorious host, and taken the chances of an obscure soldier's life? Certain old letters hinted at a different ending,—love-letters which provided for a secret meeting, preliminary perhaps to the final departure of the young Duke (who, by the usage of his realm, could only with extreme difficulty go whither, or marry whom, he pleased) to whatever worlds he had chosen, not of his own people. The minds of those still interested in the matter were now at last made up, the disposition of the remains suggesting to them the lively picture of a sullen night, the unexpected passing of the great army, and the two lovers rushing forth wildly, at the sudden tumult outside their cheerful shelter, caught in the dark and trampled out so, surprised and unseen, among the horses and heavy guns.

Time, at the court of the Grand-duke of Rosenmold, at the beginning of the eighteenth century, might seem to have been standing still almost since the Middle Age—since the days of the Emperor Charles the Fifth, at which period, by the marriage of the hereditary Grand-duke with a princess of the Imperial house, a sudden tide of wealth, flowing through the grand-ducal exchequer, had left a kind of golden architectural splendour on the place, always too ample for its population. The sloping Gothic roofs for carrying off the heavy snows still indented the sky—a world of tiles, with space uncurtailed for the awkward gambols of that very German goblin, Hans Klapper, on the long, slumberous, northern nights. Whole quarryfuls of wrought stone had been piled along the streets and around the squares, and were now grown, in truth, like nature's self again, in their rough, time-worn massiveness, with weeds and wild flowers where their decay accumulated, blossoming, always the same, beyond people's memories, every summer, as the storks came back to their platforms on the remote chimney-tops. Without, all was as it had been on the eve of the Thirty Years' War: the venerable dark-green mouldiness, priceless pearl of architectural effect, was unbroken by a single new gable. And within, human life—its thoughts, its habits, above all, its etiquette—had been put out by no matter of excitement, political or intellectual, ever at all, one might say, at any time. The rambling grand-ducal palace was full to overflowing with furniture, which, useful or useless, was all ornamental, and none of it new. Suppose the various objects, especially the contents of the haunted old lumber-rooms, duly arranged and ticketed, and their Highnesses would have had a historic museum, after which those famed "Green Vaults" at Dresden would hardly have counted as one of the glories of Augustus the Strong. An immense heraldry, that truly German vanity, had grown, expatiating, florid, eloquent, over everything, without and within—windows, house-fronts, church walls, and church floors. And one-half of the male inhabitants were big or little State functionaries, mostly of a *quasi* decorative order—the treble-singer to the town-council, the court organist, the court poet, and the like—each with his deputies and assistants, maintaining, all unbroken, a sleepy ceremonial, to make the hours just noticeable as they slipped away. At court, with a continuous round of ceremonies, which, though early in the day, must always take place under a jealous exclusion of the sun, one seemed to live in perpetual candle-light.

It was in a delightful rummaging of one of those lumber-rooms, escaped from that candle-light into the broad day of the upper-most windows, that the young Duke Carl laid his hand on an old volume of the year 1486, printed in heavy type, with frontispiece, perhaps, by Albert Dürer—*Ars Versificandi: The Art of Versification:* by Conrad Celtes. Crowned poet of the Emperor Frederick the Third, he had the right to speak on that subject; for while he vindicated as best he might old German literature against the charge of barbarism, he did also a man's part towards reviving in the Fatherland the knowledge of the poetry of Greece and Rome; and for Carl, the pearl, the golden nugget, of the volume was the Sapphic ode with which it closed—*To Apollo, praying that he would come to us from Italy, bringing his lyre with him: Ad Apolloninem, ut ab Italis cum lyra ad Germanos veniat.* The god of light, coming to Germany from some more favoured world beyond it, over leagues of rainy hill and mountain, making soft day there: that had ever been the dream of the ghost-ridden yet deep-feeling and certainly meek German soul; of the great Dürer, for instance, who had been the friend of this Conrad Celtes, and himself, all German as he was, like a gleam of real day amid that hyperborean German darkness—a darkness which clave to him, too, at that dim time, when there were violent robbers, nay, real live devils, in every German wood. And it was precisely the aspiration of Carl himself. Those verses, coming to the boy's hand at the right moment, brought a beam of effectual daylight to a whole magazine of observation, fancy, desire, stored up from the first impressions of childhood. To bring Apollo with his lyre to Germany! It was precisely what he, Carl, desired to do—was, as he might flatter himself, actually doing.

The daylight, the Apolline aurora, which the young Duke Carl claimed to be bringing to his candle-lit people, came in the somewhat questionable form of the contemporary French ideal, in matters of art and literature—French plays, French architecture, French looking-glasses—Apollo in the dandified costume of Lewis the Fourteenth. Only, confronting the essentially aged and decrepit graces of his model with his own essentially youthful temper, he invigorated what he borrowed; and with him an aspiration towards the classical ideal, so often hollow and insincere, lost all its affectation. His doating grandfather, the reigning Grand-duke, afforded readily enough, from the great store of inherited wealth which would one day be the lad's, the funds necessary for the completion of the vast unfinished Residence, with "pavilions" (after the manner of the famous Mansard) uniting its scattered parts; while a wonderful flowerage of architectural fancy, with broken attic roofs, passed over and beyond the earlier fabric; the later and lighter forms being in part carved adroitly out of the heavy masses of the old, honest, "stump-Gothic" tracery. One fault only Carl found in his French models, and was resolute to correct. He would have, at least within, real marble in place of stucco, and, if he might, perhaps solid gold for gilding. There was something in the sanguine, floridly handsome youth, with his alertness of mind turned wholly, amid the vexing preoccupations of an age of war, upon embellishment, and the softer things of life, which soothed the testy humours of the old Duke, like the quiet physical warmth of a fire or the sun. He was ready to preside with all ceremony at a presentation of Marivaux's *Death of Hannibal*, played in the original, with such imperfect mastery of the French accent as the lovers of new light in Rosenmold had at command, in a theatre copied from that at Versailles, lined with pale yellow satin, and with a picture, amid the stucco braveries of the ceiling, of the Septentrional Apollo himself, in somewhat watery red and blue. Innumerable waxlights in cut-glass lustres were a thing of course. Duke Carl himself, attired after the newest French fashion, played the part of Hannibal. The old Duke, indeed, at a council-board devoted hitherto to matters of state, would nod very early in certain long discussions on matters of art—magnificent schemes, from this or that eminent contractor, for spending his money tastefully, distinguishings of the *rococo* and the *baroque*. On the other hand, having been all his life in close intercourse with select humanity, self-conscious, and arrayed for presentation, he was a helpful judge of portraits and the various degrees of the attainment of truth therein—a phase of fine art which the grandson could not value too much. The sergeant-painter and the deputy sergeant-painter were, indeed, conventional performers enough; as mechanical in their dispensation of wigs, finger-rings, ruffles, and simpers, as the figure of the armed knight who struck the bell in the Residence tower. But scattered through its half-deserted rooms, state bed-chambers and the like, hung the works of more genuine masters, still as unadulterate as the hock, known to be two generations old, in the grand-ducal cellar. The youth had even his scheme of inviting the illustrious Antony Coppel to the court; to live there, if he would, with the honours and emoluments of a prince of the blood. The illustrious Mansard had actually promised to come, had not his sudden death taken him away from earthly glory.

And at least, if one must forego the masters, masterpieces might be had for their price. For ten thousand marks—day ever to be remembered—a genuine work of "the Urbinate," from the cabinet of a certain commercially-minded Italian grand-duke, was on its way to Rosenmold, anxiously awaited as it came over rainy mountain-passes and along the rough German roads, through doubtful weather. The tribune, the throne itself, were made ready in the presence-chamber, with hangings in the grand-ducal colours, laced with gold, together with a speech and an ode. Late at night, at last, the waggon was heard rumbling into the courtyard, with the guest arrived in safety, but, if one must confess one's self, perhaps forbidding at first sight. From a comfortless portico, with all the grotesqueness of the Middle Age, supported by brown, aged bishops, whose meditations no incident could distract, Our Lady looked out no better than an unpretending nun, with nothing to say the like of which one was used to hear. Certainly one was not stimulated by, enwrapped, absorbed in the great master's doings; only, with much private disappointment, put on one's mettle to defend him against critics notoriously wanting in sensibility, and against one's self. In truth, the painter whom Carl most unaffectedly enjoyed, the real vigour of his youthful and somewhat animal taste finding here its proper sustenance, was Rubens—Rubens reached, as he is reached at his best, in well-preserved family portraits, fresh, gay, ingenuous, as of privileged young people who could never grow old. Had not he, too, brought something of the splendour of a "better land" into those northern regions; if not the glowing gold of Titian's Italian sun, yet the carnation and yellow of roses or tulips, such as might really grow there with cultivation, even under rainy skies? And then, about this time something was heard at the grand-ducal court of certain mysterious experiments in the making of porcelain; veritable alchemy, for the turning of clay into gold. The reign of Dresden china was at hand, with one's own world of little men and women, more delightfully diminutive still, amid imitations of artificial flowers. The young Duke braced himself for a plot to steal the gifted Herr Böttcher from his enforced residence, as if in prison, at the fortress of Meissen. Why not bring pots and wheels to Rosenmold, and prosecute his discoveries there? The Grand-duke, indeed, preferred his old service of gold plate, and would have had the lad a *virtuoso* in nothing less costly than gold—gold snuff-boxes!

For, in truth, regarding what belongs to art or culture, as elsewhere, we may have a large appetite and little to feed on. Only, in the things of the mind, the appetite itself counts for so much, at least in hopeful, unobstructed youth, with the world before it. "You are the Apollo you tell us of, the northern Apollo," people were beginning to say to him, surprised from time to time by a mental purpose beyond their guesses—expressions, liftings, softly gleaming or vehement lights, in the handsome countenance of the youth, and his effective speech, as he roamed, inviting all about him to share the honey, from music to painting, from painting to the drama, all alike florid in style, yes! and perhaps third-rate. And so far consistently throughout he had held that the centre of one's intellectual system must be understood to be in France. He had thoughts of proceeding to that country, secretly, in person, there to attain the very impress of its genius.

Meantime, its more portable flowers came to order in abundance. That the roses, so to put it, were but excellent artificial flowers, redolent only of musk, neither disproved for Carl the validity of his ideal nor for our minds the vocation of Carl himself in these matters. In art, as in all other things of the mind, again, much depends on the receiver; and the higher informing capacity, if it exist within, will mould an unpromising matter to itself, will realise itself by selection, and the preference of the better in what is bad or indifferent, asserting its prerogative under the most un-likely conditions. People had in Carl, could they have understood it, the spectacle, under those superficial braveries, of a really heroic effort of mind at a disadvantage. That *rococo* seventeenth-century French imitation of the true Renaissance, called out in Carl a boundless enthusiasm, as the Italian original had done two centuries before. He put into his reception of the æsthetic achievements of Lewis the Fourteenth what young France had felt when Francis I. brought home the great Da Vinci and his works. It was but himself truly, after all, that he had found, so fresh and real, among those artificial roses.

He was thrown the more upon such outward and sensuous products of mind—architecture, pottery, presently on music—because for him, with so large intellectual capacity, there was, to speak properly, no literature in his mother-tongue. Books there were, German books, but of a dulness, a distance from the actual interests of the warm, various, coloured life around and within him, to us hardly conceivable. There was more entertainment in the natural train of his own solitary thoughts, humoured and rightly attuned by pleasant visible objects, than in all the books he had hunted through so carefully for that all-searching intellectual light, of which a pass-ing gleam of interest gave fallacious promise here or there. And still, gen-erously, he held to the belief, urging him to fresh endeavour, that the literature which might set heart and mind free must exist somewhere, though court librarians could not say where. In search for it he spent many days in those old book-closets where he had lighted on the Latin ode of Conrad Celtes. Was German literature always to remain no more than a kind of penal apparatus for the teasing of the brain? Oh! for a literature set free, conterminous with the interests of life itself.

In music, it might be thought, Germany had already vindicated its spiritual liberty. One and another of those North German towns were already aware of the youthful Sebastian Bach. The first notes had been heard of a music not borrowed from France, but flowing, as naturally as springs from their sources, out of the ever musical soul of Germany itself. And the Duke Carl was a sincere lover of music, himself playing melodiously on the violin to a delighted court. That new Germany of the spirit would be builded, perhaps, to the sound of music. In those other artistic enthusiasms, as the prophet of the French drama or the architectural taste of Lewis the Fourteenth, he had contributed himself generously, helping out with his own good faith the inadequacy of their appeal. Music alone hitherto had really helped *him*, and taken him out of himself. To music, instinctively, more and more he devoted himself; and in his desire to refine and organise the court music, from which, by leave of absence to official performers enjoying their salaries at a distance, many parts had literally fallen away, like the favourite notes of a worn-out spinet, he was ably seconded by a devoted youth, the deputy organist of the grand-ducal chapel. A member of the Roman Church amid a people chiefly of the Reformed religion, Duke Carl would creep sometimes into the curtained court pew of the Lutheran church, to which he had presented its massive golden crucifix, to listen to the *chorales*, the execution of which he had managed to time to his liking, relishing, he could hardly explain why, those passages of a pleasantly monotonous and unending melody, as it might seem,— which certainly never came to what could rightly be called an ending here on earth; and having also a sympathy with the cheerful genius of Dr. Martin Luther, with his good tunes, and that ringing laughter which sent dull goblins flitting.

At this time, then, his mind ran eagerly for awhile on the project of some musical and dramatic development of a fancy suggested by that old Latin poem of Conrad Celtes—the hyperborean Apollo, sojourning, in the revolutions of time, in the sluggish north for a season, yet Apollo still, prompting art, music, poetry, and the philosophy which interprets man's life, making a sort of intercalary day amid the natural darkness; not meridian day, of course, but a soft derivative daylight, good enough for us. It would be necessarily a mystic piece, abounding in fine touches, suggestions, innuendoes. His vague proposal was met half-way by the very practical executant power of his friend or servant, the deputy organist, already pondering, with just a satiric flavour (suppressible in actual performance, if the time for that should ever come) a musical work on Duke Carl himself; *Balder, an Interlude*. He was contented to recast and enlarge the part of the northern god of light, with a now wholly serious intention. But still, the near, the real and familiar, gave precision to, or actually superseded, the distant and the ideal. The soul of the music was but a transfusion from the fantastic but so interesting creature close at hand. And Carl was certainly true to his proposed part in that he gladdened others by an intellectual radiance which had ceased to mean warmth or animation for himself. For him the light was still to seek in France, in Italy, above all in old Greece, amid the precious things which might yet be lurking there unknown, in art, in poetry, perhaps in very life, till Prince Fortunate should come.

Yes! it was thither, to Greece, that his thoughts were turned during those romantic classical musings while the opera was made ready. That, in due time, was presented, with sufficient success. Meantime, his purpose was grown definite to visit that original country of the Muses, from which the pleasant things of Italy had been but derivative; to brave the difficulties in the way of leaving home at all, the difficulties also of access to Greece, in the present condition of the country.

At times the fancy came that he must really belong by descent to a southern race, that a physical cause might lie beneath this strange restlessness, like the imperfect reminiscence of something that had passed in earlier life. The aged ministers of heraldry were set to work (actually prolonging their days by an unexpected revival of interest in their too well-worn function) at the search for some obscure rivulet of Greek descent— later Byzantine Greek, perhaps,—in the Rosenmold genealogy. No! with a hundred quarterings, they were as indigenous, incorruptible heraldry reasserted, as the old yew-trees asquat on the heath.

And meantime those dreams of distant and probably adventurous travel lent the youth, still so healthy of body, a wing for more distant expeditions than he had ever yet inclined to, among his own wholesome German woodlands. In long rambles, afoot or on horseback, by day and night, he flung himself, for the resettling of his sanity, on the cheerful influences of their simple imagery; the hawks, as if asleep on the air below him; the bleached crags, evoked by late sunset among the dark oaks; the water-wheels, with their pleasant murmur, in the foldings of the hillside.

Clouds came across his heaven, little sudden clouds, like those which in this northern latitude, where summer is at best but a flighty guest, chill out the heart, though but for a few minutes at a time, of the warmest afternoon. He had fits of the gloom of other people—their dull passage through and exit from the world, the threadbare incidents of their lives, their dismal funerals—which, unless he drove them away immediately by strenuous exercise, settled into a gloom more properly his own. Yet at such times outward things also would seem to concur unkindly in deepening the mental shadow about him, almost as if there were indeed animation in the natural world, elfin spirits in those inaccessible hillsides and dark ravines, as old German poetry pretended, assistant cheerfully sometimes, but for the most part troublesome, to their human kindred. Of late these fits had come somewhat more frequently, and had continued. Often it was a weary, deflowered face that his favourite mirrors reflected. Yes! people were prosaic, and their lives threadbare—all but himself and organist Max, perhaps, and Fritz the treble-singer. In return, the people in actual contact with him thought him a little mad, though still ready to flatter his madness, as he could detect. Alone with the doating old grandfather in their stiff, distant, alien world of etiquette, he felt surrounded by flatterers, and would fain have tested the sincerity even of Max, and Fritz, who said, echoing the words of the other, "Yourself, Sire, are the Apollo of Germany!"

It was the desire to test the sincerity of the people about him, and unveil flatterers, which in the first instance suggested a trick he played upon the court, upon all Europe. In that complex but wholly Teutonic genealogy lately under research, lay a much-prized thread of descent from the fifth Emperor Charles, and Carl, under direction, read, with much readiness to be impressed, all that was attainable concerning the great ancestor, finding there, in truth, little enough to reward his pains. One hint he took however. He determined to assist at his own obsequies.

That he might in this way facilitate that much-desired journey occurred to him almost at once as an accessory motive, and in a little while definite motives were engrossed in the dramatic interest, the pleasing gloom, the curiosity of the thing itself. Certainly, amid the living world in Ger-

many, especially in old, sleepy Rosenmold, death made great parade of itself. Youth even, in its sentimental mood, was ready to indulge in the luxury
of decay, and amuse itself with fancies of the tomb; as in periods of deca-
dence or suspended progress, when the world seems to nap for a time,
artifices for the arrest or disguise of old age are adopted as a fashion, and
become the fopperies of the young. The whole body of Carl's relations, saving
the drowsy old grandfather, already lay buried beneath their expansive
heraldries: at times the whole world almost seemed buried thus—made
and re-made of the dead—its entire fabric of politics, of art, of custom,
being essentially heraldic "achievements," dead men's mementos, such as
these. You see he was a sceptical young man, and his kinsmen dead and
gone had passed certainly, in his imaginations of them, into no other world,
save, perhaps, into some stiffer, slower, sleepier, and more pompous phase
of ceremony—the last degree of court etiquette—as they lay there in the
great, low-pitched, grand-ducal vault, in their coffins, dusted once a year
for All Souls' Day, when the court officials descended thither, and Mass for
the dead was sung, amid an array of dropping crape and cobwebs. The lad,
with his full red lips and open blue eyes, coming as with a great cup in his
hands to life's feast, revolted from the like of that, as from suffocation.
And still the suggestion of it was everywhere. In the garish afternoon, up
to the wholesome heights of the Heiligenberg, suddenly from one of the
villages of the plain came the grinding death-knell. It seemed to come out
of the ugly grave itself, and enjoyment was dead. On his way homeward
sadly, an hour later, he enters by chance the open door of a village church,
half buried in the tangle of its churchyard. The rude coffin is lying there of
a labourer who had but a hovel to live in. The enemy dogged one's footsteps! The young Carl seemed to be flying, not from death simply, but from
assassination.

And as these thoughts sent him back, in the rebounding power of
youth, with renewed appetite to life and sense, so, grown at last familiar,
they gave additional purpose to his fantastic experiment. Had it not been
said by a wise man that after all the offence of death was in its trappings?
Well! he would, as far as might be, try the thing, while, presumably, a large
reversionary interest in life was still his. He would purchase his freedom,
at least of those gloomy "trappings," and listen while he was spoken of as

dead. The mere preparations gave pleasant proof of the devotion to him of a certain number, who entered without question into his plans. It is not difficult to mislead the world concerning what happens to those who live at the artificial distance from it of a court, with its high wall of etiquette. However the matter was managed, no one doubted, when, with a blazon of ceremonious words, the court news went forth that, after a brief illness, according to the way of his race, the hereditary Grand-duke was deceased. In momentary regret, bethinking them of the lad's taste for splendour, those to whom the arrangement of such matters belonged (the grandfather now sinking deeper into bare quiescence) backed by the popular wish, determined to give him a funeral with even more than grand-ducal measure of lugubrious magnificence. The place of his repose was marked out for him as officiously as if it had been the delimitation of a kingdom, in the ducal burial vault, through the cobwebbed windows of which, from the garden where he played as a child, the young Duke had often peered at the faded glories of the immense coroneted coffins, the oldest shedding their velvet tatters around them. Surrounded by the whole official world of Rosenmold, arrayed for the occasion in almost forgotten dresses of ceremony as if for a masquerade, the new coffin glided from the fragrant chapel where the *Requiem* was sung, down the broad staircase lined with peach-colour and yellow marble, into the shadows below. Carl himself, disguised as a strolling musician, had followed it across the square through a drenching rain, on which circumstance he overheard the old people congratulate the "blessed" dead within, had listened to a dirge of his own composing brought out on the great organ with much *bravura* by his friend, the new court organist, who was in the secret, and that night turned the key of the garden entrance to the vault, and peeped in upon the sleepy, painted, and bewigged young pages whose duty it would be for a certain number of days to come to watch beside their late master's couch.

And a certain number of weeks afterwards it was known that "the mad Duke" had reappeared, to the dismay of court marshals. Things might have gone hard with the youth had the strange news, at first as fantastic rumour, then as matter of solemn inquiry, lastly as ascertained fact, pleasing or otherwise, been less welcome than it was to the grandfather, too old, indeed, to sorrow deeply, but grown so decrepit as to propose that

ministers should possess themselves of the person of the young Duke, pro-
claim him of age and regent. From those dim travels, presenting themselves to the old man, who had never been fifty miles away from home, is
almost lunar in their audacity, he would come back—come back "in time,"
he murmured faintly, eager to feel that youthful animating life on the stir
about him once more.

Carl himself, now the thing was over, greatly relishing its satiric elements, must be forgiven the trick of the burial and his still greater enor-
mity in coming to life again. And then, duke or no duke, it was understood
that he willed that things should in no case be precisely as they had been.
He would never again be quite so near people's lives as in the past—a fitful,
intermittent visitor—almost as if he had been properly dead; the empty
coffin remaining as a kind of symbolical "coronation incident," setting forth
his future relations to his subjects. Of all those who believed him dead one
human creature only, save the grandfather, had sincerely sorrowed for him;
a woman, in tears as the funeral train passed by, with whom he had sympathetically discussed his own merits. Till then he had forgotten the incident which had exhibited him to her as the very genius of goodness and
strength: how, one day, driving with her country produce into the market,
and, embarrassed by the crowd, she had broken one of a hundred little
police rules, whereupon the officers were about to carry her away to be
fined, or worse, amid the jeers of the bystanders, always ready to deal hardly
with "the gipsy," at which precise moment the tall Duke Carl, like the flash
of a trusty sword, had leapt from the palace stair and caused her to pass
on in peace. She had half detected him through his disguise; in due time
news of his reappearance had been ceremoniously carried to her in her
little cottage, and the remembrance of her hung about him not ungrate-
fully, as he went with delight upon his way.

The first long stage of his journey over, in headlong flight night and
day, he found himself one summer morning under the heat of what seemed
a southern sun, at last really at large on the Bergstrasse, with the rich plain
of the Palatinate on his left hand; on the right hand vineyards, seen now for
the first time, sloping up into the crisp beeches of the Odenwald. By Wein-
heim only an empty tower remained of the Castle of Windeck. He lay for the
night in the great whitewashed guest-chamber of the Capuchin convent.

The national rivers, like the national woods, have a family likeness: the Main, the Lahn, the Moselle, the Neckar, the Rhine. By help of such accommodation as chance afforded, partly on the stream itself, partly along the banks, he pursued the leisurely winding course of one of the prettiest of these, tarrying for awhile in the towns, gray, white, or red, which came in his way, tasting their delightful native "little" wines, peeping into their old overloaded churches, inspecting the church furniture, or trying the organs. For three nights he slept, warm and dry, on the hay stored in a deserted cloister, and, attracted into the neighbouring minster for a snatch of church music, narrowly escaped detection. By miraculous chance the grimmest lord of Rosenmold was there within, recognised the youth and his companions—visitors naturally conspicuous, amid the crowd of peasants around them—and for some hours was upon their traces. After unclean town streets the country air was a perfume by contrast, or actually scented with pinewoods. One seemed to breathe with it fancies of the woods, the hills, and water—of a sort of souls in the landscape, but cheerful and genial now, happy souls! A distant group of pines on the verge of a great upland awoke a violent desire to be there—seemed to challenge one to proceed thither. Was there infinite view thence? It was like an outpost of some far-off fancy land, a pledge of the reality of such. Above Cassel, the airy hills curved in one black outline against a glowing sky, pregnant, one could fancy, with weird forms, which might be at their old *diableries* again among the ruins on those remote places ere night was quite come there. At last in the streets, the hundred churches, of Cologne, he feels something of a "Gothic" enthusiasm, and all a German's enthusiasm for the Rhine.

Through the length and breadth of the Rhine country the vintage was begun. The red ruins on the heights, the white-walled villages, white Saint Nepomuc upon the bridges, were but isolated high notes of contrast in a landscape, sleepy and indistinct under the flood of sunshine, with a heartiness in it like that of must, of the new wine. The noise of the vineyards came through the lovely haze, still, at times, with the sharp sound of a bell—death-bell, perhaps, or only a crazy summons to the vintagers. And amid those broad, willowy reaches of the Rhine at last, from Bingen to Mannheim, where the brown hills wander into airy, blue distance, like a little picture of paradise, he felt that France was at hand. Before him lay the road thither, easy and straight.—That well of light so close! But, unexpectedly, the capricious incidence of his own humour with the opportunity did not suggest, as he would have wagered it must, "Go, drink at once!" Was it that France had come to be of no account at all, in comparison of Italy, of Greece? or that, as he passed over the German land, the conviction had come, "For you, France, Italy, Hellas, is here!"—that the thought of the untried spiritual possibilities of meek Germany had for Carl transferred the ideal land out of space beyond the Alps or the Rhine, into future time, whither he must be the leader? A little chilly of humour, in spite of his manly strength, he was journeying partly in search of physical heat. To-day certainly, in this great vineyard, physical heat was about him in measure sufficient, at least for a German constitution. Might it be not otherwise with the imaginative, the intellectual, heat and light; the real need being that of an interpreter—Apollo, illuminant rather as the revealer than as the bringer of light? With large belief that the *Éclaircissement*, the *Aufklärung* (he had already found the name for the thing) would indeed come, he had been in much bewilderment whence and how. Here, he began to see that it could be in no other way than by action of informing thought upon the vast accumulated material of which Germany was in possession: art, poetry, fiction, an entire imaginative world, following reasonably upon a deeper understanding of the past, of nature, of one's self— an understanding of all beside through the knowledge of one's self. To understand, would be the indispensable first step towards the enlargement of the great past, of one's little present, by criticism, by imagination. Then, the imprisoned souls of nature would speak as of old. The Middle Age, in Germany, where the past has had such generous reprisals, never far from us, would reassert its mystic spell, for the better understanding of our Raffaelle. The spirits of distant Hellas would reawake in the men and women of little German towns. Distant times, the most alien thoughts, would come near together, as elements in a great historic symphony. A kind of ardent, new patriotism awoke in him, sensitive for the first time at the words *national* poesy, *national* art and literature, *German* philosophy. To the resources of the past, of himself, of what was possible for German mind, more and more his mind opens as he goes on his way. A free, open space had been determined, which something now to be created, created by him, must occupy. "Only," he thought, "if I had coadjutors! If these thoughts would awake in but one other mind!"

At Strasbourg, with its mountainous goblin houses, nine stories high, grouped snugly, in the midst of that inclement plain, like a great stork's nest around the romantic red steeple of its cathedral, Duke Carl became fairly captive to the Middle Age. Tarrying there week after week he worked hard, but (without a ray of light from others) in one long mistake, at the chronology and history of the coloured windows. Antiquity's very self seemed expressed there, on the visionary images of king or patriarch, in the deeply incised marks of character, the hoary hair, the massive proportions, telling of a length of years beyond what is lived now. Surely, past ages, could one get at the historic soul of them, were not dead, but living, rich in company, for the entertainment, the expansion, of the present: and Duke Carl was still without suspicion of the cynic after-thought that such historic soul was but an arbitrary substitution, a generous loan of one's self.

The mystic soul of Nature laid hold on him next, saying, "Come! understand, interpret me!" He was awakened one morning by the jingle of sledge-bells along the street beneath his windows. Winter had descended betimes from the mountains; the pale Rhine below the bridge of boats on the long way to Kehl was swollen with ice, and for the first time he realised that Switzerland was at hand. On a sudden he was captive to the enthusiasm of the mountains, and hastened along the valley of the Rhine by Alt Breisach and Basle, unrepelled by a thousand difficulties, to Swiss farmhouses and lonely villages, solemn still, and untouched by strangers. At Grindelwald, sleeping at last in the close neighbourhood of the greater Alps, he had the sense of an overbrooding presence, of some strange, new companions around him. Here one might yield one's self to the unalterable imaginative appeal of the elements in their highest force and simplicity—light, air, water, earth. On very early spring days the mantle was suddenly lifted, the Alps were an apex of natural glory, towards which, in broadening spaces of light, the whole of Europe sloped upwards. Through them on the right hand, as he journeyed on, were the doorways to Italy, to Como, or Venice (from yonder peak Italy's self was visible!) as, on the left hand, in the South German towns, in a high-toned, artistic fineness—in the dainty flowered ironwork, for instance—the overflow of Italian genius was traceable. These things presented themselves at last only to remind him that, in a new intellectual hope, he was already on his way home. Straight through life, straight through nature and man, with one's own self-knowledge as a light thereon, not by way of the geographical Italy or Greece, lay the road to the new Hellas, to be realised now as the outcome of home-born German genius. At times, in that early fine weather looking now not southwards, but to Germany, he seemed to trace the outspread of a faint, not wholly natural, aurora over the dark northern country. And it was in an actual sunrise that the news came which finally put him on the directest road homewards. One hardly dared breathe in the rapid uprise of all-embracing light, which seemed like the intellectual rising of the Fatherland, when up the straggling path to his high beach-grown summit (was one safe nowhere?) protesting over the roughness of the way, came the too familiar voices (*ennui* itself made audible) of certain high functionaries of Rosenmold, come to claim their new sovereign, close upon the runaway.

With news of the old Duke's decease! With a real grief at his heart, he hastened now over the ground which lay between him and the bed of death, still trying, at quieter intervals, to snatch profit by the way; peeping, at the most unlikely hours, on the objects of his curiosity, waiting for a glimpse of dawn through glowing church windows, penetrating into old church treasuries by candle-light, taxing the old courtiers to pant up, for "the view," to this or that conspicuous point in the world of hilly woodland. From one such at last, in spite of everything with pleasure to Carl, old Rosenmold was visible—the attic windows of the Residence, the storks on the chimneys, the green copper roofs baking in the long, dry German summer. The homeliness of true old Germany! He too felt it, and yearned towards his home.

And the "beggar-maid" was there. Thoughts of her had haunted his mind all the journey through, as he was aware, not unpleased, graciously overflowing towards any creature he found dependent upon him. The mere fact that she was awaiting him, at his disposition, meekly, and as though through his long absence she had never quitted the spot on which he had said farewell, touched his fancy, and on a sudden concentrated his wavering preference into a practical decision. "King Cophetua" would be hers. And his goodwill sunned her wild-grown beauty into majesty, into a kind of queenly richness. There was natural majesty in the heavy waves of golden hair folded closely above the neck, built a little massively; and she looked kind, beseeching also, capable of sorrow. She was like clear sunny weather, with bluebells and the green leaves, between rainy days, and seemed to embody *Die Ruh auf dem Gipfel*—all the restful hours he had spent of late in the woodsides and on the hilltops. One June day, on which she seemed to have withdrawn into herself all the tokens of summer, brought decision to our lover of artificial roses, who had cared so little hitherto for the like of her. Grand-duke perforce, he would make her his wife, and had already reassured her with caricature of his horrified ministers. "Go straight to life!" said his new poetic code; and here was the opportunity. Here, also, the real "adventure," in comparison of which his previous efforts that way seemed childish theatricalities, fit only to cheat a little the profound *ennui* of real life. In a hundred stolen interviews she taught the hitherto indifferent youth the art of love.

Duke Carl had made arrangements for his marriage, secret, but complete and soon to be made public. Long since he had cast complacent eyes on a strange architectural relic, an old grange or hunting-lodge on the heath, with he could hardly have defined what charm of remoteness and old romance. Popular belief amused itself with reports of the wizard who inhabited or haunted the place, his fantastic treasures, his immense age. His window lights might be seen glittering afar on stormy nights, amid a blaze of golden ornaments, said the more adventurous loiterer. It was not because he was suspicious still, but in a kind of wantonness of affection, and as if by way of giving yet greater zest to the luxury of their mutual trust, that Duke Carl added to his announcement of the purposed place and time of the event, a pretended test of the girl's devotion. He tells her the story of the aged wizard, meagre and wan, to whom she must find her way alone for the purpose of asking a question all-important to himself. The fierce old man will try to escape with terrible threats, will turn, or half turn, into repulsive animals. She must cling the faster; at last the spell will be broken; he will yield, he will become a youth once more, and give the desired answer.

The girl, otherwise so self-denying, and still modestly anxious for a private union, not to shame his high position in the world, had wished for one thing at least—to be loved amid the splendours habitual to him. Duke

Carl sends to the old lodge his choicest personal possessions. For many days the public is aware of something on hand; a few get delightful glimpses of the treasures on their way to "the place on the heath." Was he preparing against contingencies, should the great army, soon to pass through these parts, not leave the country as innocently as might be desired?

The short gray day seemed a long one to those who, for various reasons, were waiting anxiously for the darkness; the court people fretful and on their mettle, the townsfolk suspicious, Duke Carl full of amorous longing. At her distant cottage beyond the hills, Gretchen kept herself ready for the trial. It was expected that certain great military officers would arrive that night, commanders of a victorious host making its way across Northern Germany, with no great respect for the rights of neutral territory, often dealing with life and property too rudely to find the coveted treasure. It was but one episode in a cruel war. Duke Carl did not wait for the grandly illuminated supper prepared for their reception. Events precipitated themselves. Those officers came as practically victorious occupants, sheltering themselves for the night in the luxurious rooms of the great palace. The army was in fact in motion close behind its leaders, who (Gretchen warm and happy in the arms, not of the aged wizard, but of the youthful lover) are discussing terms for the final absorption of the duchy with those traitorous old councillors. At their delicate supper Duke Carl amuses his companion with caricature, amid cries of cheerful laughter, of the sleepy courtiers entertaining their martial guests in all their pedantic politeness, like people in some farcical dream. A priest, and certain chosen friends to witness the marriage, were to come ere nightfall to the grange. The lovers heard, as they thought, the sound of distant thunder. The hours passed as they waited, and what came at last was not the priest with his companions. Could they have been detained by the storm? Duke Carl gently reassures the girl—bids her believe in him, and wait. But through the wind, grown to tempest, beyond the sound of the violent thunder—louder than any possible thunder—nearer and nearer comes the storm of the victorious army, like some disturbance of the earth itself, as they flee into the tumult, out of the intolerable confinement and suspense, dead-set upon them.

*   *   *

The *Enlightening*, the *Aufklärung*, according to the aspiration of Duke Carl, was effected by other hands; Lessing and Herder, brilliant precursors of the age of genius which centered in Goethe, coming well within the natural limits of Carl's lifetime. As precursors Goethe gratefully recognised them, and understood that there had been a thousand others, looking forward to a new era in German literature with the desire which is in some sort a "forecast of capacity," awakening each other to the permanent reality of a poetic ideal in human life, slowly forming that public consciousness to which Goethe actually addressed himself. It is their aspirations I have tried to embody in the portrait of Carl.

A hard winter had covered the Main with a firm footing of ice. The liveliest social intercourse was quickened thereon. I was unfailing from early morning onwards; and, being lightly clad, found myself, when my mother drove up later to look on, fairly frozen. My mother sat in the carriage, quite stately in her furred cloak of red velvet, fastened on the breast with thick gold cord and tassels.

"Dear mother," I said, on the spur of the moment, "give me your furs, I am frozen."

She was equally ready. In a moment I had on the cloak. Falling below the knee, with its rich trimming of sables, and enriched with gold, it became me excellently. So clad I made my way up and down with a cheerful heart.

That was Goethe, perhaps fifty years later. His mother also related the incident to Bettina Brentano:—"There, skated my son, like an arrow among the groups. Away he went over the ice like a son of the gods. Anything so beautiful is not to be seen now. I clapped my hands for joy. Never shall I forget him as he darted out from one arch of the bridge, and in again under the other, the wind carrying the train behind him as he flew." In that amiable figure I seem to see the fulfilment of the *Resurgam* on Carl's empty coffin—the aspiring soul of Carl himself, in freedom and effective, at last.

GASTON DE LATOUR

I

A CLERK IN ORDERS

THE WHITE WALLS OF THE CHÂTEAU OF DEUX-MANOIRS, WITH ITS PRECINCTS, composed, before its dismantling at the Revolution, the one prominent object which towards the south-west broke the pleasant level of La Beauce, the great corn-land of central France. Abode in those days of the family of Latour, nesting there century after century, it recorded significantly the effectiveness of their brotherly union, less by way of invasion of the rights of others than by the improvement of all gentler sentiments within. From the sumptuous monuments of their last resting-place, backwards to every object which had encircled them in that warmer and more lightsome home it was visible they had cared for so much, even in some peculiarities of the very ground-plan of the house itself—everywhere was the token of their anxious estimate of all those incidents of man's pathway through the world which knit the wayfarers thereon most closely together.

Why this irregularity of ground-plan?—the traveller would ask; recognising indeed a certain distinction in its actual effect on the eye, and suspecting perhaps some conscious aim at such effect on the part of the builders of the place in an age indulgent of architectural caprices. And the traditional answer to the question, true for once, still showed the race of Latour making much, making the most, of the sympathetic ties of human life. The work, in large measure, of Gaston de Latour, it was left unfinished at his death, some time about the year 1594. That it was never completed could hardly be attributed to any lack of means, or of interest; for it is plain that to the period of the Revolution, after which its scanty remnants passed into humble occupation (a few circular turrets, a crenellated curtain wall, giving a random touch of dignity to some ordinary farm-buildings) the place had been scrupulously maintained. It might seem to have been a kind of reverence rather that had allowed the work to remain untouched for future ages precisely at this point in its growth.

And the expert architectural mind, peeping acutely into recondite motives and half-accomplished purposes in such matters, could detect the circumstance which had determined that so noticeable peculiarity of ground-plan. Its kernel was not, as in most similar buildings of that date, a feudal fortress, but an unfortified manor-house—a double *manoir*—two houses, oddly associated at a right angle. Far back in the Middle Age, said a not uncertain tradition, here had been the one point of contact between two estates, intricately interlocked with alien domain, as, in the course of generations, the family of Latour, and another, had added field to field. In the single lonely manor then existing two brothers had grown up; and the time came when the marriage of the younger to the heiress of those neighbouring lands would divide two perfect friends. Regretting over-night so dislocating a change it was the elder who, as the drowsy hours flowed away in manifold recollection beside the fire, now suggested to the younger, himself already wistfully recalling, as from the past, the kind motion and noise of the place like a sort of audible sunlight, the building of a second manor-house—the Château d'Amour, as it came to be called—that the two families, in what should be as nearly as possible one abode, might take their fortunes together.

Of somewhat finer construction than the rough walls of the older manor, the Château d'Amour stood, amid the change of years, as a visible record of all the accumulated sense of human existence among its occupants. The old walls, the old apartments, of those two associated houses still existed, with some obvious additions, beneath the delicate, fantastic surfaces of the *château* ready to speak their parts, to be almost in motion through the gloom. Many years after, Gaston de Latour, an enemy of all Gothic darkness or heaviness, returning to his home full of a later taste, changed all that. A thicket of airy spires rose above the sanctuary; the blind *triforium* broke into one continuous window; the heavy masses of stone were pared down with wonderful dexterity of hand, till not a hand's-breadth remained uncovered by delicate tracery, as from the fair white roof, touched sparingly with gold, down to the subterranean chapel of Saint Taurin, where the peasants of La Beauce came to pray for rain, not a space was left unsearched by cheerful daylight, refined, but hardly dimmed at all, by painted glass mimicking the clearness of the open sky. In the sombre old church all was in stately order now: the dusky, jewelled reliquaries, the ancient devotional ornaments from the manor—much-prized family possessions, sufficient to furnish the whole array of a great ecclesiastical function like this—the lights burning, flowers everywhere, gathered amid the last handfuls of the harvest by the peasant-women, who came to present their children for the happy chance of an episcopal blessing.

And the almost exclusively aged people, in all their old personal adornments, which now so rarely saw the light, forming the central group, expectant around the young *seigneur* they had conducted hither, seemed of one piece with those mystic figures, the old, armour-clad monumental effigies, the carved and painted imageries which ran round the outer circuit of the choir—a version of the biblical history, for the reading of those who loitered on their way from chapel to chapel. There was Joseph's dream, with the tall sheaves of the elder brethren bowing to Joseph's sheaf, like these aged heads around the youthful aspirant of to-day. There was Jacob going on his mysterious way, met by, conversing with, wrestling with, the Angels of God—rescuing the promise of his race from the "profane" Esau. There was the mother of Samuel, and, in long white ephod, the much-desired, early-consecrated child, who had inherited her religious capacity; and David, with something of his extraordinary genius for divine things written on his countenance; onward, to the sacred persons of the Annunciation, with the golden lily in the silver cup, only lately set in its place. With dress, expression, nay! the very incidents themselves innocently adapted to the actual habits and associations of the age which had produced them, these figures of the old Jewish history seemed about to take their places, for the imparting of a divine sanction, among the living actors of the day. One and all spoke of ready concurrence with religious motions, a ready apprehension of, and concurrence with, the provisions of a certain divine scheme for the improvement of one's opportunities in the world.

Would that dark-haired, fair-skinned lad concur, in his turn, and be always true to his present purpose—Gaston de Latour, standing thus, almost the only youthful thing, amid the witness of these imposing, meditative, masks and faces? Could his guardians have read below the white propriety of the youth, duly arrayed for dedication, with the lighted candle in his right hand and the surplice folded over his left shoulder, he might sorely have disturbed their placid but somewhat narrow ruminations, with the germs of what was strange to or beyond them. Certain of those shrewd old ecclesiastics had in fact detected that the devout lad, so visibly impressed, was not altogether after their kind; that, together with many characteristics obviously inherited, he possessed—had caught perhaps from some ancestor unrepresented here—some other potencies of nature, which might not always combine so accordantly as to-day with the mental requisites of an occasion such as this. One of them, indeed, touched notwithstanding by his manifest piety just then, shortly afterwards recommended him a little prayer "for peace" from the Vespers of the Roman Breviary—for the harmony of his heart with itself; advice which, except for a very short period, he ever afterwards followed, saying it every evening of his life.

Yet it was the lad's own election which had led him to this first step in a career that might take him out of the world and end the race of Latour altogether. Approaching their fourscore years, and realising almost suddenly the situation of the young Gaston, left there alone, out of what had been a large, much-promising, resonant household, they wished otherwise, but did not try to change his early-pronounced preference for the ecclesiastical calling. When he determined to seek the clericature, his proposal made a demand on all their old-fashioned religious sentiment. But the fund was a deep one, and their acquiescence in the result entire. He might indeed use his privilege of "orders" only as the stepping-stone to material advancement in a church which seemed to have gone over wholly to the world, and of which at that time one half the benefices were practically in the hands of laymen. But, actually, the event came to be a dedication on their part, not unlike those old biblical ones—an offering in old age of the single precious thing left them; the grandchild, whose hair would presently fall under the very shears which, a hundred years before, had turned an earlier, brilliant, Gaston de Latour into a monk.

Charles Guillard, Bishop of Chartres, a courtly, vivacious prelate, whose quick eyes seemed to note at a glance the whole assembly, one and all, while his lips moved silently, arrived at last, and the rite began with the singing of the Office for the Ninth Hour. It was like a stream of water crossing unexpectedly a dusty way—*Mirabilia testimonia tua!* In psalm and antiphon, inexhaustibly fresh, the soul seemed to be taking refuge, at that undevout hour, from the sordid languor and the mean business of men's lives, in contemplation of the unfaltering vigour of the divine righteousness, which had still those who sought it, not only watchful in the night but alert in the drowsy afternoon. Yes! there was the sheep astray, *sicut ovis quæ periit*—the physical world; with its lusty ministers, at work, or sleeping for a while amid the stubble, their faces upturned to the August sun—the world so importunately visible, intruding a little way, with its floating odours, in that semicircle of heat across the old over-written pavement at the great open door, upon the mysteries within. Seen from the incense-laden sanctuary, where the bishop was assuming one by one the pontifical ornaments, La Beauce, like a many-coloured carpet spread under the great dome, with the white double house-front quivering afar through the heat, though it looked as if you might touch with the hand its distant spaces, was for a moment the unreal thing. Gaston alone, with all his mystic preoccupations, by the privilege of youth, seemed to belong to both, and link the visionary company about him to the external scene.

The rite with which the Roman Church "makes a clerk," aims certainly at no low measure of difference from the coarser world around him, in its supposed scholar: and in this case the aspirant (the precise claims of the situation being well considered) had no misgiving. Discreetly, and with full attention, he answers *Adsum!* when his name is called, and advances manfully; though he kneels meekly enough, and remains, with his head bowed forward, at the knees of the seated bishop who recites the appointed prayers, between the anthems and responses of his *Schola*, or attendant singers—Might he be saved from mental blindness! Might he put on the new man, even as his outward guise was changed! Might he keep the religious habit for ever! who had thus hastened to lay down the hair of his head for the divine love. "The Lord is my inheritance" whispers Gaston distinctly, as the locks fall, cut from the thickly-grown, black head, in five places, "after the fashion of Christ's crown," the shears in the episcopal hands sounding aloud, amid the silence of the curious spectators. From the same hands, in due order, the fair surplice ripples down over him. "This is the generation of them that seek Him," the choir sings: "The Lord Himself is the portion of my inheritance and my cup." It was the Church's eloquent way of bidding unrestricted expansion to the youthful heart in its timely purpose to seek the best, to abide among the things of the spirit.

The prospect from their cheerful, unenclosed road, like a white scarf flung across the land, as the party returned home in the late August afternoon, was clear and dry and distant. The great barns at the wayside had their doors thrown back, displaying the dark, cool space within. The farmsteads seemed almost tenantless, the villagers being still at work over the immense harvest-field. Crazy bells startled them, striking out the hour from behind, over a deserted churchyard. Still and tenantless also seemed the manor as they approached, door and window lying open upon the court for the coolness; or rather it was as if at their approach certain spectral occupants started back out of the daylight—"Why depart, dear ghosts?" was what the grandparents would have cried. They had more in common with that immaterial world than with flesh and blood. There was room for the existing household, enough and to spare, in one of the two old houses. That other, the Château d'Amour, remained for Gaston, at first as a delightful, half-known abode of wonders, though with some childish fear; afterwards, as a delightful nursery of refined or fantastic sentiment, as he recalled, in this chamber or that, its old tenants and their doings, from the affectionate brothers, onwards—above all, how in one room long ago Gabrielle de Latour had died of joy.

With minds full of their recent business it was difficult to go back to common occupations; as darkness came on, the impressions of the day did but return again more vividly and concentrate themselves upon the inward sense. Observance, loyal concurrence in some high purpose for him, passive waiting on the hand one might miss in the darkness, with the gift or gifts therein of which he had the presentiment, and upon the due acceptance of which the true fortune of life would turn; these were the hereditary traits alert in Gaston, as he lay awake in the absolute, moon-lit, stillness, his outward ear attentive for the wandering footsteps which, through that wide, lightly-accentuated country, often came and went about the house, with weird suggestions of a dim passage to and fro, and of an infinite distance. He would rise, as the footsteps halted perhaps below his window, to answer the questions of the travellers, pilgrims, or labourers who had missed their way from farm to farm, or halting soldier seeking guidance; terrible or terror-stricken companies sometimes, rudely or piteously importunate to be let in—for it was the period of the Religious Wars, flaming up here and there over France, and never quite put out, during forty years.

Once, in the beginning of these troubles (he was then a child, leaning from the window, as a sound of rickety, small wheels approached) the enquiry came in broken French, *"Voulez-vous donner direction?"* from a German, one of the mercenaries of the Duc de Guise, hired for service in a civil strife of France, drawing wearily a crippled companion, so far from home. The memory of it, awakening a thousand strange fancies, had remained by him, as a witness to the power of fortuitous circumstance over the imagination.

One night there had come a noise of horns, and presently King Charles himself was standing in the courtyard, belated, and far enough now from troublesome company, as he hunted the rich-fleshed game of La Beauce through the endless corn. He entered, with a relish for the pleasant cleanliness of the place, expressed in a shrill strain of half-religious oaths, like flashes of hell-fire to Gaston's suddenly-awakened sense. It was the invincible nature of the royal lad to speak, and feel, on these mad, *alto* notes, and not unbecoming in a good Catholic; for Huguenots never swore, and these were subtly theological oaths. Well! the grandparents repressed as best they could their apprehensions as to what other hunters, what other disconcerting incident, might follow; for Catholic France very generally believed that the Huguenot leaders had a scheme for possessing themselves of the person of the young king, known to be mentally pliable. Meanwhile they led him to their daintiest apartment, with great silver *flambeaux*, that he might wash off the blood with which not his hands only were covered; for he hunted also with the eagerness of a madman—*steeped* in blood. He lay there for a few hours, after supping very familiarly on his own birds, Gaston rising from his bed to look on at a distance, and, afterwards, on his knee, serving the rose-water dish and spiced wine, as the night passed in reassuring silence; Charles himself, as usual, keenly enjoying this "gipsy" incident, with the supper after that unexpected fashion, among strange people, he hardly knew where. He was very pale, like some cunning Italian work in wax or ivory, of partly satiric character, endued by magic or crafty mechanism with vivacious movement. But as he sat thus, ever for the most part the unhappy plaything of other people's humours, escaped for a moment out of a world of demoniac politicians, the pensive atmosphere around seemed gradually to change him, touching his wild temper, pleasantly, profitably, so that he took down from the wall and struck out the notes of a lute and fell to talking of verses, leaving a stanza of his own scratched with a diamond on the window-pane—lines simpler-hearted, and more full of nature than were common at that day.

The life of Gaston de Latour was almost to coincide with the duration of the Religious Wars. The earliest public event of his memory was that famous siege of Orleans from which the young Henri de Guise rode away the head of his restless family, tormented now still further by the reality or the pretence of filial duty, seeking vengeance on the treacherous murder of his father. Following a long period of quiet progress—the tranquil and tolerant years of the Renaissance—the religious war took possession of, and pushed to strangely confused issues, a society somewhat distraught by an artificial æsthetic culture; and filled with wild passions, wildly-dramatic personalities, a scene already singularly attractive by its artistic beauty. A heady religious fanaticism was worked by every prominent egotist in turn, pondering on his chances, in the event of the extinction of the house of Valois with the three sons of Catherine de Medici, born unsound, and doomed by astrological prediction. The old manors, which had exchanged their towers for summer-houses under the softening influence of Renaissance fashions, found themselves once more medievally insecure amid a vagrant warfare of foreign mercenaries and armed peasants. It was a curiously refined people who now took down the armour, hanging high on the wall for decoration among newer things so little war-like.

A difficult age, certainly, for scrupulous spirits to move in! A perplexed network of partizan or personal interests underlay, and furnished the really directing forces in, a supposed Armageddon of contending religious convictions. The wisest perhaps, like Michel de L'Hôpital, withdrew themselves from a conflict, in which not a single actor has the air of quite pure intentions; while religion, itself the assumed ground of quarrel, seems appreciable all the while only by abstraction from the parties, the leaders, at once violent and cunning, who are most pretentious in the assertion of its rival claims. What there was of religion was in hiding, perhaps, with the so-called "Political" party, professedly almost indifferent to it, but which had at least something of humanity on its side, and some chance of that placidity of mind in which alone the business of the spirit can be done. The new sect of "Papists" were not the true Catholics: there was little of the virtue of the martyr in militant Calvinism. It is not a Catholic historian who notes with profound regret "that inauspicious day," in the year 1562, Gaston's tenth year, "when the work of devastation began, which was to strip from France that antique garniture of religious art which later ages have not been able to replace." Axe and hammer at the carved work sounded from one end of France to the other.

It was a peculiarity of this age of terror, that every one, including Charles the Ninth himself, dreaded what the accident of war might make, not merely of his enemies, but of temporary allies and pretended friends, in an evenly balanced but very complex strife—of merely personal rivals also, in some matter which had nothing to do with the assumed motives of that strife. Gaston de Latour passing on his country way one night, with a sudden flash of fierce words two young men burst from the doors of a road-side tavern. The brothers are quarrelling the division, lately effected there, of their dead father's morsel of land. "I shall hate you till death!" cries the younger, bounding away in the darkness; and two atheists part, to take opposite sides in the supposed strife of Catholic and Huguenot.

The deeds of violence which occupy the foreground of French history during the reigns of Catherine's sons might indeed lead one to fancy that little human kindness could have remained in France,—fanatical civil war of forty years, that no place at all could have been left the quiet building of character. Contempt for human life, taught us every day by nature, and alas! by man himself:—all war intensifies that. But the more permanent forces, alike of human nature and of the natural world, are on the whole in the interest of tranquillity and sanity, and of the sentiments proper to man. Like all good Catholic children, Gaston had shuddered at the name of Adretz, of Briquemaut with his great necklace of priests' ears, of that dark and fugitive Montgomeri, the slayer, as some would have it the assassin, of a king, now active, and almost ubiquitous, on the Huguenot side. Still, at Deux-manoirs, this warfare, seething up from time to time so wildly in this or that district of France, was for the most part only sensible in incidents we might think picturesque, were they told with that intention; delightful enough, certainly, to the curiosity of a boy, in whose mind nevertheless they deepened a native impressibility to the sorrow and hazard that are constant and necessary in human life, especially for the poor. The troubles of "that poor people of France"—burden of all its righteous rulers, from Saint Lewis downwards—these, at all events, would not be lessened by the struggle of Guise and Condé and Bourbon and Valois, of the Valois with each other, of those four brilliant young princes of the name of Henry. The weak would but suffer somewhat more than was usual, in the interest of the strong. If you were not sure whether that gleaming of the sun in the vast distance flashed from swords or sickles, whether that far-off curl of smoke rose from stubble-fire or village-steeple, to protect which the peasants, still lovers of their churches, would arm themselves, women and all, with fork and scythe,—still, those peasants used their scythes, in due season, for reaping their leagues of corn-land, and slept with faces as tranquil as ever towards the sky, for their noonday rest. In effect, since peace is always in some measure dependent on one's own seeking, disturbing forces do but fray their way along somewhat narrow paths over the great spaces of the quiet realm of nature. La Beauce, vast enough to present at once every phase of weather, its one landmark the twin spires of Chartres, salient as the finger of a dial, guiding, by their change of perspective, victor or vanquished on his way, offered room enough for the business both of peace and war to those enamoured of either. When Gaston, after a brief absence, was unable to find his child's garden-bed, that was only because in a fine June the corn had grown tall so quickly, through which he was presently led to it, with all its garish sweets undisturbed: and it was with the ancient growths of mind—customs, beliefs, mental preferences—as with the natural world.

It may be understood that there was a certain rudeness about the old manor, left almost untouched from age to age, with a loyalty which paid little or no heed to changes of fashion. The Château d'Amour, indeed, as the work of a later age, refined somewhat upon the rough feudal architecture; and the daintier taste had centred itself in particular upon one apartment, a veritable woman's apartment, with an effect in some degree anticipating the achievement of Gaston's own century, in which the apparatus of daily life became so eloquent of the moods of those to whom it ministered. It was the chamber of Gabrielle de Latour, who had died of joy. Here certainly she had watched, at these windows, during ten whole years, for the return of her beloved husband from a disastrous battle in the East, till against all expectation she beheld him crossing the court at last. Immense privilege! Immense distinction! Again and again Gaston tried to master the paradox, at times, in deep concentration of mind, seemed almost to touch the point of that wonderful moment.

Hither, as to an oratory, a religious place, the finer spirits of her kin had always found their way, to leave behind them there the more intimate relics of themselves. To Gaston its influence imparted early a taste for delicate things as being indispensable in all his pleasures to come; and, from the very first, with the appetite for some great distinguishing passion, the peculiar genius of his age seeming already awake spontaneously within him. Here, at least, had been one of those grand passions, such as were needed to give life its true meaning and effect. Conscious of that rudeness in his home, and feeding a strong natural instinct for outward beauty hitherto on what was barely sufficient, he found for himself in this perfumed place the centre of a fanciful world, reaching out to who could tell what refined passages of existence in that great world beyond, of which the echoes seemed to light here amid the stillness. On his first visit one pensive afternoon, fitting the lately attained key in the lock, he seemed to have drawn upon himself, yet hardly to have disturbed, the meditations of its former occupant. A century of unhindered summers had taken the heat from its colours—the couches, the curtains half shading the windows, which the rain in the south-west wind just then touched so softly. That great passion of old had been also a dainty love, leaving its impress everywhere in this magic apartment, on the musical instruments, the books lying where they might have fallen from the hands of the listless reader so long since, the fragrance which the lad's movement stirred around him. And there, on one of the windows, were the verses of King Charles, who had slept here, as in the most courtly resting-place of the house. On certain nights Gaston himself was not afraid to steal from his own bed to lie in it, though still too healthy a sleeper to be visited by the appropriate dreams he so greatly longed for.

A nature, instinctively religious, which would readily discover and give their full value to all such facts of experience as might be conformable thereto! But what would be the relation of this religious sensibility to sensibilities of another kind, now awaking in the young Gaston, as he mused in this dreamy place, surrounded by the books, the furniture, almost the very presence of the past, which had already found tongues to speak of a still living humanity—somewhere, somewhere, in the world!—waiting for him in the distance, or perchance already on its way, to explain, by its own plenary beauty and power, why wine and roses and the languorous summer afternoons were so delightful. So far indeed, the imaginative heat, that might one day enter into dangerous rivalry with simple old-fashioned faith, was blent harmoniously with it. They were hardly distinguishable elements of an amiable character, susceptible generally to the poetic side of things—two neighbourly apprehensions of a single ideal.

The great passions, the fervid sentiments, of which Gaston dreamed as the true realisation of life, have not always softened men's natures: they have been compatible with many cruelties, as in the lost spirits of that very age. They may overflow, on the other hand, in more equable natures, through the concurrence of happier circumstance, into that universal sympathy which lends a kind of amorous power to the homeliest charities. So it seemed likely to be with Gaston de Latour. Sorrow came along with beauty, a rival of its intricate omnipresence in life. In the sudden tremor of an aged voice, the handling of a forgotten toy, a childish drawing, in the tacit observance of a day, he became aware suddenly of the great stream of human tears falling always through the shadows of the world. For once the darling of old age actually more than responded in full to its tenderness. In the isolation of his life there had been little demand for sympathy on the part of those anywhere near his own age. So much the larger was the fund of superfluous affection which went forth, with a delicacy not less than their own, to meet the sympathies of the aged people who cherished him. In him, their old, almost forgotten sorrows bled anew.

Variety of affection, in a household in which many relations had lived together, had brought variety of sorrow. But they were well-nigh healed now—those once so poignant griefs—the scars remaining only as deeper lines of natural expression. It was visible, to their surprise, that he penetrated the motive of the mass said so solemnly, in violet, on the Innocents' Day, and understood why they wept at the triumphant antiphons:— "My soul is escaped as a bird out of the snare of the fowler!"—thinking intently of the little tombs which had recorded carefully almost the minutes of children's lives, Elizabeth de Latour, Cornélius de Latour, aged so many years, days, hours. Yes! the cold pavement under one's feet had once been molten lava. Surely the resources of sorrow were large in things! The fact must be duly marked and provided for, with due estimate of his own susceptibility thereto, in his scheme of life. Might he pass through the world, unriven by sorrows such as those! And already it was as if he stept softly over the earth, not to outrage its so abundant latent sensibilities.

The beauty of the world and its sorrow, solaced a little by religious faith, itself so beautiful a thing; these were the chief impressions with which he made his way outwards, at first only in longer rambles, as physical strength increased, over his native plains, whereon, as we have seen, the cruel warfare of that age had aggravated at a thousand points the everyday appeal of suffering humanity. The vast level, stretching thirty miles from east to west, thirty from north to south:—perhaps the reader may think little of its resources for the seeker after natural beauty, or its capacity to develop the imagination. A world, he may fancy, in which there could be no shadows, at best not too cheerful colours. In truth, it was all *accent*, so to speak. But then, surely, all the finer influences of every language depend mostly on accent; and he has but to think of it as Gaston actually lived in it to find a singularly companionable soul there. Gaston, at least, needed but to go far enough across it for those inward oppositions to cease, which already at times beset him; to feel at one with himself again, under the influence of a scene which had for him something of the character of the sea—its changefulness, its infinity, its pathos in the toiling human life that traversed it. Featureless, if you will, it was always under the guidance of its ample sky. Scowling back sometimes moodily enough, but almost never without a remnant of fine weather, about August it was for the most part cloudless. And then truly, under its blue dome, the great plain would as it were "laugh and sing," in a kind of absoluteness of sympathy with the sun.

II

OUR LADY'S CHURCH

"I had almost said even as they."

LIKE A SHIP FOR EVER A-SAIL IN THE DISTANCE, THOUGHT THE CHILD, EVERY-where the great church of Chartres was visible, with the passing light or shadow upon its gray, weather-beaten surfaces. The people of La Beauce were proud, and would talk often of its rich store of sacred furniture, the wonder-working relics of "Our Lady under the Earth," and her sacred veil or shift, which kings and princes came to visit, returning with a likeness thereof, replete in miraculous virtue, for their own wearing. The busy fancy of Gaston, multiplying this chance hearsay, had set the whole interior in array—a dim, spacious, fragrant place, afloat with golden lights. Lit up over the autumn fields at evening, the distant spires suggested the splendour within, with so strong an imaginative effect, that he seemed scarcely to know whether it was through the mental or bodily eye that he beheld. When he came thither at last, like many another well-born youth, to join the epis-copal household as a kind of half-clerical page, he found (as happens in the actual testing of our ideals) at once more and less than he had sup-posed; and his earlier vision was a thing he could never precisely recover, or disentangle from the supervening reality. What he *saw*, certainly, was greater far in mere physical proportion, and incommensurable at first by anything he knew—the volume of the wrought detail, the mass of the com-ponent members, the bigness of the actual stones of the masonry, contrary to the usual Gothic manner, and as if in reminiscence of those old Druidic piles amid which the Virgin of Chartres had been adored, long before the birth of Christ, by a mystic race, possessed of some prophetic sense of the grace in store for her. Through repeated dangers good-fortune has saved that unrivalled treasure of stained glass; and then, as now, the word "awful," so often applied to Gothic aisles, was for once really applicable. You enter, looking perhaps for a few minutes' cool shelter from the summer noonday; and the placid sunshine of La Beauce seems to have been transformed in a moment into imperious, angry fire.

It was not in summer, however, that Gaston first set foot there; he saw the beautiful city for the first time as if sheathed austerely in repellent armour. In his most genial subsequent impressions of the place there was always a lingering trace of that famous frost through which he made his way, wary of petrifying contact against things without, to the great western portal, on Candlemas morning. The sad, patient images by the doorways of the crowded church seemed suffering now chiefly from the cold. It was almost like a funeral—the penitential violet, the wandering taper-light, of this half-lenten feast of Purification. His new companions, at the head and in the rear of the long procession, forced every one, even the Lord Bishop himself, to move apace, bustling along, cross-bearer and acolyte, in their odd little copes, out of the bitter air, which made the jolly life Gaston now entered on, around the great fire of their hall in the episcopal palace, seem all the more winsome.

Notre-Dame de Chartres! It was a world to explore, as if one explored the entire Middle Age; it was also one unending, elaborate, religious function—a life, or a continuous drama, to take one's part in. Dependent on its structural completeness, on its wealth of well-preserved ornament, on its unity in variety, perhaps on some undefinable operation of genius, beyond, but concurrently with, all these, the church of Chartres has still the gift of a unique power of impressing. In comparison, the other famous churches of France, at Amiens for instance, at Rheims or Beauvais, may seem but formal, and to a large extent reproducible, effects of mere architectural rule on a gigantic scale. The somewhat Gothic soul of Gaston relished there something strange, or even *bizarre*, in the very manner in which the building set itself, so broadly couchant, upon the earth; in the natural richness of tone on the masonry within; in its vast echoing roof of timber, the "forest," as it was called; in the mysterious maze traced upon its pavement; its maze-like crypt, centering in the shrine of the sibylline Notre-Dame, itself a natural or very primitive grotto or cave. A few years were still to pass ere sacrilegious hands despoiled it on a religious pretext:—the Catholic Church must pay, even with the molten gold of her sanctuaries, the price of her defence in the civil war. At present, it was such a treasure-house of medieval jewellery as we have to make a very systematic effort even to imagine. The still extant register of its furniture and sacred apparel leaves the soul of the ecclesiologist athirst.

And it had another very remarkable difference from almost all Gothic churches: there were no graves there. Its emptiness in this respect is due to no revolutionary or Huguenot desecration. Once indeed, about this very time, a popular military leader had been interred with honour, within the precinct of the high altar itself. But not long afterwards, said the reverend canons, resenting on the part of their immaculate patroness this intrusion, the corpse itself, ill at ease, had protested, lifting up its hands above the surface of the pavement, as if to beg interment elsewhere; and Gaston could remember assisting, awakened suddenly one night, at the removal of the remains to a more, ordinary place of sepulture.

And yet that lavish display of jewellers' work on the altars, in the chapels, the sacristies, of Our Lady's Church, was but a framing for little else than dead people's bones. To Gaston, a piteous soul, with a touch also of that grim humour which, as we know, holds of pity, relic-worship came naturally. At Deux-manoirs too there had been relics, including certain broken children's toys and some rude childish drawings, taken forth now and then with almost religious veneration, with trembling hands and renewal of old grief, to his wondering awe at the greatness of men's sorrows. Yes! the pavement under one's feet had once been, might become again for him, molten lava. The look, the manner, of those who exposed these things, had been a revelation. The abundant relics of the church of Chartres were for the most part perished remnants of the poor human body itself; but, appertaining to persons long ago and of a far-off, immeasurable kind of sanctity, stimulated a more indifferent sort of curiosity, and seemed to bring the distant, the impossible, as with tangible evidence of fact, close to one's side. It was in one's hand—the finger of an Evangelist! The crowned head of Saint Lubin, bishop of Chartres long centuries since, but still able to preserve its wheat-stacks from fire; bones of the "Maries," with some of the earth from their grave; these, and the like of these, was what the curious eye discerned in the recesses of those variously contrived reliquaries, great and small, glittering so profusely about the dusky church, itself ministering, by its very shadows, to a certain appetite in the soul of Gaston for dimness—for a dim place like this—such as he had often prefigured to himself, albeit with some suspicion of what might seem a preference for *darkness*. Physical twilight we most of us love, in its season. To him, that perpetual twilight came in close identity with its moral or intellectual counterpart, as the welcome requisite for that part of the *soul* which loves twilight, and is, in truth, never quite at rest out of it, through some congenital uneasiness or distress, perhaps, in its processes of vision.

As complex, yet not less perfectly united under a single leading motive,—its sister volume, was the ritual order of Notre-Dame de Chartres, a year-long dramatic action, in which every one had, and knew, his part—the drama or "mystery" of Redemption, to the necessities of which the great church had shaped itself. All those various "offices" which, in Pontifical, Missal and Breviary, devout imagination had elaborated from age to age with such a range of spiritual colour and light and shade, with so much poetic tact in quotation, such a depth of insight into the Christian soul, had joined themselves harmoniously together, one office ending only where another began, in the perpetual worship of this mother of churches, which had also its own picturesque peculiarities of "use," proud of its maternal privilege therein. And the music rose—warmed, expanded, or fell silent altogether—as the order of the year, the colours, the whole expression of things changed, gathering around the full mystic effulgence of the pontiff in his own person, while the sacred theme deepened at the great ecclesiastical seasons, when the aisles overflowed with a vast multitude, and like a court, combed, starched, rustling around him, Gaston and his fellows "served" Monseigneur—they, zealous, ubiquitous, more prominent than ever, though for the most part profoundly irreverent, and, notwithstanding that, one and all, with what disdain of the un-tonsured laity!

Well! what was of the past there—the actual stones of the temple and that sacred liturgical order—entered readily enough into Gaston's mental kingdom, filling places prepared by the anticipations of his tranquil, dream-struck youth. It was the present, the uncalculated present, which now disturbed the complacent habit of his thoughts, proposing itself, importunately, in the living forms of his immediate companions, in the great clerical body of which he was become a part, in the people of Chartres itself (none the less animated because provincial) a thing, alien at a thousand points from his preconceptions of life, to be judged by him, to be rejected or located within. How vivid, how delightful, they were!—the other forty-nine of the fifty lads who had come hither, after the old-fashioned way, to serve in the household of Monseigneur by way of an "institution" in learning and good manners, as to which a grave national assembly, more than three centuries before the States-General of 1789, had judged French youth of quality somewhat behindhand, recommending king and nobles to take better care for the future of their education, "to the end that, enlightened and *moralised*, they might know their duties, and be less likely to abuse their privileges."

And how becomingly that cleric pride, that self-respecting quiet, sat upon their high-bred figures, their angelic, unspoiled faces, saddened transiently as they came under the religious spell for a moment. As for Gaston, they welcomed him with perfect friendliness, kept their best side foremost for an hour, and would not leave his very dreams. In absolute unconsciousness, they had brought from their remote old homes all varieties of hereditary gifts, vices, distinctions, dark fates, mercy, cruelty, madness. Appetite and vanity abounded, but with an abundant superficial grace, befitting a generation which, as by some æsthetic sense in the air, made the most of the pleasant outsides of life. All the various traits of the dying Middle Age were still in evidence among them, in all their crude effectiveness; only, blent, like rusty old armour wreathed in flowers, with the peculiar fopperies of the time, shrewdly divined from a distance, as happens with competent youth. To be in Paris itself, amid the full, delightful, fragrance of those dainty visible things which Huguenots despised:—that, surely, were the sum of good-fortune! Half-clerical, they loved nevertheless the touch of steel; had a laughing joy in trifling with its latent soul of destruction. In mimicry of the great world, they had their leaders, so inscrutably self-imposed:—instinctively, they felt and underwent that mystery of leadership, with its consequent heats of spirit, its tides and changes of influence.

On the other hand also, to Gaston, dreamily observant, it was quaint, likeable, the way they had of reproducing, unsuspectingly, the humours of animal nature. Does not the anthropologist tell us of a heraldry, with a large assortment of heraldic beasts, to be found among savage or half-savage peoples, as the "survival" of a period when men were nearer than they are or seem to be now, to the irrational world? Throughout the sprightly movement of the lads' daily life it was as if their "tribal" pets or monsters were with or within them. Tall Exmes, lithe and cruel like a tiger—it was pleasant to stroke him. The tiger was there, the parrot, the hare, the goat of course, and certainly much apishness. And, one and all, they were like the creatures, in their vagrant, short, memories, alert perpetually on the topmost crest of the day and hour, transferred so heartlessly, so entirely, from yesterday to to-day. Yet out of them, sure of some response, human heart did break:—in and around Camille Pontdormi, for instance, brilliant and ambitious, yet so sensitive about his threadbare home, concerning which however he had made the whole company, one by one, his confidants—so loyal to the people there, bursting into wild tears over the letter which brought the news of his younger brother's death, visibly fretting over it long afterwards. Still, for the most part, in their perfect health, nothing seemed to reach them but their own boyish ordinances, their own arbitrary "form." It was an absolute indifference; most striking when they lifted their well-trained voices to sing in choir, vacant as the sparrows, while the eloquent, far-reaching, aspiring words floated melodiously from them, sometimes, with truly medieval license, singing to the sacred music those songs from the streets (no one cared to detect) which were really in their hearts. A world of vanity and appetite, yet after all of honesty with itself! Like grown people, they were but playing a game, and meant to observe its rules. Say, rather, a world of honesty, and of courage! They, at least, were not preoccupied all day long, and, if they woke in the night, with the fear of death.

It was part of their precocious worldliness to recognise, to feel a little afraid of their new companion's intellectual power. Those obviously meditative souls, which seem "not to sleep o' nights," seldom fail to put others on their guard. Who can tell what they may be judging, planning in silence, so near to one? Looking back long afterwards across the dark period that had intervened, Gaston could trace their ways through the world. Not many of them had survived to his own middle life. Reappearing, from point to point, they connected themselves with the great crimes, the great tragedies of the time, as so many bright-coloured threads in that sombre tapestry of human passion. To recall in the obtuse, grieved, marred faces of uninteresting men or women, the disappointments, the sorrows, the tragic mistakes of the children they were long ago; that is a good trick for taking our own sympathy by surprise, which Gaston practised when he saw the last, or almost the last, of some of them, and felt a great pity, a great indulgence.

Here and now, at all events, carrying their cheerful tumult through all those quiet ecclesiastical places—the bishop's garden, the great sacristy, neat and clean in its brown, pensive lights, they seemed of a piece with the bright, simple, inanimate things, the toys, of nature. They made one lively picture with the fruit and wine they loved, the birds they captured, the buckets of clear water drawn for pastime from the great well, and Jean Sémur's painted conjuring book stolen from the old sorceress, his grandmother, out of which he told their fortunes; with the musical instruments of others; with their carefully hidden dice and playing-cards, worn or soiled by the fingers of the older gamesters who had discarded them. Like their elders, they read eagerly, in racy, new translations, old Greek and Latin books, with a delightful shudder at the wanton paganism. It was a new element of confusion in the presentment of that miniature world. The classical enthusiasm laid hold on Gaston too, but essayed in vain to thrust out of him the medieval character of his experience, or put on quite a new face, insinuating itself rather under cover of the Middle Age, still in occupation all around him. Venus, Mars, Æneas, haunted, in contemporary shape, like ghosts of folk one had known, the places with which he was familiar. Latin might still seem the fittest language for oratory, sixteen hundred years after Cicero was dead; those old Roman pontiffs, draped grandly, sat in the stalls of the choir; Propertius made love to Cynthia in the raiment of the foppish Amadée; they played Terence, and it was but a play within a play. Above all, in natural, heartfelt kinship with

their own violent though refined and cunning time, they loved every incident of soldiering; while the changes of the year, the lights, the shadows,
the flickering fires of winter, with which Gaston had first associated his
companions, so full of artificial enjoyment for the well-to-do, added themselves pleasantly, by way of shifting background, to the spectacular effect.

It was the brilliant surface with which the untried world confronted
him. Touch it where you might, you felt the resistant force of the solid matter
of human experience—of human experience, in its strange mixture of beauty
and evil, its sorrow, its ill-assorted fates, its pathetic acquiescence; above
all, in its overpowering certainty, over against his own world of echoes and
shadows, which perhaps only seemed to be so much as echoes or shadows.
A nature with the capacity of worship, he was straightway challenged, as
by a rival new religion claiming to supersede the religion he knew, to identify himself conclusively with this so tangible world, its suppositions, its
issues, its risks. Here was a world, certainly, which did not halt in meditation, but prompted one to make actual trial of it, with a liberty of heart
which might likely enough traverse this or that precept (if it were not rather
a mere scruple) of his earlier conscience. These its children, at all events,
were, as he felt, in instinctive sympathy with its motions; had shrewd divi-
nations or the things men really valued, and waited on them with unques-
tioning docility. Two worlds, two antagonistic ideals, were in evidence before
him. Could a third condition supervene, to mend their discord, or only vex
him perhaps, from time to time, with efforts towards an impossible adjustment?

At a later date, Monseigneur Charles Guillard, then Bishop of Chartres,
became something like a Huguenot, and ceased, with the concurrence of
ecclesiastical authority, from his high functions. Even now he was but a
protégé of King Charles in his relations to a more than suspicious Pope;
and a rumour of the fact, reaching somehow these brisk young ears, had
already set Gaston's mind in action, tremblingly, as to those small degrees,
scarcely realisable perhaps one by one, though so immeasurable in their
joint result, by which one might part from the "living vine"; and at times
he started back, as if he saw his own benighted footsteps pacing lightly
towards an awful precipice. At present, indeed, the assumption that there
was sanctity in everything the kindly prelate touched, was part of the well-

maintained etiquette of the little ecclesiastical court. But, as you meet in the street faces that are like a sacrament, so there are faces, looks, tones of voice, among dignified priests as among other people, to hear or look upon which is to feel the hypothesis of an unseen world impossible. As he smiled amiably out of the midst of his pontifical array on Gaston's scrupulous devotion, it was as if the old Roman augur smiled not only to his fellow augur but to the entire assistant world. In after years Gaston seemed to understand, and, as a consequence of understanding, to judge his old patron equitably; the religious sense too, had its various species. The nephew of his predecessor in the see, with a real sense of the divine world but as something immeasurably distant, Monseigneur Guillard had been brought by maladroit worldly good-fortune a little too close to its immediate and visible embodiments. From afar, you might trace the divine agency on its way. But to touch, to handle it, with these fleshly hands:—well! for Monseigneur, that was by no means to believe because the thing was "incredible, or absurd." He had smiled, not certainly from irreverence, nor (a prelate for half his life) in conscious incredulity, but only in mute surprise, at an administration of divine graces—this administration in which he was a high priest—in itself, to his quite honest thinking, so unfitting, so improbable. And was it that Gaston too was a less independent ruler of his own mental world than he had fancied, that he derived his impressions of things not directly from them, but mediately from other people's impressions about them, and he needed the pledge of their assents to ratify his own? Only, could that, after all, be a real sun, at which other people's faces were not irradiated? And sometimes it seemed, with a riotous swelling of the heart, as if his own wondrous appetite in these matters had been deadened by surfeit, and there would be a pleasant sense of liberty, of escape out-of-doors, could he be as little touched as almost all other people by Our Lady's Church, and old associations, and all those relics, and those dark, close, fragrant aisles.

At such times, to recall the winged visitant, gentle, yet withal sensitive to offence, which had settled on his youth with so deep a sense of assurance, he would climb the tower of Jean de Beauce, then fresh in all its array of airy staircase and pierced traceries, and great uncovered timbers, like some gigantic birdnest amid the stones, whence the large, quiet, country spaces became his own again, and the curious eye, at least, went home. He was become well aware of the power of those familiar influences in restoring equanimity, as he might have used a medicine or a wine. At each ascending storey, as the flight of the birds, the scent of the fields, swept past him, till he stood at last amid the unimpeded light and air of the watch-chamber above the great bells, some coil of perplexity, of unassimilable thought or fact, fell away from him. He saw the distant paths, and seemed to hear the breeze piping suddenly upon them under the cloudless sky, on its unseen, capricious way through those vast reaches of atmosphere. At this height, the low ring of blue hills was visible, with suggestions of that south-west country of peach-blossom and wine which had sometimes decoyed his thoughts towards the sea, and beyond it to "that new world of the Indies," which was held to explain a certain softness in the air from that quarter, even in the most vehement weather. Amid those vagrant shadows and shafts of light must be Deux-manoirs, the deserted rooms, the gardens, the graves. In mid-distance, even then a funeral procession was on its way humbly to one of the village churchyards. He seemed almost to hear the words across the stillness.

They identified themselves, as with his own earliest prepossessions, so also with what was apt to present itself as being the common human prepossession—a certain finally authoritative common sense upon the quiet experience of things—the oldest, the most authentic, of all voices, audible always, if one stepped aside for a moment and got one's ears into what might after all be their normal condition. It might be heard, it would seem, in proportion as men were in touch with the Earth itself, in country life, in manual work upon it, above all by the open grave, as if, reminiscent of some older, deeper, more permanent ground of fact, it whispered then oracularly a certain secret to those who came into such close contact with it. Persistent after-thought! Would it always survive, amid the indifference of others, amid the verdicts of the world, amid a thousand doubts? It seemed to have found, and filled to overflowing, the soul of one amiable little child who had a kind of genius for tranquillity, and on his first coming hither had led Gaston to what he held to be the choicest, pleasantest places, as being impregnable by noise. In his small stock of knowledge, he knew, like all around him, that he was going to die, and took kindly to the thought of a small grave in the little green close, as to a natural sleeping-place, in which he would be at home beforehand. Descending from the tower, Gaston knew he should find the child seated alone, enjoying the perfect quiet of the warm afternoon, for all the world was absent—gone forth to receive or gaze at a company of distinguished pilgrims.

Coming, sometimes with immense prelude and preparation, as when King Charles himself arrived to replace an image disfigured by profane Huguenots, sometimes with the secrecy and suddenness of an apparition vanished before the public was aware, the pilgrims to "Our Lady under the Earth" were the standing resource of those (such there were at Chartres as everywhere else) who must needs depend for the interest of their exist-ence on the doings of their neighbours. A motley host, only needing their Chaucer to figure as a looking-glass of life, type against type, they brought with them, on the one hand, the very presence and perfume of Paris, the centre of courtly propriety and fashion; on the other hand, with faces which seemed to belong to another age, curiosities of existence from remote prov-inces of France, or Europe, from distant, half-fabulous lands, remoter still. Jules Damville, who would have liked best to be a sailor, to command, not in any spiritual ark, but in the French fleet—should half-ruined France ever come to have one—led his companions one evening to inspect a strange maritime personage, stout and square, returned, contrary to all expecta-tion, after ten years' captivity among the savages of Florida, kneeling among the lights at the shrine, with the frankness of a good child, his hair like a mat, his hands tattooed, his mahogany face seamed with a thousand weather-wrinklings, his outlandish offerings lying displayed around him.

Looking, listening, as they served them in the episcopal guest-cham-ber, those young clerks made wonderful leaps, from time to time, in manly knowledge. With what eager shrewdness they noted, discussed, reproduced, the manners and attire of their pilgrim guests, sporting what was to their liking therein in the streets of Chartres. The more cynical or supercilious pilgrim would sometimes present himself—a personage oftenest of high ecclesiastical station, like the eminent translator of Plutarch, Amyot, af-terwards Bishop of Auxerre, who seemed to care little for shrine or relic, but lingered long over certain dim manuscripts in the canonical library, where our scholarly Gaston was of service, helping him directly to what he desired to see. And one morning early, visible at a distance to all the world, risen betimes to gaze, the Queen-mother and her three sons were kneeling there—yearning, greedy, as ever, for a hundred diverse, perhaps incompatible, things. It was at the beginning of that winter of the great siege of Chartres, the morning on which the child Guy Debreschescourt died in his sleep. His tiny body—the placid, massive, baby head still one broad smile, the rest of him wrapped round together like a chrysalis—was put to rest finally, in a fold of the winding-sheet of a very aged person, deceased at the same hour.

For a hard winter, like that famous winter of 1567, the hardest that had been known for fifty years, makes an end of the weak—the aged, the very young. To the robust, how pleasant had the preparation for it seemed the scent of the first wood-fire upon the keen October air; the earth turning from gray to black under the plough; the great stacks of fuel, come down lazily from the woods of Le Perche, along the winding Eure; its wholesome perfume; the long, soothing nights, and early twilight. The mind of Gaston, for one, was touched by the sense of some remote and delicate beauty in these things, like magicians' work, like an effect of magic as being extorted from unsuspected sources.

What winter really brought however, was the danger and vexation of a great siege. The householders of Catholic Chartres had watched the forces of their Huguenot enemies gathering from this side and that; and at last the dreaded circle was complete. They were prisoners like the rest, Gaston and the grandparents, shut up in their little hotel; and Gaston, face to face with it, understood at last what war really means. After all, it took them by surprise. It was early in the day. A crowd of worshippers filled the church of Sainte-Foy, built partly upon the ramparts; and at the conclusion of the mass, the Sacrament was to be carried to a sick person. Touched by unusual devotion at this perilous time, the whole assembly rose to escort the procession on its way, passing out slowly, group after group, as if by mechanical instinct, the more reluctant led on by the general consent. Gaston, the last lingerer, halting to let others proceed quietly before him, turned himself about to gaze upon the deserted church, half tempted to remain, ere he too stepped forth lightly and leisurely, when under a shower of massy stones from the *coulevrines* or great cannon of the besiegers, the entire roof of the place sank into the empty space behind him. But it was otherwise in a neighbouring church, crushed, in a similar way, with all its good people, not long afterwards.

And in the midst of the siege, with all its tumult about her, the old grandmother died, to the undissembled sorrow of Gaston, bereft, unexpectedly as it seemed, of the gentle creature, to whom he had always turned for an affection, that had been as no other in its absolute incapacity of offence. A tear upon the cheek, like the bark of a tree, testified to some unfulfilled hope, something wished for but not to be, which left resignation, by nature or grace, still imperfect, and made death at fourscore years and ten seem, after all, like a premature summons in the midst of one's days. For a few hours, the peace which followed brought back to the face a protesting gleam of youth, far antecedent to anything Gaston could possibly have remembered there, moving him to a pity, a peculiar sense of pleading helplessness, which to the end of his life was apt to revive at the sight (it might be in an animal) of what must perforce remember that it had been young but was old.

That broken link with life seemed to end some other things for him. As one puts away the toys of childhood, so now he seemed to discard what had been the central influence of his earlier youth, what more than anything else had stirred imagination and brought the consciousness of his own life warm and full. Gazing now upon the "holy and beautiful place," as he had gazed on the dead face, for a moment he seemed to anticipate the indifference of age. And when not long after the rude hands of Catholics themselves, at their wits' end for the maintenance of the "religious war," spoiled it of the accumulated treasure of centuries, leaving Notre-Dame de Chartres in the bareness with which we see it to-day, he had no keen sense of personal loss.

III

MODERNITY

THE BESIEGING ARMIES DISAPPEARED LIKE THE SNOW, LEAVING CITY AND SUB-
urb in all the hardened soilure of war and winter, which only the torrents
of spring would carry away. And the spring came suddenly: it was pleasant, after that long confinement, to walk afar securely through its early
fervours. Gaston too went forth on his way home, not alone. Three chosen
companions went with him, pledged to the old manor for months to come;
its lonely ancient master welcoming readily the tread of youth about him.

"The Triumvirate":—so their comrades had been pleased to call the
three; that term (delightful touch of classic colour on one's own trite but
withal pedantic age) being then familiar, as the designation of three conspicuous agents on the political scene of the generation just departing.
Only, these young Latinists went back for the associations of the word to
its Roman original, to the three gallants of the distant time, rather than to
those native French heroes—Montmorenci, Saint-André, Guise—too close
to them to seem really heroic. Mark Antony, knight of Venus, of Cleopatra;
shifty Lepidus; bloody, yellow-haired Augustus, so worldly and so fine; you
might find their mimic semblance, more easily than any suggestion of that
threadbare triad of French adventurers, in the unfolding manhood of Jasmin,
Amadée, and Camille.

They had detached themselves by an irresistible natural effective-

ness from the surface of that youthful scholastic world around the episcopal throne of Chartres, carrying its various aptitudes as if to a perfect triple
flower; restless Amadée de l'Autrec, who was to be a soldier, dazzled early
into dangerous, rebellious paths by the iron ideal of the soldiers of "the
religion," and even now fitting his blond prettiness to airs of Huguenot
austerity; Camille Pontdormi, who meant to be a lawyer in an age in which
certain legists had asserted an audacity of genius after a manner very cap-
tivating to youth with any appetite for predominance over its fellows—
already winsomely starched a little, amid his courtly finery, of garb, and
manner, and phrase; Jasmin de Villebon, who hardly knew what he meant
to be, except perhaps a poet—himself, certainly, a poem for any competent reader. Vain,—yes! a little; and mad, said his companions, of course,
with his clinging, exigent, lover's ways. It was he who had led the others on
this visit to Gaston de Latour. Threads to be cut short, one by one, before
his eyes, the three would cross and recross, gaily, pathetically, in the tapestry of Gaston's years; and, divided far asunder afterwards, seemed at this
moment, moving there before him in the confidential talk he could not
always share, inseparably linked together, like some complicated pictorial
arabesque, under the common light, of their youth, and of the morning,
and of their sympathetic understanding of the visible world.

So they made their way, under the rows of miraculous white thorn-
blossom, and through the green billows, at peace just then, though the war
still blazed or smouldered along the southern banks of the Loire and far
beyond, and it was with a delightful sense of peril, of prowess attested in
the facing of it, that they passed from time to time half-ruined or deserted
farm-buildings where the remnants of the armies might yet be lingering. It
was Jasmin, poetic Jasmin, who, in giving Gaston the book he now carried
ever ready to hand, had done him perhaps the best of services, for it had
proved the key to a new world of seemingly boundless intellectual resources,
and yet with a special closeness to visible or sensuous things;—the scent
and colour of the field-flowers, the amorous business of the birds, the flush
and re-fledging of the black earth itself in that fervent springtide, which
was therefore unique in Gaston's memory. It was his intellectual springtide;
as people look back to a physical spring, which for once in ten or fifteen
years, for once in a lifetime, was all that spring could be.

The book was none other than Pierre de Ronsard's "Odes," with "*Mignonne! allons voir si la Rose*," and "The Skylark" and the lines to April—itself verily like nothing so much as a jonquil, in its golden-green binding and yellow edges and perfume of the place where it had lain—sweet, but with something of the sickliness of all spring flowers since the days of Proserpine. Just eighteen years old, and the work of the poet's own youth, it took possession of Gaston with the ready intimacy of one's equal in age, fresh at every point; and he experienced what it is the function of contemporary poetry to effect anew for sensitive youth in each succeeding generation. The truant and irregular poetry of his own nature, all in solution there, found an external and authorised mouthpiece, ranging itself rightfully, as the latest achievement of human soul in this matter, along with the consecrated poetic voices of the past.

Poetry! Hitherto it had seemed hopelessly chained to the bookshelf, like something in a dead language, "dead, and shut up in reliquaries of books," or like those relics "one may only see through a little pane of glass," as one of its recent "liberators" had said. Sure, apparently, of its own "niche in the temple of Fame," the recognised poetry of literature had had the anticipation! Here was a poetry which boldly assumed the dress, the words, the habits, the very trick, of contemporary life, and turned them into gold. It took possession of the lily in one's hand, and projecting it into a visionary distance, shed upon the body of the flower the soul of its beauty. Things were become at once more deeply sensuous and more deeply ideal. As at the touch of a wizard, something more came into the rose than its own natural blush. Occupied so closely with the visible, this new poetry had so profound an intuition of what can only be felt, and maintained that mood in speaking of such objects as wine, fruit, the plume in the cap, the ring on the finger. And still that was no dubious or generalised form it gave to flower or bird, but the exact pressure of the jay at the window; you could count the petals,—of the exact natural number; no expression could be too faithful to the precise texture of things; words, too, must embroider, be twisted and spun, like silk or golden hair. Here were real people, in their real, delightful attire, and you understood how they moved; the visible was more visible than ever before, just because soul had come to its surface. The juice in the flowers, when Ronsard named them, was like wine or blood. It was such a coloured thing; though the gray things also, the cool things, all the fresher for the contrast—with a freshness, again, that seemed to touch and cool the soul—found their account there; the clangorous passage of the birds at night foretokening rain, the moan of the wind at the door, the wind's self made visible over the yielding corn.

It was thus Gaston understood the poetry of Ronsard, generously expanding it to the full measure of its intention. That poetry, too, lost its thaumaturgic power in turn, and became mere literature in exchange for life, partly in the natural revolution of poetic taste, partly for its faults. Faults and all, however, Gaston loyally accepted it; those faults—the lapse of grace into affectation, of learning into pedantry, of exotic fineness into a trick—counting with him as but the proof of faith to its own dominant positions. They were but characteristics, needing no apology with the initiated, or welcome even, as savouring of the master's peculiarities of perfection. He listened, he looked round freely, but always now with the ear, the eye, of his favourite poet. It had been a lesson, a doctrine, the communication of an art,—the art of placing the pleasantly æsthetic, the welcome, elements of life at an advantage, in one's view of it, till they seemed to occupy the entire surface; and he was sincerely grateful for an undeniable good service.

And yet the gifted poet seemed but to have spoken what was already in Gaston's own mind, what he had longed to say, had been just going to say; so near it came, that it had the charm of a discovery of one's own. That was an illusion, perhaps; it was because the poet told one so much about himself, making so free a display of what though personal was very contagious; of his love-secrets especially, how love and nothing else filled his mind. He was in truth but "love's secretary," noting from hour to hour its minutely changing fortunes. Yes! that was the reason why visible, audible, sensible things glowed so brightly, why there was such luxury in sounds, words, rhythms, of the new light come on the world, of that wonderful freshness. With a masterly appliance of what was near and familiar, or again in the way of bold innovation, he found new words for perennially new things, and the novel accent awakened long-slumbering associations. Never before had words, single words, meant so much. What expansion, what liberty of heart, in speech: how associable to music, to singing, the written lines! He sang of the lark, and it was the lark's voluble self. The physical beauty of humanity lent itself to every object, animate or inanimate, to the very hours and lapses and changes of time itself. An almost burdensome fulness of expression haunted the gestures, the very dress, the personal ornaments, of the people on the highway. Even Jacques Bonhomme at his labour, or idling for an hour, borrowed from his love, homely as it was, a touch of dignity or grace, and some secret of utterance, which made one think of Italy or Greece. The voice of the shepherd calling, the chatter of the shepherdess turning her spindle, seemed to answer, or wait for answer,—to be fragments of love's ideal and eternal communing.

It was the power of "modernity," as renewed in every successive age for genial youth, protesting, defiant of all sanction in these matters, that the true "classic" must be of the present, the force and patience of present time. He had felt after the thing, and here it was,—the one irresistible poetry there had ever been, with the magic word spoken in due time, transforming his own age and the world about him, presenting its everyday touch, the very trick one knew it by, as an additional grace, asserting the latent poetic rights of the transitory, the fugitive, the contingent. Poetry need no longer mask itself in the habit of a bygone day: Gaston could but pity the people of bygone days for not being above-ground to read. Here, was a discovery, a new faculty, a privileged apprehension, to be conveyed in turn to one and to another, to be propagated for the imaginative regeneration of the world. It was a manner, a habit of thought, which would invade ordinary life, and mould that to its intention. In truth, all the world was already aware, and delighted. The "school" was soon to pay the penalty of that immediate acceptance, that intimate fitness to the mind of its own time, by sudden and profound neglect, as a thing preternaturally tarnished and tame, like magic youth, or magic beauty, turned in a moment by magic's own last word into withered age. But then, to the liveliest spirits of that time it had seemed nothing less than "impeccable," after the manner of the great sacred products of the past, though in a living tongue. Nay! to Gaston for one, the power of the old classic poetry itself was explained by the reflex action of the new, and might seem to justify its pretensions at last.

From the poem fancy wandered to the poet, and curious youth would fain see the writer in person,—what a poet was like, with anxious surmises, this way and that, as to the degree in which the precious mental particles might be expected to have wrought up the outward presence to their own high quality. A creature of the eye, in this case at least, the intellectual hold on him being what it was, Gaston had no fear of disillusion. His poetic readings had borrowed an additional relish from the genial, companionable, manner of his life at this time, taking him into the remotest corners of the vast level land, and its outer ring of blue up-lands; amid which, as he rode one day with "the three," towards perfectly new prospects, he had chanced on some tangible rumour of the great poet's present abode. The hill they had mounted at leisure, in talk with a village priest, dropped suddenly upon a vague tract of wood and pasture, with a dark ridge beyond towards the south-west; and the black notch, which broke its outline against the mellow space of evening light, was the steeple of the priory of Croix-val, of which reverend body Pierre de Ronsard, although a layman, was, by special favour of King Charles, Superior.

Though a formal peace was come, though the primary movers of war had taken hands or kissed each other, and were exchanging suspicious courtesies, yet the unquiet temper of war was still abroad everywhere, with an after-crop of miserable incidents. The captainless national and mercenary soldiers were become in large number thieves or beggars, and the peasant's hand sank back to the tame labour of the plough reluctantly. Relieved a little by the sentimental humour of the hour, lending, as Ronsard prompted, a poetic and always amorous interest to everything around him, poor Gaston's very human soul was vexed nevertheless at the spectacle of the increased hardness of human life, with certain misgivings from time to time at the contrast of his own luxurious tranquillity. The homeless woman suckling her babe at the road-side, the gray-beard hasting before the storm, the tattered fortune-teller who, when he shook his head at her proposal to "read his hand," assured him (perhaps with some insight into his character) "You do *that*"—you shake your head, negatively—"too much!" these, and the like, might count as fitting human accidents in an impassioned landscape picture. And his new imaginative culture had taught him to value "surprises" in nature itself; the quaint, exciting charm of the mistletoe in the wood, of the blossom before the leaf, the cry of passing birds at night. Nay! the most familiar details of nature, its daily routine of light and darkness, beset him now with a kind of troubled and troubling eloquence. The rain, the first streak of dawn, the very sullenness of the sky, had a power, only to be described by saying that they seemed to be *moral facts*.

On his way at last to gaze on the abode of the new hero or demi-god of poetry, Gaston perceives increasingly, as another excellence of his verse, how truthful, how close it is to the minute fact of the scene around; as there are pleasant wines which, expressing the peculiar quality of their native soil, lose their special pleasantness away from home. The physiognomy of the scene was changed; the plain of La Beauce had ruffled itself into low green hills and gently winding valleys, with clear, quick water, and fanciful patches of heath and woodland. Here and there a secular oak tree maintained a solitude around it. It was the district of the "little river Loir"— the Vendomois; and here, in its own country, the new poetry, notwithstanding its classic elegance, might seem a native wild flower, modest enough.

He came riding with his companions towards evening along the road which had suddenly abandoned its day-long straightness for wanton curves and ascents; and there, as an owl on the wing cried softly, beyond the tops of the spreading poplars was the west front, silver-gray, and quiet, inexpressibly quiet, with its worn, late-gothic "flamings" from top to bottom, as full of reverie to Gaston's thinking as the enchanted castle in a storybook. The village lay thinly scattered around the wide, grass-grown space; below was the high espaliered garden-wall, and within it, visible through the open doors, a gaunt figure, hook-nosed, like a wizard, at work with the spade, too busily to turn and look. Or was it that he did not hear at all the question repeated thrice:—Could one see His Reverence the Prior, at least in his convent church? "You see him" was the answer, as a face, all nerve, distressed nerve, turned upon them not unkindly, the vanity of the great man aware and pleasantly tickled. The unexpected incident had quickened a prematurely aged pulse, and in reward for their good service the young travellers were bidden carry their equipment, not to the village inn, but to the guest-chamber of the half-empty priory. The eminent man of letters, who had been always an enthusiastic gardener though busy just now not with choice flowers but with salutary kitchen-stuff, working indeed with much effort, to counteract the gout, was ready enough in his solitude to make the most of chance visitors, especially youthful ones. A bell clanged; he laid aside the spade, and casting an eye at the whirling weather-vanes announced that it would snow. There had been no "sunset." They had travelled away imperceptibly from genial afternoon into a world of ashen evening.

The enemies of the lay Prior, satirists literary and religious, falsely made a priest of him, a priest who should have sacrificed a goat to pagan Bacchus. And in truth the poet, for a time a soldier, and all his life a zealous courtier, had always been capable, as a poet should be, of long-sustained meditation, adapting himself easily enough to the habits of the "religious," following attentively the choir-services in their church, of which he was a generous benefactor, and to which he presently proceeded for vespers. Gaston and "the three" sat among the Brethren, tempting curious eyes, in the stalls of the half-lighted choir, while in purple cope and jaunty biretta the lay Prior "assisted," his *confidentiaire*, or priestly substitute, officiating at the altar. The long, sad, Lenten office over, an invitation to supper followed, for Ronsard still loved, in his fitful retirements at one or another of his numerous benefices, to give way to the chance recreation of flattering company, and these gay lads' enthusiasm for his person was obvious. And as for himself, the great poet, with his bodily graces and airs of court, had always possessed the gift of pleasing those who encountered him.

The snow was falling now in big, slow flakes, a great fire blazing under the chimney with its cipher and enigmatic motto, as they sat down to the leek-soup, the hard eggs, and the salad grown and gathered by their host's own hands. The long stone passages through which they passed from church, with the narrow brown doors of the monks' dormitories one after another along the whitewashed wall, made the coquetries of the Prior's own distant apartment all the more reassuring. You remembered that from his ninth year he had been the pet of princesses, the favourite of kings. Upon the cabinets, chests, book-cases, around, were ranged the *souvenirs* received from various royal persons, including three kings of France, the fair Queen of Scots, Elizabeth of England; and the conversation fell to, and was kept going by, the precious contents of the place where they were sitting, the books printed and bound as they had never been before—books which meant assiduous study, the theory of poetry with Ronsard always accompanying its practice—delicate things of art, which beauty had handled or might handle, the pictured faces on the walls, in their frames of reeded ebony or jewelled filigree. There was the Minerva, decreed him at a conference of the elegant, pedantic "Jeux Floraux," which had claimed Pierre de Ronsard "Prince of Poets." The massive silver image Ronsard had promptly offered to his patron King Charles; but in vain, for, though so greatly in want of ready-money that he melted down church ornaments and exacted "black" contributions from the clergy, one of the things in which Charles had ever been sincere was a reverence for literature.

So there it stood, doing duty for Our Lady, with gothic crown and a fresh sprig of consecrated box, bringing the odd, enigmatic physiognomy, preferred by the art of that day, within the sphere of religious devotion. The King's manuscript, declining, in verse really as good as Ronsard's, the honour not meant for him, might be read, attached to the pedestal. The ladies of his own verse, Marie, Cassandre, and the rest, idols one after another of a somewhat artificial and for the most part unrequited love, from the Angevine maiden—*La petite pucelle Angevine*—who had vexed his young soul by her inability to yield him more than a faint Platonic affection, down to Helen, to whom he had been content to propose no other, gazed, more impassibly than ever, from the walls.

They might have been sisters, those many successive loves, or one and the same lady over and over again, in slightly varied humour and attire perhaps, at the different intervals of some rather lengthy, mimetic *masque* of love, to which the theatrical dress of that day was appropriate; for the mannered Italian, or Italianised, artists, including the much-prized, native Janet, with his favourite water-green backgrounds, aware of the poet's predilection, had given to all alike the same brown eyes and tender eyelids and golden hair and somewhat ambered paleness, varying only the curious artifices of the dress—knots, and nets, and golden spider-work, and clear, flat stones. Dangerous guests in that simple, cloistral place, Sibyls of the Renaissance on a mission from Italy to France, to Gaston one and all seemed under the burden of some weighty message concerning a world unknown to him; the stealthy lines of cheek and brow contriving to express it, while the lips and eyes only smiled, not quite honestly. It had been a learned love, with undissembled "hatred of the vulgar." Three royal Margarets, much-praised *pearls* of three succeeding generations (for to the curious in these objects purity is far from being the only measure of value) asserted charms a thought more frank, or French, though still gracefully pedantic, with their quaintly kerchiefed books—books of what?—in their pale hands. Among the ladies, on the pictured wall as in life, were the poet's male companions, stirring memories of a more material sort, though their common interest had been poetry—memories of that "Bohemia," which even a prince of court poets had frequented when he was young, of his cruder youthful vanities. In some cases the date of death was inscribed below.

One there was among them, the youngest, of whose genial fame to come this experienced judge of men and books, two years before "St. Bartholomew's," was confident—a crowned boy, King Charles himself. Here perhaps was the single entirely disinterested sentiment of the poet's life, wholly independent of a long list of benefits, or benefices; for the younger had turned winsomely, appealingly, to the elder, who, forty years of age, feeling chilly at the thought, had no son. And of one only of those companions did the memory bring a passing cloud. It was long ago, on a journey, that he had first spoken, accidentally, with Joachim du Bellay, whose friendship had been the great intellectual fortune of his life. For a moment one saw the encounter at the wayside inn, in the broad, gay morning, a quarter of a century since; and there was the face—deceased at thirty-five. Pensive, plaintive, refined by sickness, of exceeding delicacy, it must from the first have been best suited to the grayness of an hour like this.—To-morrow, where will be the snow?

The leader in that great poetic battle of the Pleiad, their host himself (he explained the famous device, and named the seven chief stars in the constellation) was depicted appropriately, in veritable armour, with antique Roman cuirass of minutely inlaid gold, and flowered mantle; the crisp, ceremonial, laurel-wreath of the Roman conqueror lying on the audacious, over-developed brows, above the great hooked nose of practical enterprise. In spite of his pretension to the Epicurean conquest of a kingly indifference of mind, the portrait of twenty years ago betrayed, not less than the living face with its roving, astonished eyes, the haggard soul of a haggard generation, whose eagerly-sought refinements had been after all little more than a theatrical make-believe—an age of wild people, of insane impulse, of homicidal mania. The sweet-souled songster had no more than others attained real calm in it. Even in youth nervous distress had been the chief facial characteristic. Triumphant, nevertheless, in his battle for Greek beauty—for the naturalisation of Greek beauty in the brown cloud-lands of the North—he might have been thinking, contemptuously, of barking little Saint-Gelais, or of Monsieur Marot's pack-thread poems. He, for his part, had always held that poetry should be woven of delicate silk, or of fine linen, or at least of good home-spun worsted.

To Gaston, yielding himself to its influence, for a moment the scene around seemed unreal: an exotic, embalming air, escaped from some old Greek or Roman pleasure-place, had turned the poet's workroom into a strange kind of private sanctuary, amid these rude conventual buildings, with the March wind aloud in the chimneys. Notwithstanding, what with the long day's ride, the keen evening, they had done justice to the monastic fare, the "little" wine of the country, the cream, the onions,—fine Camille, and dainty Jasmin, and the poet turned to talk upon gardening, concerning which he could tell them a thing or two—of early salads, and those special apples the king loved to receive from him, *millefleurs* pippins, painted with a thousand tiny streaks of red, yellow, and green. A dish of them came to table now, with a bottle, at the right moment, from the darkest corner of the cellar. And then, in nasal voice, well-trained to Latin intonation, giving a quite medieval amplitude to the poet's sonorities of rhythm and vocabulary, the Sub-prior was bidden to sing, after the notation of Goudimel, the "Elegy of the Rose"; the author girding cheerily at the clerkly man's assumed ignorance of such compositions.

It was but a half-gaiety, in truth, that awoke in the poet even now, with the singing and the good wine, as the notes echoed windily along the passages. On his forty-sixth year the unaffected melancholy of his later life was already gathering. The dead!—he was coming to be on their side. The fact came home to Gaston that this evocator of "the eternally youthful" was visibly old before his time; his work being done, or centered now for the most part on amendments, not invariably happy, of his earlier verse.

The little panelled drawers were full of them. The poet pulled out one, and as it stood open for a moment there lay the first book of the *Franciade*, in silken cover, white and gold, ready for the king's hands, but never to be finished.

Gaston, as he turned from that stolen reading of the opening verse in jerky, feverish, gouty manuscript, to the writer, let out his soul perhaps; for the poet's face struck fire too, and seeming to detect on a sudden the legible document of something by no means conventional below the young man's well-controlled manner and expression, he became as if paternally anxious for his intellectual furtherance, and in particular for the addition of "manly power" to a "grace" of mind, obviously there already in due sufficiency. Would he presently carry a letter with recommendation of himself to Monsieur Michel de Montaigne? Linked they were, in the common friendship of the late Etienne de la Boetie yonder! Monsieur Michel could tell him much of the great ones—of the Greek and Latin masters of style. Let his study be in them! With what justice, by the way, had those Latin poets dealt with winter, and wintry charms, in their bland Italy! And just then, at the striking of a rickety great bell of the Middle Age, in the hands of a cowled brother came the emblazoned grace-cup, with which the Prior de Ronsard had enriched his "house," and the guests withdrew.

"Yesterday's snow" was nowhere, a surprising sunlight everywhere; through which, after gratefully bidding adieu to the great poet, almost on their knees for a blessing, our adventurers returned home. Gaston, intently pondering as he lingered behind the others, was aware that this new poetry, which seemed to have transformed his whole nature into half-sensuous imagination, was the product not of one or more individual writers, but (it might be in the way of a response to their challenge) a general direction of men's minds, a delightful "fashion" of the time. He almost anticipated our modern idea, or platitude, of the *Zeit-geist*. A social instinct was involved in the matter, and loyalty to an intellectual *movement*. As its leader had himself been the first to suggest, the actual authorship belonged not so much to a star as to a constellation, like that hazy Pleiad he had pointed out in the sky, or like the swarm of larks abroad this morning over the corn, led by a common instinct, a large element in which was sympathetic trust in the instinct of others. Here, truly, was a doctrine to propa-

gate, a secret open to every one who would learn, towards a new manage-
ment of life,—nay! a new religion, or at least a new worship, maintaining
and visibly setting forth a single overpowering apprehension.

The worship of physical beauty a religion, the proper faculty of which
would be the bodily eye! Looked at in this way, some of the well-marked
characteristics of the poetry of the Pleiad assumed a hieratic, almost an
ecclesiastical air. That rigid correctness; that gracious unction, as of the
medieval Latin psalmody; that aspiring fervour; that jealousy of the profane "vulgar"; the sense, flattering to one who was in the secret, that this
thing, even in its utmost triumph, could never be really popular:—why were
these so welcome to him but from the continuity of early mental habit? He
might renew the overgrown tonsure, and wait, devoutly, rapturously, in this
goodly sanctuary of earth and sky about him, for the manifestation, at the
moment of his own worthiness, of flawless humanity, in some undreamed-
of depth and perfection of the loveliness of bodily form.

And therewith came the consciousness, no longer of mere bad-
neighbourship between what was old and new in his life, but of incompat-
ibility between two rival claimants upon him, of two ideals. Might that
new religion be a religion not altogether of goodness, a profane religion,
in spite of its poetic fervours? There were "flowers of evil," among the rest.
It came in part, avowedly, as a kind of consecration of evil, and seemed to
give it the beauty of holiness. Rather, good and evil were distinctions inap-
plicable in proportion as these new interests made themselves felt. For a
moment, amid casuistical questions as to one's indefeasible right to liberty of heart, he saw himself, somewhat wearily, very far gone from the
choice, the consecration, of his boyhood. If he could but be rid of that altogether! Or if that would but speak with irresistible decision and effect!
Was there perhaps somewhere, in some penetrative mind in this age of
novelties, some scheme of truth, some science about men and things, which
might harmonise for him his earlier and later preference, "the sacred and
the profane loves," or, failing that, establish, to his pacification, the exclusive supremacy of the latter?

IV

PEACH-BLOSSOM AND WINE

THOSE SEARCHINGS OF MIND BROUGHT FROM TIME TO TIME CRUEL STARTS FROM sleep, a sudden shudder at any wide outlook over life and its issues, draughts of mental east-wind across the hot mornings, into which the voices of his companions called him, to lose again in long rambles every thought save that of his own firm, abounding youth. These rambles were but the last, sweet, wastefully-spent remnants of a happy season. The letter for Monsieur Michel de Montaigne was to hand, with preparations for the distant journey which must presently break up their comradeship. Nevertheless, its actual termination overtook them at the last as if by surprise: on a sudden that careless interval of time was over.

The carelessness of "the three" at all events had been entire. Secure, on the low, warm, level surface of things, they talked, they rode, they ate and drank, with no misgivings, mental or moral, no too curious questions as to the essential nature of their so palpable well-being, or the rival standards thereof, of origins and issues. And yet, with all their gaiety, as its last triumphant note in truth, they were ready to trifle with death, welcoming, by way of a foil to the easy character of their days, a certain luxurious sense of danger—the night-alarm, the arquebuse peeping from some quiet farm-building across their way, the rumoured presence in their neighbourhood of this or that great military leader—delightful premonitions of the adventurous life soon to be their own in Paris. What surmises they had of any vaguer sort of danger, took effect, in that age of wizardry, as a quaintly *practical* superstition, the expectation of cadaverous "churchyard things" and the like, intruding themselves where they should not be, to be dissipated in turn by counter-devices of the dark craft which had evoked them. Gaston, then, as in after years, though he saw no ghosts, could not bear to trifle with such matters: to his companions it was a delight, as they supped, to note the indication of nameless terrors, if it were only in the starts and crackings of the timbers of the old place. To the turbid spirits of that generation the midnight heaven itself was by no means a restful companion; and many were the hours wasted by those young astrophiles in puzzling out the threats, or the enigmatic promises, of a starry sky.

The fact that armed persons were still abroad, thieves or assassins, lurking under many disguises, might explain what happened on the last evening of their time together, when they sat late at the open windows as the night increased, serene but covered summer night, aromatic, velvet-footed. What coolness it had was pleasant after the wine; and they strolled out, fantastically muffled in certain old heraldic dresses of parade, caught up in the hall as they passed through, Gaston alone remaining to attend on his grandfather. In about an hour's time they returned, not a little disconcerted, to tell a story of which Gaston was reminded (seeing them again in thought as if only half real, amid the bloomy night, with blood upon their boyish flowers) as they crossed his path afterwards at three intervals. Listening for the night-hawk, pushing aside the hedge-row to catch the evening breath off the honeysuckle, they had sauntered on, scarcely looking in advance, along the causeway. Soft sounds came out of the distance, but footsteps on the hard road they had not heard, when three others fronted them face to face—Jasmin, Amadée, and Camille—their very selves, visible in the light of the lantern carried by Camille: they might have felt the breath upon their cheeks: real, close, definite, cap for cap, plume for plume, flower for flower, a light like their own flashed up counter-wise, but with blood, all three of them, fresh upon the bosom, or in the mouth. It was well to draw the sword, be one's enemy carnal or spiritual; even devils, as wise men know, taking flight at its white glitter through the air. Out flashed the brave youths' swords, still with mimic counter-motion, upon nothing—upon the empty darkness before them.

Curdled at heart for an hour by that strange encounter, they went on their way next morning no different. There was something in the mere belief that peace was come at last. For a moment Huguenots were, or pretended to be, satisfied with a large concession of liberty; to be almost light of soul. The French, who can always pause in the very midst of civil bloodshed to eulogise the reign of universal kindness, were determined to treat a mere armistice as nothing less than realised Utopia. To bear offensive weapons became a crime; and the sense of security at home was attested by vague schemes of glory to be won abroad, under the leadership of "The Admiral," the great Huguenot Coligni, anxious to atone for his share in the unhappiness of France by helping her to foreign conquests. Philip of Spain had been watching for the moment when Charles and Catherine should call the Duke of Alva into France to continue his devout work there. Instead, the poetic mind of Charles was dazzled for a moment by the dream of wrestling the misused Netherlands from Spanish rule altogether.

Under such genial conditions, then, Gaston set out towards those south-west regions he had always yearned to, as popular imagination just now set thither also, in a vision of French ships going forth from the mouths of the Loire and the Gironde, from Nantes, Bordeaux, and La Rochelle, to the Indies, in rivalry of Spanish adventure. The spasmodic gaiety of the time blent with that of the season of the year, of his own privileged time of life, and allowed the opulent country through which he was to pass all its advantages. Ever afterwards that low ring of blue hills beyond La Beauce meant more for him, not less, than of old. After the reign of his native apple-blossom and corn, it was that of peach-blossom and wine. Southwards to Orleans and the Loire then, with the course of the sunny river, to Blois, to Amboise, to Tours, he traversed a region of unquestioned natural charm, heightened greatly by the mental atmosphere through which it reached him. Black Angers, white Saumur, with its double in the calm broad water below, the melancholy seigneurial woods of Blois, ranged themselves in his memory as so many distinct types of what was dignified or pleasant in human habitations. Frequently, along the great historic stream, as along some vast street, contemporary genius was visible (a little prematurely as

time would show) in a novel and seductive architecture, which, by its en-
graving of exotic grace on homely native forms, spoke of a certain restless
aspiration to be what one was not but might become—the old Gaulish desire to be refined, to be mentally enfranchised by the sprightlier genius of
Italy. With their terraced gardens, their airy galleries, their triumphal chim-
ney-pieces, their spacious stairways, their conscious provision for the elegant enjoyment of all seasons in turn, here surely were the new abodes
for the new humanity of this new, poetic, picturesque age. What but flawless
bodies, duly appointed to typically developed souls, could move on the
daily business of life through these dreamy apartments into which he entered from time to time, finding their very garniture like a personal presence in them? Was there light here in the earth itself? It was a landscape,
certainly, which did not merely accept the sun, but flashed it back gratefully from the white, gracious, carven houses, that were like a natural part
of it. As he passed below, fancy would sometimes credit the outlook from
their lofty gables with felicities of combination beyond possibility. What
prospects of mountain and sea-shore from those aerial window-seats!

And still, as in some sumptuous tapestry, the architecture, the landscape, were but a setting for the human figures: these palatial abodes, never
out of sight, high on the river bank, challenged continual speculation as to
their inhabitants—how they moved, read poetry and romance, or wrote
the memoirs which were like romance, passed through all the hourly changes
of their all-accomplished, intimate life. The Loire was the river pre-eminently of the monarchy, of the court; and the fleeting human interests, fact
or fancy, which gave its utmost value to the liveliness of the natural scene,
found a centre in the movements of Catherine and her sons, still roving,
after the eccentric habit inherited from Francis the First, from one "house
of pleasure" to another, in the pursuit at once of amusement and of that
political intrigue which was the serious business of their lives. Like some
fantastic company of strolling players amid the hushed excitement of a
little town, the royal family, with all its own small rivalries, would be housed
for the night under the same roof with some of its greater enemies—Henri
de Guise, Condé, "The Admiral," all alike taken by surprise—but courte-
ously, and therefore ineffectively. And Gaston, come thus by chance so close
to them, had the sense not so much of nearness to the springs of great

events, as of the likeness of the whole matter to a stage-play with its ingeniously contrived encounters, or the assortments of a game of chance.

And in a while the dominant course of the river itself, the animation
of its steady, downward flow, even amid the sand-shoals and whispering
islets of the dry season, bore his thoughts beyond it, in a sudden irresistible appetite for the sea; and he determined, varying slightly from the pre-
scribed route, to reach his destination by way of the coast. From Nantes
he descended imperceptibly along tall hedge-rows of acacia, till on a sudden, with a novel freshness in the air, through a low archway of laden fruit-
trees it was visible—sand, sea, and sky, in three quiet spaces, line upon
line. The features of the landscape changed again, and the gardens, the
rich orchards, gave way to bare, grassy undulations: only, the open sandy
spaces presented their own native flora, for the fine silex seemed to have
crept into the tall, wiry stalks of the ixias, like grasses the seeds of which
had expanded, by solar magic, into veritable flowers, crimson, green, or
yellow patched with black.

It was pleasant to sleep as if in the sea's arms, amid the low mur-
murs, the salt odour mingled with the wild garden scents of a little inn or
farm, forlorn in the wide enclosure of an ancient manor, deserted as the
sea encroached—long ago, for the fig-trees in the riven walls were tough
and old. Next morning he must turn his back betimes, with the freshness
of the outlook still undimmed, all colours turning to white on the shell-
beach, the wrecks, the children at play on it, the boat with its gay stream-
ers dancing in the foam. Bright as the scene of his journey had been, it had
had from time to time its grisly touches; a forbidden fortress with its steel-
clad inmates thrust itself upon the way; the village church had been ruined too recently to count as picturesque; and at last, at the meeting-point
of five long causeways across a wide expanse of marshland, where the wholesome sea turned stagnant, La Rochelle itself scowled through the heavy
air, the dark ramparts still rising higher around its dark townsfolk:—La
Rochelle, the "Bastion of the Gospel" according to John Calvin, the conceded capital of the Huguenots. They were there, and would not leave it,
even to share the festivities of the marriage of King Charles to his little
Austrian Elizabeth about this time—the armed chiefs of Protestantism,
dreaming of a "dictator" after the Roman manner, who should set up a re-

ligious republic. Serried closely together on land, they had a strange mixed
following on the sea. Lair of heretics, or shelter of martyrs, La Rochelle
was ready to protect the outlaw. The corsair, of course, would be a Protes-
tant, actually armed perhaps by sour old Jeanne of Navarre—the ship he
fell across, of course, Spanish. A real Spanish ship of war, gay, magnificent,
was gliding even then, stealthily, through the distant haze; and nearer lay
what there was of a French navy. Did the enigmatic "Admiral," the coming
dictator, Coligni, really wish to turn it to foreign adventure, in rivalry of
Spain, as the proper patriotic outcome of this period, or breathing-space,
of peace and national unity?

Undoubtedly they were still there, even in this halcyon weather, those
causes of disquiet, like the volcanic forces beneath the massive chestnut-
woods, spread so calmly through the breathless air, on the ledges and lev-
els of the red heights of the Limousin, under which Gaston now passed on
his way southwards. On his right hand a broad, lightly diversified expanse
of vineyard, of towns and towers innumerable, rolled its burden of fat things
down the slope of the Gironde towards the more perfect level beyond. In
the heady afternoon an indescribable softness laid hold on him, from the
objects, the atmosphere, the lazy business, of the scene around. And was
that the quarter whence the dry daylight, the intellectual iron, the chaly-
beate influence, was to come?—those coquettish, well-kept, vine-wreathed
towers, smiling over a little irregular old village, itself half-hidden in gad-
ding vine, pointed out by the gardeners (all labourers here were gardeners) as the end of his long, pleasant journey, as the abode of Monsieur Michel
de Montaigne, the singular but not unpopular gentleman living there among
his books, of whom Gaston hears so much over-night at the inn where he
rests, before delivering the great poet's letter, entering his room at last in a
flutter of curiosity.

In those earlier days of the Renaissance, a whole generation had been
exactly in the position in which Gaston now found himself. An older ideal
moral and religious, certain theories of man and nature actually in the
possession, still haunted humanity, at the very moment when it was called,
through a full knowledge of the past, to enjoy the present with an unrestricted expansion of its own capacities.—Might one enjoy? Might one eat
of all the trees?—Some had already eaten, and needed, retrospectively, a

theoretic justification, a sanction of their actual liberties, in some new reading of human nature itself and its relation to the world around it.— Explain to us the propriety, on the full view of things, of this bold course we have taken, or know we shall take!

Ex post facto, at all events, that justification was furnished by the *Essays* of Montaigne. The spirit of the essays doubtless had been felt already in many a mind, as, by a universal law of reaction, the intellect *does* supply the due theoretic equivalent to an inevitable course of conduct. But it was Montaigne certainly who turned that emancipating ethic into current coin. To Pascal, looking back upon the sixteenth century as a whole, Montaigne was to figure as the impersonation of its intellectual licence; while Shakespeare, who represents the free spirit of the Renaissance moulding the drama, hints, by his well-known preoccupation with Montaigne's writings, that just there was the philosophic counterpart to the fulness and impartiality of his own artistic reception of the experience of life.

Those essays, as happens with epoch-marking books, were themselves a life, the power which makes them what they are having been accumulated in them imperceptibly by a thousand repeated modifications, like character in a person: at the moment when Gaston presented himself, to go along with the great "egotist" for a season, that life had just begun. Born here, at the place whose name he took, *Montaigne*—the acclivity—of Saint Michael, just thirty-six years before, brought up simply, earthily, at nurse in one of the neighbouring villages, to him it was doubled strength to return thither, when, disgusted with the legal business which had filled his days hitherto, seeing that "France had more laws than all the rest of the world," and was what one saw, he began the true work of his life, a continual journey in thought, "a continual observation of new and unknown things," his bodily self remaining, for the most part, with seeming indolence at home.

It was Montaigne's boast that throughout those invasive times his house had lain open to all comers, that his frankness had been rewarded by immunity from all outrages of war, of the crime war shelters: and openness—that all was wide open, searched through by light and warmth and air from the soil—was the impression it made on Gaston, as he passed from farmyard to garden, from garden to court, to hall, up the wide winding stair, to the uppermost chamber of the great round tower; in which sun-baked place the studious man still lingered over a late breakfast, telling, like all around, of a certain homely epicureanism, a rare mixture of luxury with a preference for the luxuries that after all were home-grown and savoured of his native earth.

Sociable, of sociable intellect, and still inclining instinctively, as became his fresh and agreeable person, from the midway of life, towards its youthful side, he was ever on the alert for a likely interlocutor to take part in the conversation, which (pleasantest, truly! of all modes of human commerce) was also of ulterior service as stimulating that endless *inward* converse from which the essays were a kind of abstract. For him, as for Plato, for Socrates whom he cites so often, the essential dialogue was that of the mind with itself; but this dialogue throve best with, often actually needed, outward stimulus—physical motion, some text shot from a book, the queries and objections of a living voice.—"My thoughts sleep, if I sit still." Neither "thoughts," nor "dialogues," exclusively, but thoughts still partly implicate in the dialogues which had evoked them, and therefore not without many seemingly arbitrary transitions, many links of connexion to be supposed by the reader, constituting their characteristic difficulty, the *Essays* owed their actual publication at last to none of the usual literary motives—desire for fame, to instruct, to amuse, to sell—but to the sociable desire for a still wider range of conversation with others. He wrote for companionship, "if but one sincere man would make his acquaintance"; speaking on paper, as he "did to the first person he met."—"If there be any person, any knot of good company, in France or elsewhere, who can like my humour, and whose humours I can like, let them but whistle, and I will run!"

Notes of expressive facts, of words also worthy of note (for he was a lover of style), collected in the first instance for the help of an irregular memory, were becoming, in the quaintly labelled drawers, with labels of wise old maxim or device, the primary, rude stuff, or "protoplasm," of his intended work, and already gave token of its scope and variety. "All motion discovers us"; if to others, so also to ourselves. Movement, rapid movement of some kind, a ride, the hasty survey of a shelf of books, best of all a conversation like this morning's with a visitor for the first time,—amid the felicitous chances of that, at some random turn by the way, he would become aware of shaping purpose: the beam of light or heat would strike down, to illuminate, to fuse and organise the coldly accumulated matter, of reason, of experience. Surely, some providence over thought and speech led one finely through those haphazard journeys! But thus dependent to so great a degree on external converse for the best fruit of his own thought, he was also an efficient evocator of the thought of another—himself an original spirit more than tolerating the originality of others,—which brought it into play. Here was one who (through natural predilection, reinforced by theory) would welcome one's very self, undistressed by, while fully observant of, its difference from his own—one's errors, vanities, perhaps fatuities. Naturally eloquent, expressive, with a mind like a rich collection of the choice things of all times and countries, he was at his best, his happiest, amid the magnetic contacts of an easy conversation. When Gaston years afterwards came to read the famous *Essays*, he found many a delightful actual conversation re-set, and had the key we lack to their surprises, their capricious turns and lapses.—Well! Montaigne had opened the letter, had forthwith passed his genial criticism on the writer, and then, characteristically, forgetting all about it, turned to the bearer as if he had been intimate with him from childhood. And the feeling was mutual. Gaston in half an hour seemed to have known his entertainer all his life.

In unimpeded talk with sincere persons of what quality soever—there, rather than in shadowy converse with even the best books—the flower, the fruit, of mind was still in life-giving contact with its root. With books, as indeed with persons, his intercourse was apt to be desultory. Books!—He was by way of asserting his independence of them, was their *very candid* friend:—they were far from being an unmixed good. He would observe (the fact was its own scornful comment) that there were more books upon books than upon any other subject. Yet books, more than a thousand volumes, a handsome library for that day, nicely representative not only of literature but of the owner's taste therein, lay all around; and turning now to this, now to that, he handled their pages with nothing less than tenderness: it was the first of many inconsistencies which yet had about them a singularly taking air, of reason, of equity. Plutarch and Seneca were soon in the foreground: they would "still be at his elbow to test and be tested": masters of the autumnal wisdom that was coming to be his own, ripe and placid—from the autumn of old Rome, of life, of the world, the very genius of second thoughts, of exquisite tact and discretion, of judgment upon knowledge.

But the books dropped from his hands in the very midst of enthusiastic quotation; and the guest was mounting a little turret staircase, was on the leaden roof of the old tower, amid the fat, noonday Gascon scenery. He saw, in bird's-eye view, the country he was soon to become closely acquainted with, a country (like its people) of passion and capacity, though at that moment emphatically lazy. Towards the end of life some conscientious pangs seem to have touched Montaigne's singularly humane and sensitive spirit, when he looked back on the long intellectual entertainment he had had, in following, as an inactive spectator, "the ruin of his country," through a series of chapters, every one of which had told emphatically in his own immediate neighbourhood. With its old and new battlefields, its business, its fierce changes, and the old perennial sameness of men's ways beneath them all, it had been certainly matter of more assiduous reading than even those choice, incommensurable, books, of ancient Greek and Roman experience. The variableness, the complexity, the miraculous surprises of man, concurrent with the variety, the complexity, the surprises of nature, making all true knowledge of either wholly relative and provisional; a like insecurity in one's self, if one turned thither for some ray of clear and certain evidence; this, with an equally strong sense all the time of the interest, the power and charm, alike of man and nature and of the individual mind;—such was the sense of this open book, of all books and things. That was what this quietly enthusiastic reader was ready to assert as the sum of his studies; disturbingly, as Gaston found, reflecting on his long unsuspicious sojourn there, and detaching from the habits, the random traits of character, his concessions and hints and sudden emphatic statements, the soul and potency of the man.

How imperceptibly had darkness crept over them, effacing everything but the interior of the great circular chamber, its book-shelves and enigmatic mottoes and the tapestry on the wall,—Circe and her sorceries, in many parts—to draw over the windows in winter. Supper over, the young wife entered at last. Always on the lookout for the sincerities of human nature (sincerity counting for life-giving *form*, whatever the *matter* might be) as he delighted in watching children, Montaigne loved also to watch grown people when they were most like children; at their games, therefore, and in the mechanical and customary parts of their existence, as discovering the real soul in them. Abstaining from the dice himself, since for him such "play was not play enough, but too grave and serious a diversion," and remarking that "the play of children is not performed in play, but to be judged as their most serious action," he set Gaston and the amiable, unpedantic, lady to play together, where he might observe them closely; the game turning still, irresistibly, to conversation, the last and sweetest if somewhat drowsy relics of this long day's recreations.—Was Circe's castle here? If Circe could turn men into swine, could she also release them again? It was frailty, certainly, that Gaston remained here week after week, scarce knowing why; the conversation begun that morning lasting for nine months, over books, meals, in free rambles chiefly on horseback, as if in the waking intervals of a long day-sleep.

V

SUSPENDED JUDGMENT

THE DIVERSITY, THE UNDULANCY, OF HUMAN NATURE!—SO DEEP A SENSE OF IT
went with Montaigne always that himself too seemed to be ever changing
colour sympathetically therewith. Those innumerable differences, mental
and physical, of which men had always been aware, on which they had so
largely fed their vanity, were ultimate. That the surface of humanity presented an infinite variety was the tritest of facts. Pursue that variety below the surface!—the lines did but part further and further asunder, with
an ever-increasing divergency, which made any common measure of truth
impossible. Diversity of custom!—What was it but diversity in the moral
and mental view, diversity of opinion? and diversity of opinion, what but
radical diversity of mental constitution? How various in kind and degree
had he found men's thoughts concerning death, for instance, "some (ah
me!) even running headlong upon it, with a real affection"? Death, life;
wealth, poverty; the whole sum of contrasts; nay! duty itself, "the relish of
right and wrong"; all depend upon the opinion each one has of them, and
"receive no colour of good or evil but according to the application of the
individual soul." Did Hamlet learn of him that "there is nothing either good
or bad but thinking makes it so"?—"What we call evil is not so of itself: it
depends only upon us, to give it another taste and complexion.—Things,
in respect of themselves, have peradventure their weight, measure, and

conditions; but when once we have taken them into us, the soul forms them as she pleases.—Death is terrible to Cicero, courted by Cato, indifferent to Socrates.—Fortune, circumstance, offers but the matter: 'tis the soul adds the form.—Every opinion, how fantastic soever to some, is to another of force enough to be espoused at the risk of life."

For opinion was the projection of individual *will*, of a native original predilection. Opinions!—they are like the clothes we wear, which warm us, not with their heat, but with ours. Track your way (as he had learned to do) to the remote origin of what looks like folly; at home, on its native soil, it was found to be justifiable, as a proper growth of wisdom. In the vast conflict of taste, preference, conviction, there was no real inconsistency. It was but that the soul looked "upon things with another eye, and represented them to itself with another kind of face; reason being a tincture almost equally infused into all our manners and opinions; though there never were in the world two opinions exactly alike." And the practical comment was, not as one might have expected, towards the determination of some common standard of truth amid that infinite variety, but to this effect rather, that we are not bound to receive every opinion we are not able to refute, nor to accept another's refutation of our own; these diversities being themselves ultimate, and the priceless pearl of truth lying, if anywhere, not in large theoretic apprehension of the general, but in minute vision of the particular; in the perception of the concrete phenomenon, at this particular moment, and from this unique point of view—that for you, this for me—now, but perhaps not then.

Now; and not then! For if men are so diverse, not less disparate are the many men who keep discordant company within each one of us, "every man carrying in him the entire form of human condition." "That we taste nothing pure": the variancy of the individual in regard to himself: the complexity of soul which there, too, makes "all judgments in the gross" impossible or useless, certainly inequitable, he delighted to note. Men's minds were like the grotesques which some artists of that day loved to joint together, or like one of his own inconstant essays, never true for a page to its proposed subject. "Nothing is so supple as our understanding: it is double and diverse; and the matters are double and diverse, too."

Here, as it seemed to Gaston, was one for whom exceptions had taken the place of law: the very genius of qualification followed him through all his keen, constant, changeful consideration of men and things. How many curious moral variations he had to show!—"vices that are lawful": vices in us which "help to make up the seam in our piecing, as poisons are useful for the conservation of health": "actions good and excusable that are not lawful in themselves": "the soul discharging her passions upon false objects where the true are wanting": men doing more than they propose, or they hardly know what, at immense hazard, or pushed to do well by vice itself, or working for their enemies: "condemnations more criminal than the crimes they condemn": the excuses that are self-accusations: instances, from his own experience, of a hasty confidence in other men's virtue which "God had favoured": and how, "even to the worst people, it is sweet, their end once gained by a vicious act, to foist into it some show of justice." In the presence of this indefatigable analyst of act and motive all fixed outlines seemed to vanish away. The healthful pleasure of motion, of thoughts in motion!—Yes! Gaston felt them, the oldest of them, moving, as he listened, under and away from his feet, as if with the ground he stood on. And this was the vein of thought which oftenest led the master back contemptuously to emphasise the littleness of man.—"I think we can never be despised according to our full desert."

By way of counterpoise, there were admirable surprises in man. That cross-play of human tendencies determined from time to time in the forces of unique and irresistible character, "moving all together," pushing the world around it to phenomenal good or evil. For such as "make it their business to oversee human actions, it seems impossible they should proceed from one and the same person." Consolidation of qualities supposed, this did but make character, already the most attractive, because the most dynamic, phenomenon of experience, more interesting still. So tranquil a spectator of so average a world, a too critical minimiser, it might seem, of all that pretends to be of importance, Montaigne was constantly, gratefully, announcing his contact, in life, in books, with undeniable power and greatness, with forces full of beauty in their vigour, like lightning, the sea, the torrents:—overpowering desire augmented, yet victorious, by its very difficulty; the bewildering constancy of martyrs; single-hearted virtue not to be resolved into anything less surprising than itself; the devotion of that famed, so companionable, wife, dying cheerfully by her own act along with the sick husband "who could do no better than kill himself"; the grief, the joy, of which men suddenly die; the unconscious Stoicism of the poor; that stern self-control with which Jacques Bonhomme goes as usual to his daily labour with a heart tragic for the dead child at home; nay! even the boldness and strength of "those citizens who sacrifice honour and conscience, as others of old sacrificed their lives, for the good of their country." So carefully equable, his mind nevertheless was stored with, and delighted in, incidents, personalities, of barbarous strength—Esau, in all his phases— the very rudest children or "our great and powerful mother, nature." As Plato had said, " 'twas to no purpose for a sober-minded man to knock at the door of poesy," or, if truth were spoken, of any other high matter of doing or making. That was consistent with his sympathetic belief in the capability of mere impetuous youth as such. Even those unexpected traits in ordinary people which seem to hint at larger laws and deeper forces of character, disconcerting any narrow judgment upon them, he welcomed as akin to his own indolent, but suddenly kindling, nature:—the mere self-will of men, the shrewd wisdom of an un-lettered old woman, the fount of goodness in a cold or malicious heart. "I hear every day fools say things far from foolish." Those invincible prepossessions of humanity, or of the individual, which Bacon reckoned "idols of the cave" are no offence to him; are direct informations, it may be, beyond price, from a kindly spirit of truth in things.

For him there had been two grand surprises, two pre-eminent manifestations of the power and charm of man, not to be explained away,— one, within the compass of general and public observation: the other, a matter of special intimacy to himself. There had been the greatness of the old Greek and Roman life, so greatly recorded: there had been the wisdom and kindness of Etienne de la Boetie, as made known in all their fulness to him alone. That his ardent devotion to the ancients had been rewarded with minute knowledge concerning them, was the privilege of the age in which he was born, late in the Revival of Letters. But the classical reading, which with others was often but an affectation, seducing them from the highest to a lower degree of reality, from men and women to their mere shadows in old books, had been for him nothing less than personal con-

tact. "The qualities and fortunes" of the old Romans, especially, their wonderful straight ways through the world, the straight passage of their armies
upon them, the splendour of their armour, of their entire external presence and show, their "riches and embellishments," above all, "the suddenness of Augustus," in that grander age for which *decision* was justifiable
because really possible, had ever been "more in his head than the fortunes
of his own country." If "we have no hold even on things present but by
imagination," as he loved to observe,—then, how much more potent,
steadier, larger, the imaginative substance of the world of Alexander and
Socrates, of Virgil and Caesar, than that of an age, which seemed to him,
living in the midst of it, respectable mainly by its docility, by an imitation
of the ancients which after all left untouched the real sources of their greatness. They had been indeed great, at the least dramatically, redeemed in
part by magnificent courage and tact, in their very sins. "Our force is no
more able to reach them in their vicious than in their virtuous qualities;
for both the one and the other proceed from a vigour of soul which was
without comparison greater in them than in us."

And yet, thinking of his friendship with the "incomparable Etienne
de la Boetie, so perfect, inviolate and entire, that the like is hardly to be
found in story," he had to confess that the sources of greatness must still
be quick in the world. That had remained with him as his one fixed standard of value in the estimate of men and things. On this single point, antiquity itself had been surpassed; the discourses it had left upon friendship
seeming to him "poor and flat in comparison of the sense he had of it." For
once, his sleepless habit of analysis had been checked by the inexplicable,
the absolute; amid his jealously guarded indifference of soul he had been
summoned to yield, and had yielded, to the magnetic power of another.
"We were halves throughout, so that methinks by outliving him I defraud
him of his part. I was so grown to be always his double in all things that
methinks I am no more than half of myself. There is no action or thought
of mine wherein I do not miss him, as I know that he would have missed
me." Tender yet heroic, impulsive yet so wise, he might have done what the
survivor (so it seemed to himself) was but vainly trying to do. It was worth
his while to become famous, if that hapless memory might but be embalmed
in one's fame. It had been better than love,—that friendship! to the build-

ing of which so much "concurrence" had been requisite, that "'twas much if fortune brought the like to pass once in three ages." Actually, we may think, the "sweet society" of those four years, in comparison with which the rest of his so pleasant life "was but smoke," had touched Montaigne's nature with refinements it might otherwise have lacked. He would have wished "to speak concerning it, to those who had experience" of what he said, could such have been found. In despair of that, he loved to discourse of it to all comers,—how it had come about, the circumstances of its sudden and wonderful growth. Yet after all were he pressed to say why he had so loved Etienne de la Boetie, he could but answer, "Because it was He! Because it was I!"

And the surprises there are in man, his complexity, his variancy, were symptomatic of the changefulness, the confusion, the surprises, of the earth under one's feet, of the whole material world. The irregular, the unforeseen, the inconsecutive, miracle, accident, he noted lovingly: it had a philosophic import. It was habit rather than knowledge of them that took away the strangeness of the things actually about one. How many unlikely matters there were, testified by persons worthy of faith, "which, if we cannot persuade ourselves to believe, we ought at least to leave in suspense.— Though all that had arrived by report of past time should be true, it would be less than nothing in comparison of what is unknown."

On all sides we are beset by the incalculable:—walled up suddenly, as if by malign trickery, in the open field, or shed forward senseless by the crowd around us, to good-fortune. In art, as in poetry, there are the "transports" which lift the artist out of, as they are not of, himself; for orators also, "those extraordinary motions which sometimes carry them above their design." Himself, "in the necessity and heat of combat," had sometimes made answers, that went "through and through," beyond hope. The work, by its own force and fortune, sometimes outstrips the workman. And then, in defiance of the proprieties, whereas poets sometimes "flag, and languish in a prosaic manner," prose will shine with the lustre, vigour and boldness, with "the fury" of poetry.

And as to "affairs,"—how spasmodic the mixture, collision or coincidence, of the mechanic succession of things with men's volition! Mere rumour, so large a factor in events,—who could trace out its ways? Various events (he was never tired of illustrating the fact) "followed from the same counsel." Fortune, chance, that is to say, the incalculable contribution of mere matter to man, "would still be mistress of events"; and one might think it no un-wisdom to commit everything to fortuity. But no! "fortune too is oft-times observed to act by the rule of reason: chance itself comes round to hold of justice;" war, above all, being a matter in which fortune was inexplicable, though men might seem to have made it the main business of their lives. If "the force of all counsel lies in the occasion," that is because things perpetually shift. If man—his taste, his very conscience—change with the habit of time and place, that is because habit is the emphatic determination, the tyranny, of changing external and material circumstance. So it comes about that every one gives the name of barbarism to what is not in use round about him, excepting perhaps the Greeks and Romans, somewhat conventionally; and Montaigne was fond of assuring people, suddenly, that could we have those privileged Greeks and Romans actually to sit beside us for a while, they would be found to offend our niceties at a hundred points. We have great power of taking ourselves in, and "pay ourselves with words." Words too, language itself, and therewith the more intimate physiognomy of thought, "slip every day through our fingers." With his eye on his own labour, wistfully, he thought on the instability of the French language in particular—a matter, after all, so much less "perennial than brass." In no respect was nature more stable, more consecutive, than man.

In nature, indeed, as in one's self, there might be no ultimate inconsequence: only, "the soul looks upon things with another eye, and represents them to itself with another kind of face: for everything has many faces and several aspects. There is nothing single and rare in respect of itself, but only in respect of our knowledge, which is a wretched foundation whereon to ground our rules, and one that represents to us a very false image of things." Ah! even in so "dear" a matter as bodily health, immunity from physical pain, what doubts! what variations of experience, of learned opinion! Already, in six years of married life, of four children treated so carefully, never, for instance, roughly awaked from sleep, "wherein," he would observe, "children are much more profoundly involved than we,"—of four children, two were dead, and one even now miserably sick. Seeing the doctor depart one morning a little hastily, on the payment of his fee, he was tempted to some nice questions as to the money's worth. "There are so many maladies, and so many circumstances, presented to the physician, that human sense must soon be at the end of its lesson:—the many complexions in a melancholy person; the many seasons in winter; the many nations in the French; the many ages in age; the many celestial mutations in the conjunction of Venus and Saturn; the many parts in man's body, nay, in a finger. And suppose the cure effected, how can we assure ourselves that it was not because the disease was arrived at its period, or an effect of chance, or the operation of something else that the child had eaten, drunk, or touched that day, or by virtue of his mother's prayers? We suppose we see one side of a thing when we are really looking at another. As for me, I never see all of anything; neither do they who so largely promise to show it to others. Of the hundred faces that everything has I take one, and am for the most part attracted by some new light I find in it."

And that new light was sure to lead him back very soon to his "governing method, ignorance"—an ignorance "strong and generous, and that yields nothing in honour and courage to knowledge; an ignorance, which to conceive requires no less knowledge than to conceive knowledge itself"—a sapient, instructed, shrewdly ascertained ignorance, suspended judgment, doubt everywhere.—Balances, very delicate balances; he was partial to that image of equilibrium, or preponderance, in things. But was there, after all, so much as preponderance anywhere? To Gaston there was a kind of fascination, an actually æsthetic beauty, in the spectacle of that keen-edged intelligence, dividing evidence so finely, like some exquisite steel instrument with impeccable sufficiency, always leaving the last word loyally to the central intellectual faculty, in an entire disinterestedness. If on the one hand he was always distrustful of things that he wished, on the other he had many opinions he would endeavour to make his son dislike, if he had one. What if the truest opinions were not always the most commodious to man, "being of so wild a composition"? He would say nothing to one party that he might not on occasion say to the other, "with a little alteration of accent." Yes! Doubt, everywhere! doubt in the far background, as the proper intellectual equivalent to the infinite possibilities of things: doubt, shrewdly economising the opportunities of the present hour, in the very spirit of the traveller who walks only for the walk's sake,—"every day concludes my expectation, and the journey carried on after the same fashion": doubt finally, as "the best of pillows to sleep on." And in fact Gaston did sleep well after those long days of physical and intellectual movement, in that quiet world, till the spring came round again.

But beyond and above all the various interests upon which the philosopher's mind was for ever afloat, there was one subject always in prominence—himself. His minute peculiarities, mental and physical, what was constitutional with him as well as his transient humours, how things affected him, what they really *were* to him, Michael, much more than man, all this Gaston came to know, as the world knew it afterwards in the *Essays*, often amused, sometimes irritated, but never suspicious of postures, or insincerity. Montaigne himself admitted his egotism with frank humour:—"in favour of the Huguenots, who condemn our private confession, I confess myself in public." And this outward egotism of manner was but the symptom of a certain deeper doctrinal egotism:—"I have no other end in writing but to discover *myself.*" And what was the purport, what the justification, of this undissembled egotism? It was the recognition, over against, or in continuation of, that world of floating doubt, of the individual mind, as for each one severally, at once the unique organ, and the only matter, of knowledge,—the wonderful energy, the reality and authority of that, in its absolute loneliness, conforming all things to its law, without witnesses as without judge, without appeal, save to itself. Whatever truth there might be, must come for each one from within, not from without. To that wonderful microcosm of the individual soul, of which, for each one, all other worlds are but elements,—to himself,—to what was apparent immediately to him, what was "properly of his own having and substance": he confidently dismissed the inquirer. His own egotism was but the pattern of the true intellectual life of every one. "The greatest thing in the world is for a man to know that he is his own. If the world find fault that I speak too much of myself, I find fault that they do not so much as think of themselves." How it had been "lodged in its author":—that, surely, was the essential question, concerning every opinion that comes to one man from another.

Yet, again, even on this ultimate ground of judgment, what undulancy, complexity, surprises!—"I have no other end in writing but to discover my-self, who also shall peradventure be another thing to-morrow." The great work of his life, the *Essays*, he placed "now high, now low, with great doubt and inconstancy." "What are we but sedition? like this poor France, fac-tion against faction, within ourselves, every piece playing every moment its own game, with as much difference between us and ourselves as be-tween ourselves and others. Whoever will look narrowly into his own bo-som will hardly find himself twice in the same condition. I give to myself sometimes one face and sometimes another, according to the side I turn to. I have nothing to say of myself, entirely and without qualification. One grows familiar with all strange things by time. But the more I frequent myself and the better I know myself, the less do I understand myself. If others would consider themselves as I do, they would find themselves full of caprice. Rid myself of it I cannot without making myself away. They who are not aware of it have the better bargain. And yet I know not whether they have or no!"

One's own experience!—that, at least, *was* one's own: low and earthy, it might be; still, the earth was, emphatically, good, good-natured; and he loved, emphatically to recommend the wisdom, amid all doubts, of keep-ing close to it. Gaston soon knew well a certain threadbare garment worn by Montaigne in all their rides together, sitting quaintly on his otherwise gallant appointments,—an old mantle that had belonged to his father. Retained, as he tells us, in spite of its inconvenience, "because it seemed to envelope me in him," it was the symbol of a hundred natural, perhaps somewhat material, pieties. Parentage, kinship, relationship through earth,—the touch of that was everywhere like a caress to him. His fine taste notwithstanding, he loved, in those long rambles, to partake of homely fare, paying largely for it. Everywhere it was as if the earth in him turned kindly to earth. "Under the sun," the sturdy purple thistles, the blossom-ing burrs also, were worth knowing. Let us grow together with you! they seem to say. Himself was one of those whom he thought "Heaven favoured" in making them die, so naturally, by degrees. "I shall be blind before I am sensible of the decay of my sight, with such kindly artifice do the Fatal Sisters entwist our lives. I melt, and steal away from myself. How *variously* is it no longer I!" It was not he who would carry a furry robe at midsummer, because he might need it in the winter.—"In fine, we must live among the living, and let the river flow under the bridge without our care, above all things avoiding fear, that great disturber of reason. The thing in the world I am most afraid of is fear."

And still, health, the invincible survival of youth, "admonished him to a better wisdom than years and sickness." Was there anything better, fairer, than the beautiful light of health? To be in health was itself the sign, perhaps the essence, of wisdom—a wisdom, rich in counsels regarding all one's contacts with the earthy side of existence. And how he could laugh!— at that King of Thrace, for instance, who had a religion and a god all to himself, which his subjects might not presume to worship; at that King of Mexico, who swore at his coronation not only to keep the laws, but also to make the sun run his annual course; at those followers of Alexander, who all carried their heads on one side as Alexander did.

The natural second-best, the intermediate and unheroic virtue (even the Church, as we know, by no means *requiring* "heroic" virtue), was perhaps actually the best, better than any kind of heroism, in an age whose very virtues were apt to become insane; an age "guilty and extravagant" in its very justice; for which, as regards all that belongs to the spirit, the one thing needful was moderation. And it was characteristic of Montaigne, a note of the real helpfulness there was in his thoughts, that he preferred to base virtue on low, safe, ground. "The lowest walk is the safest: 'tis the seat of constancy." The wind about the tower, coming who knows whence and whither?—could one enjoy its music, unless one knew the foundations safe, twenty feet below-ground? Always he loved to hear such words as "soften and modify the temerity of our propositions." To say less than the truth about it, to dissemble the absoluteness of its claim, was agreeable to his confidence in the natural charm, the gaiety of goodness, "that fair and beaten path nature has traced for us," over against any difficult, militant, or chimerical virtue.—"Never had any morose and ill-looking physician done anything to purpose." In that age, it was a great thing to be just blameless. Virtue had its bounds, "which once transgressed, the next step was into the territories of vice." "All decent and honest means of securing ourselves from harm, were not only permitted but commendable." Any man who despises his own life, might "always be master of that of another." He would not condemn "a magistrate who *sleeps*; provided the people under his charge sleep as well as he." Though a blundering world, in collusion with a prejudiced philosophy, has "a great suspicion of facility," there was a certain easy taking of things which made life the richer for others as well as for one's self, and was at least an excellent makeshift for disinterested service to them. With all his admiration for the antique greatness of character, he would never commend "so savage a virtue, and one that costs so dear," as that, for instance, of the Greek mother, the Roman father, who assisted to put their own erring sons to death. More truly commendable was the custom of the Lacedæmonians, who when they went to battle sacrificed always to the Muses, that "these might, by their sweetness and gaiety, soften martial fury." How had divine philosophy herself been discredited by the sour mask, the sordid patches, with which, her enemies surely! had sent her abroad into the world. "I love a gay and civil philosophy. There is nothing more *cheerful* than wisdom: I had like to have said more wanton."

Was that why his conversation was sometimes coarse? "All the contraries are to be found in me, in one corner or another"; if delicacy, so also coarseness. Delicacy there was, certainly,—a wonderful fineness of sensation. "To the end," he tells us, "that sleep should not so stupidly escape from me, I have caused myself to be disturbed in my sleep, so that I might the better and more sensibly taste and relish it.—Of scents, the simple and natural seem to me the most pleasing, and I have often observed that they cause an alteration in me, and work upon my spirits according to their several virtues.—In excessive heats I always travel by night, from sunset to sunrise.—I am betimes sensible of the little breezes that begin to sing and whistle in the shrouds, the forerunners of the storm.—When I walk alone in a beautiful orchard, if my thoughts are for a while taken up with foreign occurrences, I some part of the time call them back again to my walk, to the orchard, to the sweetness of the solitude, and to myself.—There is nothing in us either purely corporeal, or purely spiritual." 'Tis an inhuman wisdom that would have us despise and hate the culture of the body. 'Tis not a soul, 'tis not a body, we are training up, but a man; and we ought not to divide him. Of all the infirmities we have, the most savage is to despise our being."

There was a fineness of sensation in these unpremeditated thoughts, which to Gaston seemed to connect itself with the exquisite words he had found to paint his two great affections, for his father and for Etienne de la Boetie—a fineness of sensation perhaps quite novel in that age, but still of *physical* sensation: and in pursuit of fine physical sensation he came, on his broad, easy, indifferent passage through the world, across the coarsest growths which also thrive "under the sun," and was not revolted. They were akin to that ruder earth within himself, of which a kind of undissembled greed was symptomatic; the love of "meats little roasted, very high, and even, as to several, quite gone"; while, in drinking, he loved "clear glass, that the eye might taste too, according to its capacity"; akin also to a certain slothfulness:—"Sleeping," he says, "has taken up a great part of my life." And there was almost nothing he would not say: no fact, no story, from his curious half-medical reading, he would not find some plausible pretext to tell. Man's kinship to the animal, the material, and all the proofs of it:—he would never blush at them! In truth, he led the way to the immodesty of French literature; and had his defence, a sort of defence, ready. "I know very well that few will quarrel with the licence of my writings, who have not more to quarrel with in the licence of their own thoughts."

Yet when Gaston, twenty years afterwards, heard of the seemingly pious end of Monsieur de Montaigne, he recalled a hundred, always quiet but not always insignificant, acts of devotion, noticeable in those old days, on passing a village church, or at home, in the little chapel—superstitions, concessions to others, strictly appropriate recognitions rather, as it might seem, of a certain great possibility, which might lie among the conditions of so complex a world. That was a point which could hardly escape so reflective a mind as Gaston's: and at a later period of his life, at the harvest of his own second thoughts, as he pondered on the influence over him of that two-sided thinker, the opinion that things as we find them would bear a certain old-fashioned construction, seemed to have been the consistent motive, however secret and subtle in its working, of Montaigne's sustained intellectual activity. A lowly philosophy of ignorance would not be likely to disallow or discredit whatever intimations there might be, in the experience of the wise or of the simple, in favour of a venerable religion, which from its long history had come to seem like a growth of nature. Somewhere, among men's seemingly random and so inexplicable apprehensions, might lie the grains of a wisdom more precious than gold, or even its price-less pearl. That "free and roving thing," the human soul—what might it not have found out for itself, in a world so wide? To deny, at all events, would be only "to *limit* the mind, by negation."

It was not however this side of that double philosophy which recom-mended itself just now to Gaston. The master's wistful tolerance, so ex-traordinary a characteristic in that age, attracted him, in his present humour, not so much in connexion with those problematic heavenly lights that might find their way to one from infinite skies, as with the pleasant, quite finite, objects and experiences of the indubitable world of sense, so close around him. Over against the world's challenge to make trial of it, here was that general licence, which his own warm and curious appetite just then de-manded of the moral theorist. For so pronounced a lover of sincerity as Monsieur de Montaigne, there was certainly a strange ambiguousness in the result of his lengthy inquiries, on the greatest as well as on the lightest matters, and it was inevitable that a listener should accept the dubious lesson in his own sense. Was this shrewd casuist only bringing him by a round-about way to principles he would not have cared to avow? To the great religious thinker of the next century, to Pascal, Montaigne was to figure as emphatically on the wrong side, not merely because "he that is not *with* us, is *against* us." It was something to have been, in the matter of religious tolerance, as on many other matters of justice and gentleness, the solitary conscience of the age. But could one really care for truth, who never even seemed to find it? Did he fear, perhaps, the practical responsi-bility of getting to the very bottom of certain questions? That the actual discourse of so keen a thinker appeared often inconsistent or inconsecu-tive, might be a hint perhaps that there was some deeper ground of thought in reserve; as if he were really moving, securely, over ground you did not see.—What might that ground be? As to Gaston himself,—had this kindly entertainer only been drawing the screws of a very complex piece of ma-chinery which had worked well enough hitherto for all practical purposes?—Was this all that had been going on, while he lingered there, week after week, in a kind of devout attendance on theories, and, for his part, feeling no reverberation of actual events around him, still less of great events in preparation? These were the questions Gaston had in mind, as, at length, he thanked his host one morning with real regret, and took his last look around that meditative place, the manuscripts, the books, the emblems,— the house of Circe on the wall.

VI

SHADOWS OF EVENTS

WE ALL FEEL, I SUPPOSE, THE PATHOS OF THAT MYTHIC SITUATION IN HOMER, where the Greeks at the last throb of battle around the body of Patroclus find the horror of supernatural darkness added to their other foes; feel it through some touch of truth to our own experience how the malignancy of the forces against us may be doubled by their uncertainty and the resultant confusion of one's own mind—blindfold night there too, at the moment when daylight and self-possession are indispensable.

In that old dream-land of the Iliad such darkness is the work of a propitiable deity, and withdrawn at its pleasure; in life, it often persists obstinately. It was so with the agents on the terrible Eve of St. Bartholomew, 1572, when a man's foes were those of his own household. An ambiguity of motive and influence, a confusion of spirit amounting, as we approach the centre of action, to physical madness, encompasses those who are formally responsible for things; and the mist around that great crime, or great "accident," in which the gala weather of Gaston's coming to Paris broke up, leaving a sullenness behind it to remain for a generation, has never been penetrated. The doubt with which Charles the Ninth would seem to have left the world, doubt as to his own complicity therein, as well as to the precise nature, the course and scope, of the event itself, is still unresolved. So it was with Gaston also. The incident in his life which opened for him the profoundest sources of regret and pity, shaped as it was in a measure by those greater historic movements, owed its tragic significance there to an unfriendly shadow precluding knowledge how certain facts had really gone, a shadow which veiled from others a particular act of his and the true character of its motives.

For, the scene of events being now contracted very closely to Paris, the predestined actors therein were gradually drawn thither as into some narrow battlefield or slaughter-house or fell trap of destiny, and Gaston, all unconsciously, along with them—he and his private fortunes involved in those larger ones. Result of chance, or fate, or cunning prevision, there are in the acts great and little—the acts and the words alike—of the king and his associates, at this moment, coincidences which give them at least superficially the colour of an elaborate conspiracy. Certainly, as men looked back afterwards, all the seemingly random doings of those restless months ending in the Noces Vermeilles marriage of Henry of Navarre with Margaret of France, lent themselves agreeably to the theory of a great plot to crush out at one blow, in the interest of the reigning Valois, not the Huguenots only but the rival houses of Guise and Bourbon. The word, the act, from hour to hour through what presented itself at the time as a long-continued season of frivolity, suggested in retrospect alike to friend and foe the close connexion of a mathematical problem. And yet that damning coincidence of date, day and hour apparently so exactly timed, in the famous letter to the Governor of Lyons, by which Charles, the trap being now ready, seems to shut all the doors upon escaping victims, is admitted even by Huguenot historians to have been fortuitous. Gaston recalling to mind the actual mien of Charles as he passed to and fro across the chimeric scene, timid, and therefore constitutionally trustful towards older persons, filially kissing the hand of the grim Coligni—*Mon père! Mon père!*— all his *câlineries* in that age of courtesy and assassinations—would wonder always in time to come, as the more equitable sort of historians have done, what amount of guilty foresight the young king had carried in his bosom. And this ambiguity regarding the nearest agent in so great a crime, adding itself to the general mystery of life, touched Gaston duly with a sense of the dim melancholy of man's position in the world. It might seem the function of some cruel or merely whimsical power, thus, by the flinging of mere dust through the air, to double our actual misfortunes. However carefully the critical intelligence in him might trim the balance, his imagination at all events would never be clear of the more plausible construction of events. In spite of efforts not to misjudge, in proportion to the clearness with which he recalled the visible footsteps of the "accursed" Valois, he saw them, irresistibly, in connexion with the end actually reached, moving to the sounds of wedding music, through a world of dainty gestures, amid sonnets and flowers, and perhaps the most refined art the world has seen, to their surfeit of blood.

And if those "accursed" Valois might plead to be judged refinedly, so would Gaston, had the opportunity come, have pleaded not to be misunderstood. Of the actual event he was not a spectator, and his sudden absence from Paris at that moment seemed to some of those he left there only a cruelly characteristic incident in the great treachery. Just before that delirious night set in, the news that his old grandfather lay mortally sick at Deux-manoirs had snatched him away to watch by the dying bed, amid the peaceful ministries the religion which was even then filling the houses of Paris with blood. But the yellow-haired woman, light of soul, whose husband he had become by dubious and irregular Huguenot rites, the religious sanction of which he hardly recognised—flying after his last tender kiss, with the babe in her womb, from the ruins of her home, and the slaughter of her kinsmen, supposed herself treacherously deserted. For him, on the other hand, "the pity of it," the pity of the thing supplied all that had been wanting in its first consecration, and made the lost mistress really a wife. His recoil from that damaging theory of his conduct brought home to a sensitive conscience the fact that there had indeed been a measure of self-indulgent weakness in his acts, and made him the creature for the rest of his days of something like remorse.

The gaiety, the strange devils' gaiety of France, at least in all places whither its royalty came, ended appropriately in a marriage—a marriage of "The Reform" in the person of Prince Henry of Navarre, to Catholicism in the person of Margaret of Valois, Margaret of the "Memoirs," Charles's sister, in tacit defiance of, or indifference to, the Pope. With the great Huguenot leaders, with the princes of the house of Guise, and the Court, like one united family, all in gaudy evidence in its streets, Paris, ever with an eye for the chance of amusement, always preoccupied with the visible side of things, always Catholic—was bidden to be tolerant for a moment, to carry no fire-arms under penalties, "to renew no past quarrels," and draw no sword in any new one. It was the perfect stroke of Catherine's policy, the secret of her predominance over her sons, thus, with a flight of purchaseable fair women ever at command, to maintain perpetual holiday, perpetual idleness, with consequent perpetual, most often idle, thoughts about marriage, amid which the actual conduct of affairs would be left to herself. Yet for Paris thus Catholic, there was certainly, even if the Pope were induced to consent, and the Huguenot bridegroom to "conform," something illicit and inauspicious about this marriage within the prohibited degrees of kinship. In fact, the cunningly sought papal dispensation never came; Charles, with apparent unconcern, fulfilled his threat, and did without it; must needs however trick the old Cardinal de Bourbon into performing his office, not indeed, "in the face of the Church," but in the open air outside the doors of the cathedral of Notre-Dame, the Catholics quietly retiring into the interior, when that starveling ceremony was over, to hear the nuptial mass. Still, the open air, the August sunshine, had lent the occasion an irresistible physical gaiety in this hymeneal Assumption weather. Paris, suppressing its scruples, its conscientious and unconscientious hatreds, at least for a season, had adorned herself as that fascinating city always has been able to adorn herself, if with something of artifice, certainly with great completeness almost to illusion. Whatever gloom the Middle Age with its sins and sorrows might have left there, was under gallant disguise to-day. In the train of the young married people, *jeunes premiers* in an engagement which was to turn out almost as transitory as a stage-play, a long month of masquerade meandered night and day through the public places. His carnality and hers, so startling in their later developments, showed now in fact but as the engaging force of youth, since youth, however unpromising its antecedents, can never have sinned irretrievably. Yet to curious retrospective minds not long afterwards, these graceful follies would seem tragic or allegoric, with an undercurrent of infernal irony throughout. Charles and his two brothers, keeping the gates of a mimic paradise in the court of the Louvre, while the fountains ran wine—were they already thinking of a time when they would keep those gates, with iron purpose, while the gutters ran blood?

If Huguenots were disgusted with the frivolities of the hour, passing on the other side of the street in sad attire, plotting, as some have thought, as their enemies will persuade the Pope, a yet more terrible massacre of their own, only anticipated by the superior force and shrewdness of the Catholics, on the very eve of its accomplishment—they did but serve just now to relieve the predominant white and red, and thereby double the brilliancy, of a gay picture. Yet a less than Machiavellian cunning might perhaps have detected, amid all this sudden fraternity—as in some unseasonably fine weather signs of coming distress—a risky element of exaggeration in those precipitately patched-up amities, a certain hollow ring in those improbable religious conversions, those unlikely reconciliations in what was after all an age of treachery as a fine art. With Gaston, however, the merely receptive and poetic sense of life was abundantly occupied with the spectacular value of the puissant figures in motion around him. If he went beyond the brilliancy of the present moment in his wonted pitiful equitable after-thoughts, he was still concerned only with the more general aspects of the human lot, and did not reflect that every public movement, however generous in its tendency, is really flushed to active force by identification with some narrower personal or purely selfish one. Coligni, "the Admiral," centre of Huguenot opposition, just, kind, grim, to the height of inspired genius, the grandest character his faith had yet produced—undeterred by those ominous voices (of aged women and the like) which are apt to beset all great actions, yielded readily to the womanish endearments of Charles, his filial words and fond touching of the hands, the face, aged at fifty-five—just this portion of his conduct let us hope being exclusive of his precise share in the "conspiracy." And the opportune death in Paris of the Huguenot Queen of Navarre only stirred question for a moment: autopsy revealed no traces of unfair play, though at a time credulous as to impossible poisoned perfumes and such things, romantic in its very suspicions.

Delirium was in the air already charged with thunder, and laid hold on Gaston too. It was as if through some unsettlement in the atmospheric medium the objects around no longer acted upon the senses with the normal result. Looking back afterwards, this singularly self-possessed person had to confess that under its influence he had lost for a while the exacter view of certain outlines, certain real differences and oppositions of things in that hotly coloured world of Paris (like a shaken tapestry about him) awaiting the Eve of Saint Bartholomew. Was the "undulant" philosophy of Monsieur de Montaigne, in collusion with this dislocating time, at work upon him, that, following with only too entire a mobility the *experience* of the hour, he found himself more than he could have thought possible the toy of external accident? Lodged in Abelard's quarter, he all but repeats Abelard's typical *experience*. His new Heloise, with capacities doubtless, as he reflected afterwards regretfully, for a refined and serious happiness, although actually so far only a man's plaything, sat daintily amid her posies and painted potteries in the window of a house itself as forbidding and stern as her kinsmen, busy Huguenot printers, well-to-do at a time not only fertile in new books and new editions, but profuse of tracts, sheets, satiric handbills for posting all over France. Gaston's curiosity, a kind of fascination he finds in their dark ways, takes him among them on occasion, to feel all the more keenly the contrast of that picture-like prettiness in this framing of their grim company, their grim abode. Her frivolity is redeemed by a sensitive affection for these people who protect her, by a self-accusing respect for their religion, for the somewhat surly goodness, the hard and unattractive pieties into which she cannot really enter; and she yearns after her like, for those harmless forbidden graces towards which she has a natural aptitude, loses her heart to Gaston as he goes to and fro, wastes her days in reminiscence of that bright passage, notes the very fineness of his linen. To him, in turn, she seems, as all longing creatures ever have done, to have some claim upon him—a right to consideration— to an effort on his part: he finds a sister to encourage: she touches him, clings where she touches. The gloomy, honest, uncompromising Huguenot brothers interfere just in time to save her from the consequence of what to another than Gaston might have counted as only a passing fondness to be soon forgotten; and the marriage almost forced upon him seemed under its actual conditions no binding sacrament. A marriage really indissoluble in itself, and for the heart of Colombe sacramental, as he came afterwards to understand—for his own conscience at the moment, the transaction seemed to have but the transitoriness, as also the guilt of a vagrant love. A connexion so light of motive, so inexpressive of what seemed the leading forces of his character, he might, but for the sorrow which stained its actual issue, have regarded finally as a mere mistake, or an unmeaning accident in his career.

Coligni lay suffering in the fiery August from the shot of the ambiguous assassin which had missed his heart, amid the real or feigned regrets of the Guises, of the royal family, of his true friends, wondering as they watched whether the bullet had been a poisoned one. The other Huguenot leaders had had their warnings to go home, as the princes of the house of Navarre, Condé and Henry of Bearn, would fain have done—the gallant world about them being come just now to have certain suspicious resemblances to a prison or a *trap*. Under order of the king the various quarters of Paris had been distributed for some unrevealed purpose of offence or defence. To the officers in immediate charge it was intimated that "those of the new religion" designed "to rise against the king's authority, to the trouble of his subjects and the city of Paris. For the prevention of which conspiracy the king enjoined the Provost to possess himself of the keys of the various city gates, and seize all boats plying on the river, to the end that none might enter or depart." And just before the lists close around the doomed, Gaston has bounded away on his road homeward to the bed of the dying grandfather, after embracing his wife, anxious, if she might, to share his journey, with some forecast of coming evil among those dark people.

The white badges of Catholicism had been distributed, not to every Catholic (a large number of Catholics perished), to some Huguenots such as La Rochefoucauld, *brave guerrier et joyeux compagnon*, dear to Charles, hesitating still with some last word of conscience in his ear at the very gate of the Louvre, when a random pistol-shot, in the still undisturbed August night, rousing sudden fear for himself, precipitates the event, and as if in delirium he is driven forth on the scent of human blood. He has always hunted like a madman. It was thus "the matins of Paris" began, in which not religious zealots only assisted, but the thieves, the wanton, the unemployed, the reckless children, *les enfants massacreurs* like those seen dragging an insulted dead body to the Seine, greed or malice or the desire for swift settlement of some long-pending law-suit finding here an opportunity. A religious pretext had brought into sudden evidence all the latent ferocities of a corrupt though dainty civilisation, and while the stairways of the Louvre, the streets, the vile trap-doors of Paris, run blood, far away at Deux-manoirs Gaston watches as the light creeps over the silent cornfields, the last sense of it in those aged eyes now ebbing softly away. The village priest, almost as aged, assists patiently with his immemorial consolations at this long, leisurely, scarce perceptible ending to a long, leisurely life, on the quiet double-holiday morning.*

The wild news of public disaster, penetrating along the country-roads now bristling afresh with signs of universal war, seemed of little consequence in comparison with that closer grief at home, which made just then the more effective demand on his sympathy, till the thought came of the position of Colombe—his wife left behind there in Paris. Immediate rumour, like subsequent history, gave variously the number—the number of thousands—who perished. The great Huguenot leader was dead, one party at least, the royal party, safe for the moment and in high spirits. As Charles himself put it, the ancient private quarrel between the houses of Guise and Châtillon was ended by the decease of the chief of the latter, Coligni de Châtillon—a death so saintly after its new fashion that the long-delayed vengeance of Henri de Guise on the presumed instigator of the murder of his father seemed a martyrdom. And around that central barbarity the slaughter had spread over Paris in widening circles. With conflicting thoughts, in wild terror and grief, Gaston seeks the footsteps of Colombe, of her people, from their rifled and deserted house to the abodes of their various acquaintance, like the traces of wrecked men under deep water. Yet even amid his private distress, queries on points of more general interest in the *event* would not be excluded. With whom precisely, in whose interest had the first guilty motion been?—Gaston on the morrow asked in vain as the historian asks still. And more and more as he picked his way

---

* Sunday, August 24, Feast of St. Bartholomew.

among the direful records of the late massacre, not the cruelty only but the obscurity, the accidental character, yet, alas! also the treachery, of the public event seemed to identify themselves tragically with his own personal action. Those queries, those surmises were blent with the enigmatic sense of his own helplessness amid the obscure forces around him, which would fain compromise the indifferent, and had made him so far an accomplice in their unfriendly action that he felt certainly not quite guiltless, thinking of his own irresponsible, self-centered, passage along the ways, through the weeks that had ended in the public crime and his own private sorrow. Pity for those unknown or half-known neighbours whose faces he must often have looked on—*ces pauvres morts!*—took an almost remorseful character from his grief for the delicate creature whose vain longings had been perhaps but a rudimentary aptitude for the really high things himself had represented to her fancy, the refined happiness to which he might have helped her. The being whose one claim had lain in her incorrigible lightness, came to seem representative of the suffering of the whole world in its plenitude of piteous detail, in those unvalued caresses, that desire towards himself, that patient half-expressed claim not to be wholly despised, poignant now for ever. For he failed to find her: and her brothers being presumably dead, all he could discover of a certainty from the last survivor of her more distant kinsmen was the fact of her flight into the country, already in labour it was thought, and in the belief that she had been treacherously deserted, like many another at that great crisis. In the one place in the neighbourhood of Paris with which his knowledge connected her he seeks further tidings, but hears only of her passing through it, as of a passage into vague infinite space; a little onward, dimly of her death, with the most damaging view of his own conduct presented with all the condemnatory resources of Huguenot tongues, but neither of the place nor the circumstances of that event, nor whether, as seemed hardly probable, the child survived. It was not till many years afterwards that he stood by her grave, still with no softening of the cruel picture driven then as with fire into his soul; her affection, her confidence in him still contending with the suspicions, the ill-concealed antipathy to him of her hostile brothers, the distress of her flight, half in dread to find the husband she was pursuing with the wildness of some lost child, who seeking its parents begins to suspect treacherous abandonment. That most mortifying view of his actions had doubtless been further enforced on her by others, the worst possible reading, to her own final discomfiture, of a not unfaithful heart.

VII

THE LOWER PANTHEISM

Jetzo, da ich ausgewachsen,
Viel gelesen, viel gereist,
Schwillt mein Herz, und ganz von Herzen,
Glaub' ich an den Heilgen Geist.

—Heine

THOSE WHO WERE CURIOUS TO TRACE THE SYMMETRIES OF CHANCE OR DESTINY felt now quite secure in observing that, of nine French kings of the name, every third Charles had been a madman. Over the exotic, nervous creature who had inherited so many delicacies of organisation, the coarse rage or *rabies* of the wolf, part, doubtless, of an inheritance older still, had asserted itself on that terrible night of Saint Bartholomew, at the mere sight, the scent, of blood, in the crime he had at least allowed others to commit; and it was not an unfriendly witness who recorded that, the fever once upon him, for an hour he had been less a man than a beast of prey. But, exemplifying that exquisite fineness of cruelty proper to an ideal tragedy, with the work of his madness all around him, he awoke sane next day, to remain so—aged at twenty-one—seeking for the few months left him to forget himself in his old out-of-door amusements, rending a consumptive bosom with the perpetual horn-blowing which could never rouse again the gay morning of life.

"I have heard," says Brantome, of Elisabeth, Charles's queen, "that on the Eve of Saint Bartholomew, she, having no knowledge of the matter, went to rest at her accustomed hour, and, sleeping till the morning, was told, as she arose, of the brave mystery then playing. 'Alas!' she cried; 'the king! my husband! does he know it?' 'Ay! Madam,' they answered; 'the king himself has ordained it.' 'God!' she cried; 'how is this? and what counsellors be they who have given him this advice? O God, be pitiful! for unless Thou art pitiful I fear this offence will never be pardoned unto him'; and asking for her 'Hours,' suddenly betook herself to prayer, weeping."

Like the shrinking, childish Elisabeth, the Pope also wept at that dubious service to his Church from one who was, after all, a Huguenot in belief; and Huguenots themselves pitied his end.— *"Ah! ces pauvres morts! que j'ai eu un meschant conseil! Ah! ma nourrice! ma mie, ma nourrice! que de sang, et que de meurtres!"*

It was a peculiarity of the naturally devout Gaston that, habituated to yield himself to the poetic guidance of the Catholic Church in her wonderful, year-long dramatic version of the story of redemption, he had ever found its greatest day least evocative of proportionate sympathy. The sudden gaieties of Easter morning, the congratulations to the Divine Mother, the sharpness of the recoil from one extreme of feeling to the other, for him never cleared away the Lenten preoccupation with Christ's death and passion: the empty tomb, with the white clothes lying, was still a tomb: there was no human warmth in the "spiritual body": the white flowers, after all, were those of a funeral, with a mortal coldness, amid the loud Alleluias, which refused to melt at the startling summons, any more than the earth will do in the March morning because we call it Spring. It was altogether different with that other festival which celebrates the Descent of the Spirit, the tongues, the nameless impulses gone all abroad, to soften slowly, to penetrate, all things, as with the winning subtlety of nature, or of human genius. The gracious Pentecostal fire seemed to be in alliance with the sweet, warm, relaxing winds of that later, securer, season, bringing their spicy burden from unseen sources. Into the close world, like a walled garden, about him, influences from remotest time and space found their way, travelling unerringly on their long journeys, as if straight to him, with the assurance that things were not wholly left to themselves; yet so unobtrusively that, a little later, the transforming spiritual agency would be discernible at most in the grateful cry of an innocent child, in some good deed of a bad man, or unlooked-for gentleness of a rough one, in the occasional turning to music of a rude voice. Through the course of years during which Gaston was to remain in Paris, very close to other people's sins, interested, all but entangled, in a world of corruption in flower (pleasantly enough to the eye), those influences never failed him. At times it was as if a legion of spirits besieged his door: *"Open unto me! Open unto me! My sister, my love, my dove, my undefiled!"* And one result, certainly, of this constant prepossession was, that it kept him on the alert concerning theories of the divine assistance to man, and the world,—theories of inspiration.

On the Feast of Pentecost, on the afternoon of the thirtieth of May, news of the death of Charles the Ninth had gone abroad promptly, with large rumours as to the manner of it. Those streams of blood blent themselves fantastically in Gaston's memory of the event with the gaudy colours of the season—the crazy red trees in blossom upon the heated sky above the old gray walls; like a fiery sunset, it might seem, as he looked back over the ashen intervening years. To Charles's successor (he and the Queen-mother now delightfully secure from fears, however unreasonable, of Charles's jerking dagger) the day became a sweet one, to be noted unmistakably by various pious and other observances, which still further fixed the thought of that Sunday on Gaston's mind, with continual surmise as to the tendencies of so complex and perplexing a scene.

The last words of Charles had asserted his satisfaction in leaving no male child to wear his crown. But the brother, whose obvious kingly qualities, the chief facts really known of him so far, Charles was thought to have envied—the gallant feats of his youth, *de ses jeunes guerres*, his stature, his high-bred beauty, his eloquence, his almost pontifical refinement and grace,—had already promptly deserted the half-barbarous kingdom, his acceptance of which had been but the mask of banishment; though he delayed much on his way to the new one, passing round through the cities of Venice and Lombardy, seductive schools of the art of life as conceived by Italian epicures, of which he became only too ready a student. On Whit-Monday afternoon, while Charles "went in lead, amid very little private or public concern, to join his kinsfolk at Saint-Denys, Paris was already looking out for its new king, following, through doubtful rumour, his circuitous journey to the throne, by Venice, Padua, Ferrara, Mantua, Turin, over Mont Cenis, by Lyons, to soil, still building confidently on the prestige of his early manhood. Seeing him at last, all were conscious in a moment of the inversion of their hopes. Had the old witchcrafts of Poland, the old devilries of his race, laid visible hold on the hopeful young man, that he must now take purely satiric estimate of so great an opportunity, with a programme which looked like formal irony on the kingly position, a premeditated mockery of those who yielded him, on demand, a servile reverence never before paid to any French monarch? Well! the amusement, or business, of Parisians, at all events, would still be that of spectators, assisting at the last act of the Valois tragedy, in the course of which fantastic traits and incidents would naturally be multiplied. Fantastic humour seemed at its height in the institution of a new order of knighthood, the enigmatic splendours of which were to be a monument of Henry's superstitious care, or, as some said, of his impious contempt, of the day which had made him master of his destiny,—that great Church festival, towards the emphatic marking of which he was ever afterwards ready to welcome any novel or striking device for the spending of an hour.

It was on such an occasion, then,—on a Whitsunday afternoon, amid the gaudy red hues of the season, that Gaston listened to one, who, as if with some intentional new version of the sacred event then commemorated, had a great deal to say concerning the Spirit; above all, of the freedom, the indifference, of its operations; and who would give a strangely altered colour, for a long time to come, to the thoughts, to the very words, associated with the celebration of Pentecost. The speaker, though understood to be a brother of the Order of Saint Dominic, had not been present at the mass—the daily University red mass, *De Spiritu Sancto*, but said today according to the proper course of the season in the chapel of the Sorbonne, with much pomp, by the Italian Bishop of Paris. It was the reign of the Italians just then, a doubly refined, somewhat morbid, somewhat ash-coloured, Italy in France, more Italian still. What our Elisabethan poets imagined about Italian culture—forcing all they knew of Italy to an ideal of dainty sin such as had never actually existed there,—that the court of Henry, so far as in it lay, realised in fact. Men of Italian birth, "to the great suspicion of simple people," swarmed in Paris, already "flightier, less constant, than the girouettes on its steeples"; and it was love for Italian fashions that had brought king and courtiers here this afternoon, with great *éclat*, as they said, frizzed and starched, in the beautiful, minutely considered, dress of the moment, pressing the learned University itself into the background; for the promised speaker, about whom tongues had been busy, not only in the Latin quarter, had come from Italy. In an age in which all things about which Parisians much cared must be Italian, there might be a hearing for Italian philosophy. Courtiers at least would understand Italian; and this speaker was rumoured to possess in perfection all the curious arts of his native language. And of all the kingly qualities of Henry's youth, the single one which had held by him was that gift of eloquence he was able also to value in others; an inherited gift perhaps, for amid all contemporary and subsequent historic gossip about his mother, the two things certain are, that the hands credited with so much mysterious ill-doing were fine ones, and that she was an admirable speaker.

Bruno himself tells us, long after he had withdrawn himself from it, that the monastic life promotes the freedom of the intellect by its silence and self-concentration. The prospect of such freedom sufficiently explains why a young man who, however well-found in worldly and personal advantages, was above all conscious of great intellectual possessions, and of fastidious spirit also, with a remarkable distaste for the vulgar, should have espoused poverty, chastity, and obedience, in a Dominican cloister. What liberty of mind may really come to, in such places, what daring new departures it may suggest even to the strictly monastic temper, is exemplified by the dubious and dangerous mysticism of men like John of Parma and Joachim of Flora, the reputed author of a new "Everlasting Gospel"; strange dreamers, in a world of sanctified rhetoric, of that later dispensation of the Spirit, in which all law will have passed away; or again by a recognised tendency, in the great rival Order of Saint Francis, in the so-called "spiritual" Franciscans, to understand the dogmatic words of faith, *with a difference.*

The three convents in which successively Bruno had lived, at Naples, at Città di Campagna, and finally the *Minerva* at Rome, developed freely, we may suppose, all the mystic qualities of a genius, in which, from the first, a heady southern imagination took the lead. But it was from beyond monastic bounds that he would look for the sustenance, the fuel, of an ardour born or bred within them. Amid such artificial religious stillness the air itself becomes generous in under-tones. The vain young monk (vain, of course) would feed his vanity by puzzling the good, sleepy heads of the average sons of Dominic with his neology, putting new wine into old bottles, teaching them their own business, the new, higher, truer sense of the most familiar terms, of the chapters they read, the hymns they sang; above all, as it happened, every word that referred to the Spirit, the reign of the Spirit, and its excellent freedom. He would soon pass beyond the utmost possible limits of his brethren's sympathy, beyond the largest and freest interpretation such words would bear, to words and thoughts on an altogether different plane, of which the full scope was only to be felt in certain old pagan writers,—pagan, though approached, perhaps, at first, as having a kind of natural, preparatory, kinship with Scripture itself. The Dominicans would seem to have had well-stocked, and liberally-selected, libraries; and this curious youth, in that age of restored letters, read eagerly, easily, and very soon came to the kernel of a difficult old author, Plotinus or Plato,—to the real purpose of thinkers older still, surviving by glimpses only in the books of others, Empedocles, for instance, and Pythagoras, who had been nearer the original sense of things; Parmenides, above all, that most ancient assertor of God's identity with the world. The affinities, the unity, of the visible and the invisible, of earth and heaven, of all things whatever, with one another, through the consciousness, the person, of God the Spirit, who was at every moment of infinite time, in every atom of matter, at every point of infinite space; aye! *was* everything, in turn: that doctrine— *l'antica filosofia Italiana*—was in all its vigour there, like some hardy growth out of the very heart of nature, interpreting itself to congenial minds with all the fulness of primitive utterance. A big thought! yet suggesting, perhaps, from the first, in still, small, immediately practical, voice, a freer way of taking, a possible modification of, certain moral precepts. A primitive morality,—call it! congruous with those larger primitive ideas, with that larger survey, with the earlier and more liberal air.

Returning to this ancient "pantheism," after the long reign of a seemingly opposite faith, Bruno unfalteringly asserts "the vision of all things in God" to be the aim of all metaphysical speculation, as of all enquiry into nature. The Spirit of God, in countless variety of forms, neither above, nor in any way without, but intimately within, all things, is really present, with equal integrity and fulness, in the sunbeam ninety millions of miles long, and the wandering drop of water as it evaporates therein. The divine consciousness has the same relation to the production of things as the human intelligence to the production of true thoughts concerning them. Nay! those thoughts are themselves actually God in man: a loan to man also of His assisting Spirit, who, in truth, is the Creator of things, in and by His contemplation of them. For Him, as for man in proportion as man thinks truly, thought and being are identical, and things existent only in so far as they are known. Delighting in itself, in the sense of its own energy, this sleepless, capacious, fiery intelligence, evokes all the orders of nature, all the revolutions of history, cycle upon cycle, in ever new types. And God the Spirit, the soul of the world, being therefore really identical with the soul of Bruno also, as the universe shapes itself to Bruno's reason, to his imagination, ever more and more articulately, he too becomes a sharer of the divine joy in that process of the formation of true ideas, which is really parallel to the process of creation, to the evolution of things. In a certain mystic sense, which some in every age of the world have understood, he, too, is the creator; himself actually a participator in the creative function. And by such a philosophy, Bruno assures us, it was his experience that the soul is greatly expanded: *con questa filosofia l'anima mi s'aggrandisce: mi se magnifica l'intelletto!*

For, with characteristic largeness of mind, Bruno accepted this theory in the whole range of its consequences. Its more immediate corollary was the famous axiom of "indifference," of "the coincidence of contraries." To the eye of God, to the philosophic vision through which God sees in man, nothing is really alien from Him. The differences of things, those distinctions, above all, which schoolmen and priests, old or new, Roman or Reformed, had invented for themselves, would be lost in the length and breadth of the philosophic survey: nothing, in itself, being really either great or small; and matter certainly, in all its various forms, not evil but divine. Dare one choose or reject this or that? If God the Spirit had made, nay! was, all things indifferently, then, matter and spirit, the spirit and the flesh, heaven and earth, freedom and necessity, the first and the last, good and evil, would be superficial rather than substantial differences. Only, were joy and sorrow also, together with another distinction, always of emphatic reality to Gaston, for instance, to be added to the list of phenomena really "coincident," or "indifferent," as some intellectual kinsmen of Bruno have claimed they should?

The Dominican brother was at no distant day to break far enough away from the election, the seeming "vocation," of his youth, yet would remain always, and under all circumstances, unmistakably a monk in some predominant qualities of temper. At first it was only by way of thought that he asserted his liberty—delightful, late-found, privilege!—traversing, in strictly mental journeys, that spacious circuit, as it broke away before him at every moment upon ever-new horizons. Kindling thought and imagination at once, the prospect draws from him cries of joy, of a kind of religious joy, as in some new "canticle of the creatures," some new hymnal, or antiphonary. "Nature" becomes for him a sacred term.—"Conform thyself to Nature!" with what sincerity, what enthusiasm, what religious fervour, he enounces that precept, to others, to himself! Recovering, as he fancies, a certain primeval sense of Deity broadcast on things, a sense in which Pythagoras and other "inspired" theorists of early Greece had abounded, in his hands philosophy becomes a poem, a sacred poem, as it had been with them. That Bruno himself, in "the enthusiasm of the idea," drew from his axiom of the "indifference of contraries" the practical consequence which is in very deed latent there, that he was ready to sacrifice to the antinomianism, which is certainly a part of its rigid logic, the austerities, the purity of his own youth, for instance, there is no proof. The service, the sacrifice, he is ready to bring to the great light that has dawned for him, occupying his entire conscience with the sense of his responsibilities to it, is the sacrifice of days and nights spent in eager study, of plenary, disinterested utterance of the thoughts that arise in him, at any hazard, at the price, say! of martyrdom. The work of the divine Spirit, as he conceives it, exalts, inebriates him, till the scientific apprehension seems to take the place of prayer, oblation, communion. It would be a mistake, he holds, to attribute to the human soul capacities merely passive or receptive. She, too, possesses initiatory power as truly as the divine soul of the world, to which she responds with the free gift of a light and heat that seem her own.

Yet a nature so opulently endowed can hardly have been lacking in purely physical or sensuous ardours. His pantheistic belief that the Spirit of God is in all things, was not inconsistent with, nay! might encourage, a keen and restless eye for the dramatic details of life and character however minute, for humanity in all its visible attractiveness, since there too, in truth, divinity lurks. From those first fair days of early Greek specula-tion, love had occupied a large place in the conception of philosophy; and in after days Bruno was fond of developing, like Plato, like the Christian Platonists, combining something of the peculiar temper of each, the anal-ogy between the flights of intellectual enthusiasm and those of physical love, with an animation which shows clearly enough the reality of his ex-perience in the latter. The *Eroici Furori*, his book of books, dedicated to Philip Sidney, who would be no stranger to such thoughts, presents a sin-gular blending of verse and prose, after the manner of Dante's *Vita Nuova*. The supervening philosophic comment reconsiders those earlier, physi-cally erotic, impulses which had prompted the sonnet in voluble Italian, entirely to the advantage of their abstract, incorporeal, theoretic, equiva-lents. Yet if it is after all but a prose comment, it betrays no lack of the natural stuff out of which such mystic transferences must be made. That there is no single name of preference, no Beatrice, or Laura, by no means proves the young man's earlier desires to have been merely Platonic; and if the colours of love inevitably lose a little of their force and propriety by such deflexion from their earlier purpose, their later intellectual purpose as certainly finds its opportunity thereby, in the matter of borrowed fire and wings. A kind of old scholastic pedantry creeping back over the ar-dent youth who had thrown it off so defiantly (as if love himself went in now for a University degree), Bruno develops, under the mask of amo-rous verse, all the various stages of abstraction, by which, as the last step of a long ladder, the mind attains actual "union." For, as with the purely religious mystics, "union," the mystic union of souls with one other and their Lord, nothing less than union between the contemplator and the contemplated—the reality, or the sense, or at least the name of such union—was always at hand. Whence that instinctive tendency towards union if not from the Creator of things Himself, who has doubtless prompted it in the physical universe, as in man? How familiar the thought that the whole creation, not less than the soul of man, longs for God, "as the hart for the water-brooks"! To unite oneself to the infinite by largeness and lucidity of intellect, to enter, by that admirable faculty, into eternal life—this was the true vocation of the spouse, of the rightly amorous soul. *A filosofia è necessario amore.* There would be degrees of progress therein, as of course also of relapse: joys and sorrows, therefore. And, in interpreting these, the philosopher, whose intellectual ardours have superseded religion and physical love, is still a lover and a monk. All the influences of the convent, the sweet, heady incense, the pleading sounds, the sophisticated light and air, the grotesque humours of old gothic carvers, the thick stratum of pagan sentiment beneath all this,—*Santa Maria sopra Minervam!*—are indelible in him. Tears, sympathies, tender inspirations, attraction, repulsion, zeal, dryness, recollection, desire:—he finds a place for them all: knows them all well in their unaffected simplicity, while he seeks the secret and secondary, or, as he fancies, the primary, form and purport of each.

Whether as a light on actual life, or as a mere barren scholastic subtlety, never before had the pantheistic doctrine been developed with such completeness, never before connected with so large a sense of nature, so large a promise of the knowledge of it as it really is. The eyes that had not been wanting to visible humanity turned now with equal liveliness on the natural world, in that region of his birth, where all the colour and force of nature are at least two-fold. Nature is not only a thought or meditation in the divine mind; it is also the perpetual energy of that mind, which, ever identical with itself, puts forth and absorbs in turn all the successive forms of life, of thought, of language even. What seemed like striking transformations of matter were in truth only a chapter, a clause, in the great volume of the transformations of the divine Spirit. The mystic recognition that all is indeed divine had accompanied a realisation of the largeness of the field of concrete knowledge, the infinite extent of all there was actually to know. Winged, fortified, by that central philosophic faith, the student proceeds to the detailed reading: of nature, led on from point to point by manifold lights, which will surely strike on him by the way, from the divine intelligence in it, speaking directly, sympathetically, to a like intelligence in him. The earth's wonderful animation, as divined by one who anticipates by a whole generation the Baconian "philosophy of experience": in that, those bold, flighty, pantheistic speculations become tangible matter of fact. Here was the needful book for man to read; the full revelation, the story in detail, of that one universal mind, struggling, emerging, through shadow, substance, manifest spirit, in various orders of being,—the veritable history of God. And nature, together with the true pedigree and evolution of man also, his gradual issue from it, was still all to learn. The delightful tangle of *things!*—it would be the delightful task of man's *thoughts* to disentangle that. Already Bruno had measured the space which Bacon would fill, with room, perhaps, for Darwin also. That Deity is everywhere, like all such abstract propositions, is a two-edged force, depending for its practical effect on the mind which admits it on the peculiar perspective of that mind. To Dutch Spinosa, in the next century, faint, consumptive, with a naturally faint hold on external things, the theorem that God was in all things whatever, annihilating their differences, suggested a somewhat chilly withdrawal from the contact of all alike. But in Bruno, eager and impassioned, an Italian of the Italians, it awoke a constant, inextinguishable appetite for every form of experience,—a fear, as of the one sin possible, of limiting, for one's self or another, the great stream flowing for thirsty souls, that wide pasture set ready for the hungry heart.

Considered from the point of view of a minute observation of nature, the Infinite might figure as "the infinitely little"; no blade of grass being like another, as there was no limit to the complexities of an atom of earth,—cell, sphere, within sphere. And the earth itself, hitherto seemingly the privileged centre of a very limited universe, was, after all, but an atom in an infinite world of starry space, then lately divined by candid intelligence, which the telescope was one day to present to bodily eyes. For if Bruno must needs look forward to the future, to Bacon, for adequate knowledge of the earth, the infinitely little, he could look backwards also gratefully to another daring mind which had already put that earth into its modest place and opened the full view of the heavens. If God is eternal, then, the universe is infinite and worlds innumerable. Yes! one might well have divined what reason now demonstrated, indicating those endless spaces which a real sidereal science would gradually occupy.

That the stars are suns: that the earth is in motion: that the earth is of like stuff with the stars:—now the familiar knowledge of children—dawning on Bruno as calm assurance of reason on appeal from the prejudice of the eye, brought to him an inexpressibly exhilarating sense of enlargement in the intellectual, nay! the physical atmosphere. And his consciousness of unfailing unity and order did not desert him in that broader survey, which made the utmost one could ever know of the earth seem but a very little chapter in the endless history of God the Spirit, rejoicing so greatly in the admirable spectacle that it never ceases to evolve from matter new conditions. The immoveable earth, as we term it, beneath one's feet!—Why, one almost felt the movement, the respiration, of God in it. And yet how greatly even the physical eye, the *sensible* imagination (so to term it) was flattered by the theorem. What joy in that motion, in the prospect, the music! "The music of the spheres!"—he could listen to it in a perfection such as had never been conceded to Plato, to Pythagoras even.—

> Veni, Creator Spiritus,
> Mentes tuorum visita,
> Imple superna gratia,
> Quæ tu creasti pectora.

Yes! The grand old Christian hymns, perhaps the grandest of them all, seemed to blend themselves in the chorus, to be deepened immeasurably under this new intention. It is not always, or often, that men's abstract ideas penetrate the temperament, touch the animal spirits, affect conduct. It was what they did with Bruno. The ghastly spectacle of the endless material universe—infinite *dust*, in truth, starry as it may look to our terrestrial eyes—that prospect from which the mind of Pascal recoiled so painfully, induced in Bruno only the delightful consciousness of an ever-widening kinship and sympathy, since every one of those infinite worlds must have its sympathetic inhabitants. Scruples of conscience, if he felt such, might well be pushed aside for the "excellency" of such knowledge as this. To shut the eyes, whether of the body or the mind, would be a kind of sullen ingratitude;—the one sin to believe, directly or indirectly, in any absolutely dead matter anywhere, as being implicitly a denial of the indwelling spirit.—A free spirit, certainly, as of old! Through all his pantheistic flights, from horizon to horizon, it was still the thought of liberty that presented itself, to the infinite relish of this "prodigal son" of Dominic. God the Spirit had made all things indifferently, with a largeness, a beneficence, impiously belied by any theory of restrictions, distinctions, of absolute limitation. Touch! see! listen! eat freely of all the trees of the garden of Paradise, with the voice of the Lord God literally everywhere!—

here was the final counsel of perfection. The world was even larger than youthful appetite, youthful capacity. Let theologian and every other theorist beware how he narrowed either. "The plurality of worlds!"—How petty in comparison seemed those sins, the purging of which was men's chief motive in coming to places like this convent, whence Bruno, with vows broken, or for him obsolete, presently departed. A sonnet, expressive of the joy with which he returned to so much more than the liberty of ordinary men, does not suggest that he was driven from it. Though he must have seemed to those who surely had loved so loveable a creature there to be departing, like the "prodigal" of the Gospel, into the farthest of possible far countries, there is no proof of harsh treatment on their part, or even of an effort to detain him.

It happens most naturally of course that those who undergo the shock of spiritual or intellectual change sometimes fail to recognise their debt to the deserted cause:—How much of the heroism, or other high quality, of their rejection has really been the product of what they reject? Bruno, the escaped monk, is still a monk; and his philosophy, impious as it might seem to some, a religion; very new indeed, yet a *religion*. He came forth well-fitted by conventual influences to play upon men as he had been played upon. A challenge, a war-cry, an alarum, everywhere he seemed to be but the instrument of some subtly materialised spiritual force, like that of the old Greek prophets, that "enthusiasm" he was inclined to set so high, or like impulsive Pentecostal fire. His hunger to know, fed dreamily enough at first within the convent walls, as he wandered over space and time, an indefatigable reader of books, would be fed physically now by ear and eye, by large matter-of-fact experience, as he journeys from university to university; less as a teacher than a courtier, a citizen of the world, a knight-errant of intellectual light. The philosophic need to try all things had given reasonable justification to the stirring desire for travel common to youth, in which, if in nothing else, that whole age of the later Renaissance was invincibly young. The theoretic recognition of that mobile spirit of the world, ever renewing its youth, became the motive of a life as mobile, as ardent, as itself, of a continual journey, the venture and stimulus of which would be the occasion of ever-new discoveries, of renewed conviction.

The unity, the spiritual unity, of the world:—that must involve the alliance, the congruity, of all things with one another, of the teacher's personality with the doctrine he had to deliver, of the spirit of that doctrine with the fashion of his utterance, great reinforcements of sympathy. In his own case, certainly, when Bruno confronted his audience at Paris, himself, his theme, his language, were alike the fuel of one clear spiritual flame, which soon had hold of his audience also; alien, strangely alien, as that audience might seem from the speaker. It was *intimate* discourse, in magnetic touch with every one present, with his special point of impressibility; the sort of speech which, consolidated into literary form as a book, would be a dialogue according to the true Attic genius, full of those diversions, passing irritations, unlooked-for appeals, in which a solicitous missionary finds his largest range of opportunity, and takes even dull wits unaware. In Bruno, that abstract theory of the perpetual motion of the world was become a visible person talking with you.

And as the runaway Dominican was still in temper a monk, so he presented himself to his audience in the comely Dominican habit. The reproachful eyes were to-day for the most part kindly observant, registering every detail of that singular company, all the physiognomic effects which come, by the way, on people, and through them, on things,—the "shadows of ideas" in men's faces—his own pleasantly expressive with them, in turn. *De Umbris Idearum:* it was the very title of his discourse. There was "heroic gaiety" there: only, as usual with gaiety, it made the passage of a peevish cloud seem all the chillier. Lit up, in the agitation of speaking, by many a harsh or scornful beam, yet always sinking, in moments of repose, to an expression of high-bred melancholy, the face was one that looked, after all, made for suffering,—already half pleading, half defiant, as of a creature you could hurt, but to the last never shake a hair's-breadth from its estimate of yourself.

Like nature, like nature in that opulent country of his birth which the "Nolan," as he delighted to call himself, loved so well that, born wanderer as he was, he must perforce return thither sooner or later at the risk of life, he gave *plenis manibus*, but without selection, and was hardly more fastidious in speech than the "asinine" vulgar he so deeply contemned. His rank, un-weeded eloquence, abounding in play of words, rabbinic allegories, verses defiant of prosody, in the kind of erudition he professed to despise, with here and there a shameless image,—the product not of formal method, but of Neapolitan improvisation—was akin to the heady wine, the sweet, coarse odours, of that fiery, volcanic soil, fertile in such irregularities as manifest power. Helping himself indifferently to all religions for rhetoric illustration, his preference was still for that of the soil, the old pagan religion, and for the primitive Italian gods, whose names and legends haunt his speech, as they do the carved and pictorial work of that age of the Renaissance. To excite, to surprise, to move men's minds, like the volcanic earth as if in travail, and, according to the Socratic fancy, to bring them to the birth, was after all the proper function of the teacher, however unusual it might seem in so ancient a university. "Fantastic!"—from first to last, that was the descriptive epithet; and the very word, carrying us to Shakespeare, reminds one how characteristic of the age such habit was, and that it was pre-eminently due to Italy. A man of books, he had yet so vivid a hold on people and things, that the traits and tricks of the audience seemed to strike from his memory all the graphic resources of his old readings. He seemed to promise some greater matter than was then actually exposed by him; to be himself enjoying the fulness of a great outlook, the vague suggestion of which did but sustain the curiosity of the listeners. And still, in hearing him speak you seemed to see that subtle spiritual fire to which he testified kindling from word to word. What Gaston then heard was, in truth, the first fervid expression of all those contending views out of which his written works would afterwards be compacted, of course with much loss of heat in the process. Satyric or hybrid growths, things due to ὕβρις, insult, insolence, to what the old satyrs of fable embodied,—the volcanic South is kindly prolific of these, and Bruno abounded in mockery; though it was by way of protest. So much of a Platonist, for Plato's genial humour he had nevertheless substituted the harsh laughter of Aristophanes. Paris, teeming, beneath a very courtly exterior, with mordant words, in unabashed criticism of all real or suspected evil, provoked his utmost powers of scorn for the "Triumphant Beast," the "installation of the ass," shining even there amid the university folk,—those intellectual bankrupts of the Latin Quarter, who had so long passed between them, however gravely, a worthless "parchment and paper" currency. In truth, Aristotle, the supplanter of Plato, was still in possession, pretending, as

Bruno conceived, to determine heaven and earth by precedent, hiding the proper nature of things from the eyes of men. "Habit"—the last word of his practical philosophy—indolent habit! what would this mean, in the intellectual life, but just that sort of dead judgments which, because the mind, the eye, were no longer really at work in them, are most opposed to the essential quickness and freedom of the spirit?

The *Shadows* of Ideas: *De Umbris Idearum:* such, in set terms, have been the subject of Bruno's discourse, appropriately to the still only half emancipated intellect of his audience:—on approximations to truth: the divine imaginations, as seen, darkly, more bearably by weaker faculties, in words, in visible facts, in their shadows merely. According to the doctrine of "Indifference," indeed, there would be no real distinction between substance and shadow. In regard to man's feeble wit, however, varying degrees of knowledge constituted such a distinction. "Ideas, and Shadows of Ideas": the phrase recurred often; and, as such mystic phrases will, fixed itself in Gaston's fancy, though not quite according to the mind of the speaker; accommodated rather to the thoughts which just then preoccupied his own. As already in his life there had been the *Shadows of Events,*—the indirect yet fatal influence there of deeds in which he had no part, so now, for a time, he seemed to fall under the spell, the power, of the *Shadows of Ideas,* of Bruno's Ideas; in other words, of those indirect suggestions, which, though no necessary part of, yet inevitably followed upon, his doctrines. What, for instance, might be the proper practical limitations of that telling theory of "the coincidence, the indifference, of opposites"?

To that true son of the Renaissance, in the light of his large, antique, pagan ideas, the difference between Rome and the Reform would figure, of course, as but an insignificant variation upon some deeper and more radical antagonism, between two tendencies of men's minds. But what about an antagonism deeper still? Between Christ and the world, say!—Christ and the flesh!—or about that so very ancient antagonism between good and evil. Was there any place really left for imperfection, moral or otherwise, in a world, wherein the minutest atom, the lightest thought, could not escape from God's presence? Who should note the crime, the sin, the mistake, in the operation of that eternal spirit, which was incapable of mis-shapen births? In proportion as man raised himself to the ampler survey of the divine work around him, just in that proportion did the very notion of evil disappear. There were no weeds, no "tares," in the endless field. The truly illuminated mind, discerning spiritually, might do what it would. Even under the shadow of monastic walls, that had sometimes been the precept, which larger theories of "inspiration" had bequeathed to practice. "Of all the trees of the garden thou mayest freely eat!—If ye take up any deadly thing, it shall not hurt you!—And I think that I, too, have the spirit of God."

Bruno, a citizen of the world, Bruno at Paris, was careful to warn off the vulgar from applying the decisions of philosophy beyond its proper speculative limits. But a kind of secrecy, an ambiguous atmosphere, encompass from the first, alike the speaker and the doctrine; and in that world of fluctuating and ambiguous characters the alerter mind certainly, pondering on this novel "reign of the spirit"—what it might actually be—would hardly fail to find in Bruno's doctrines a method of turning poison into food, to live and thrive thereon; an art, to Paris, in the intellectual and moral condition of that day, hardly less opportune than had it related to physical poisons. If Bruno himself was cautious not to suggest the ethic or practical equivalent to his theoretic positions, there was that in his very manner of speech, in that rank, un-weeded eloquence of his, which seemed naturally to discourage any effort at selection, any sense of fine difference, of *nuances* or proportion, in things. The loose sympathies of his genius were allied to nature, nursing, with equable maternity of soul, good, bad, and indifferent alike, rather than to art, distinguishing, rejecting, refining. Commission and omission! sins of the former surely had the natural preference. And how would Paolo and Francesca have read this lesson? How would Henry, and Margaret of the "Memoirs," and other susceptible persons then present, read it, especially if the opposition between practical good and evil traversed diametrically another distinction, the "opposed points" of which, to Gaston for instance, could never by any possibility become "indifferent,"—the distinction, namely, between the precious and the base, æsthetically; between what was right and wrong in the matter of art?

APPENDIX

Diaphaneitè

There are some unworldly types of character which the world is able to estimate. It recognises certain moral types, or categories, and regards whatever falls within them as having a right to exist. The saint, the artist, even the speculative thinker, out of the world's order as they are, yet work, so far as they work at all, in and by means of the main current of the world's energy. Often it gives them late, or scanty, or mistaken acknowledgment; still it has room for them in its scheme of life, a place made ready for them in its affections. It is also patient of doctrinaires of every degree of littleness. As if dimly conscious of some great sickness and weariness of heart in itself, it turns readily to those who theorise about its unsoundness. To constitute one of these categories, or types, a breadth and generality of character is required. There is another type of character, which is not broad and general, rare, precious above all to the artist, a character which seems to have been the supreme moral charm in the Beatrice of the *Commedia*. It does not take the eye by breadth of colour; rather it is that fine edge of light, where the elements of our moral nature refine themselves to the burning point. It crosses rather than follows the main current of the world's life. The world has no sense fine enough for those evanescent shades, which fill up the blanks between contrasted types of character—delicate provision in the organisation of the moral world for the transmission to every part of it of the life quickened at single points! For this nature there is no place ready in its affections. This colourless, unclassified purity of life it can neither use for its service, nor contemplate as an ideal.

"Sibi unitus et simplificatus esse," that is the long struggle of the Imitatio Christi. The spirit which it forms is the very opposite of that which regards life as a game of skill, and values things and persons as marks or counters of something to be gained, or achieved, beyond them. It seeks to value everything at its eternal worth, not adding to it, or taking from it, the amount of influence it may have for or against its own special scheme of life. It is the spirit that sees external circumstances as they are, its own power and tendencies as they are, and realises the given conditions of its life, not disquieted by the desire for change, or the preference of one part in life rather than another, or passion, or opinion. The character we mean to indicate achieves this perfect life by a happy gift of nature, without any struggle at all. Not the saint only, the artist also, and the speculative thinker, confused, disintegrated in the world, as sometimes they inevitably are, aspire for this simplicity to the last. The struggle of this aspiration with a lower practical aim in the mind of Savonarola has been subtly traced by the author of *Romola*. As language, expression, is the function of intellect, as art, the supreme expression, is the highest product of intellect, so this desire for simplicity is a kind of indirect self-assertion of the intellectual part of such natures. Simplicity in purpose and act is a kind of determinate expression in dexterous outline of one's personality. It is a kind of moral expressiveness; there is an intellectual triumph implied in it. Such a simplicity is characteristic of the repose of perfect intellectual culture. The artist and he who has treated life in the spirit of art desires only to be shown to the world as he really is; as he comes nearer and nearer to perfection, the veil of an outer life not simply expressive of the inward becomes thinner and thinner. This intellectual throne is rarely won. Like the religious life, it is a paradox in the world, denying the first conditions of man's ordinary existence, cutting obliquely the spontaneous order of things. But the character we have before us is a kind of prophecy of this repose and simplicity, coming as it were in the order of grace, not of nature, by some happy gift, or accident of birth or constitution, showing that it is indeed within the limits of man's destiny. Like all the higher forms of inward life this character is a subtle blending and interpenetration of intellectual, moral and spiritual elements. But it is as a phase of intellect, of culture, that it is most striking and forcible. It is a mind of taste lighted up by some spiritual ray within. What is meant by taste is an imperfect intellectual state; it is but a sterile kind of culture. It is the mental attitude, the intellectual manner of perfect culture, assumed by a happy instinct. Its beautiful way of handling everything that appeals to the senses and the intellect is really directed by the laws of the higher intellectual life, but while culture is able to trace those laws, mere taste is unaware of them. In the character before us, taste, without ceasing to be instructive, is far more than a mental attitude or manner. A magnificent intellectual force is latent within it. It is like the reminiscence of a forgotten culture that once adorned the mind; as if the mind of one φιλοσοφήσας ποτε μετ' ἔρωτος, fallen into a new cycle, were beginning its spiritual progress over again, but with a certain power of anticipating its stages. It has the freshness without the shallowness of taste, the range and seriousness of culture without its strain and over-consciousness. Such a habit may be described as wistfulness of mind, the feeling that there is "so much to know," rather as a longing after what is unattainable, than as a hope to apprehend. Its ethical result is an intellectual guilelessness, or integrity, that instinctively prefers what is direct and clear, lest one's own confusion and intransparency should hinder the transmission from without of light that is not yet inward. He who is ever looking for the breaking of a light he knows not whence about him, notes with a strange heedfulness the faintest paleness in the sky. That truthfulness of temper, that receptivity, which professors often strive in vain to form, is engendered here less by wisdom than by innocence. Such a character is like a relic from the classical age, laid open by accident to our alien modern atmosphere. It has something of the clear ring, the eternal outline of the antique. Perhaps it is nearly always found with a corresponding outward semblance. The veil or mask of such a nature would be the very opposite of the "dim blackguardism" of Danton, the type Carlyle has made too popular for the true interest of art. It is just this sort of entire transparency of nature that lets through unconsciously all that is really lifegiving in the established order of things; it detects without difficulty all sorts of affinities between its own elements, and the nobler elements in that order. But then its wistfulness and a confidence in perfection it has makes it love the lords of change. What makes revolutionists is either self-pity, or indignation for the sake of others, or a sympathetic perception of the dominant undercurrent of progress in things. The nature before us is revolutionist from the direct sense of personal worth, that χλιδή, that pride of life, which to the Greek was a heavenly grace. How can he value what comes of accident, or usage, or convention, whose individual life nature itself has isolated and perfected? Revolution is often impious. They who prosecute revolution have to violate again and again the instinct of reverence. That is inevitable, since after all progress is a kind of violence. But in this nature revolutionism is softened, harmonised, subdued as by distance. It is the revolutionism of one who has slept a hundred years. Most of us are neutralised by the play of circumstances. To most of us only one chance is given in the life of the spirit and the intellect, and circumstances prevent our dexterously seizing that one chance. The one happy spot in our nature has no room to burst into life. Our collective life, pressing equally on every part of every one of us, reduces nearly all of us to the level of a colourless uninteresting existence. Others are neutralised, not by suppression of gifts, but by just equipoise among them. In these no single gift, or virtue, or idea, has an unmusical predominance. The world easily confounds these two conditions. It sees in the character before us only indifferentism. Doubtless the chief vein of the life of humanity could hardly pass through it. Not by it could the progress of the world be achieved. It is not the guise of Luther or Spinoza; rather it is that of Raphael, who in the midst of the Reformation and the Renaissance, himself lighted up by them, yielded himself to neither, but stood still to live upon himself, even in outward form a youth, almost an infant, yet surprising all the world. The beauty of the Greek statues was a sexless beauty; the statues of the gods had the least traces of sex. Here there is a moral sexlessness, a kind of impotence, an ineffectual wholeness of nature, yet with a divine beauty and significance of its own.

Over and over again the world has been surprised by the heroism, the insight, the passion, of this clear crystal nature. Poetry and poetical history have dreamed of a crisis, where it must needs be that some human victim be sent down into the grave. These are they whom in its profound emotion humanity might choose to send. "What," says Carlyle, of Charlotte Corday, "What if she had emerged from her secluded stillness, suddenly like a star; cruel-lovely, with half-angelic, half-dæmonic splendour; to gleam for a moment, and in a moment be extinguished; to be held in memory, so bright complete was she, through long centuries!"

Often the presence of this nature is felt like a sweet aroma in early manhood. Afterwards, as the adulterated atmosphere of the world assimilates us to itself, the savour of it faints away. Perhaps there are flushes of it in all of us; recurring moments of it in every period of life. Certainly this is so with every man of genius. It is a thread of pure white light that one might disentwine from the tumultuary richness of Goethe's nature. It is a natural prophecy of what the next generation will appear, renerved, modified by the ideas of this. There is a violence, an impossibility about men who have ideas, which makes one suspect that they could never be the type of any widespread life. Society could not be conformed to their image but by an unlovely straining from its true order. Well, in this nature the idea appears softened, harmonised as by distance, with an engaging naturalness, without the noise of axe or hammer.

People have often tried to find a type of life that might serve as a basement type. The philosopher, the saint, the artist, neither of them can be this type; the order of nature itself makes them exceptional. It cannot be the pedant, or the conservative, or anything rash and irreverent. Also the type must be one discontented with society as it is. The nature here indicated alone is worthy to be this type. A majority of such would be the regeneration of the world.

About Walter Pater*

PATER, WALTER HORATIO (1839–1894), ENGLISH MAN OF LETTERS, WAS BORN at Shadwell on the 4th of August 1839. He was the second son of Richard Glode Pater, a medical man, of Dutch extraction, born in New York. Jean-Baptiste Pater, the painter, was probably of the same family. Richard Pater moved from Olney to Shadwell early in the century, and continued to practise there among the poorer classes. He died while his son Walter was yet an infant, and the family then moved to Enfield, where the children were brought up. In 1853 Walter Pater was sent to King's School, Canterbury, where he was early impressed by the aesthetic beauties of the cathedral. These associations remained with him through life. As a schoolboy he read *Modern Painters,* and was attracted to the study of art, but he did not make any conspicuous mark in school studies, and showed no signs of the literary taste which he was afterwards to develop. His progress was always gradual. He gained a school exhibition, however, with which he proceeded in 1858 to Queen's College, Oxford. His undergraduate life was unusually uneventful; he was a shy, "reading man," making few friends. Jowett, however, was struck by his promise, and volunteered to give him private tuition. But Pater's class was a disappointment, and he only took a second in

*From *The Encyclopædia Britannica,* Eleventh Edition, University Press, Cambridge, England, 1910.

literae humaniores in 1862. After taking his degree he settled in Oxford and read with private pupils. As a boy he had cherished the idea of entering the Anglican Church, but, under the influence of his Oxford reading, his faith in Christianity became shaken, and by the time he took his degree he had thoughts of graduating as a Unitarian minister. This project, too, he resigned; and when, in 1864, he was elected to a fellowship at Brasenose, he had settled down easily into a university career. But it was no part of his ambition to sink into academic torpor. With the assumption of his duties as fellow the sphere of his interests widened rapidly; he became acutely interested in literature, and even began to write articles and criticisms himself. The first of these to be printed was a brief essay upon Coleridge, which he contributed in 1866 to the *Westminster Review*. A few months later (January 1867) appeared in the same review his now well-known essay on Winckelmann, the first expression of his idealism. In the following year, his study of "Aesthetic Poetry" appeared in the *Fortnightly Review*, to be succeeded by essays on Leonardo da Vinci, Sandro Botticelli, Pico della Mirandola, and Michelangelo. These, with other studies of the same kind, were in 1878 collected in his *Studies in the History of the Renaissance*. Pater was now the centre of a small but very interesting circle in Oxford. Such men as cherished aesthetic tastes were naturally drawn to him; and, though always retiring and, in a sense, remote in manner, he was continually spreading his influence, not only in the university, but among men of letters in London and elsewhere. The little body of Pre-Raphaelites were among his friends, and by the time that *Marius the Epicurean* appeared he had quite a following of disciples to hail it as a gospel. This fine and polished work, the chief of all his contributions to literature, was published early in 1885. In it Pater displays, with perfected fullness and loving elaboration, his ideal of the aesthetic life, his cult of beauty as opposed to bare asceticism, and his theory of the stimulating effect of the pursuit of beauty as an ideal of its own. In 1887 he published *Imaginary Portraits,* a series of essays in philosophic fiction; in 1889, *Appreciations, with an Essay on Style;* in 1893, *Plato and Platonism;* and in 1894, *The Child in the House.* His *Greek Studies* and his *Miscellaneous Studies* were collected posthumously in 1895; his posthumous romance of *Gaston de Latour* in 1896; and his *Essays from the "Guardian"* were privately printed in 1897. A collected edition of Pater's works was issued in 1901. Pater changed his residence from time to time, living sometimes at Kensington and in different parts of Oxford; but the centre of his work and influence was always his rooms at Brasenose. Here he laboured, with a wonderful particularity of care and choice, upon perfecting the expression of his theory of life and art. He wrote with difficulty, correcting and recorrecting with imperturbable assiduity. His mind, moreover, returned to the religious fervour of his youth, and those who knew him best believed that had he lived longer he would have resumed his boyish intention of taking holy orders. He was cut off, however, in the prime of his powers. Seized with rheumatic fever, he rallied, and sank again, dying on the staircase of his house, in his sister's arms, on the morning of Monday the 30th of July 1894. Pater's nature was so contemplative, and in a way so centred upon reflection, that he never perhaps gave full utterance to his individuality. His peculiar literary style, too, burnished like the surface of hard metal, was too austerely magnificent to be always persuasive. At the time of his death Pater exercised a remarkable and a growing influence among that necessarily restricted class of persons who have themselves something of his own love for beauty and the beautiful phrase. But the cumulative richness and sonorous depth of his language harmonized intimately with his deep and earnest philosophy of life; and those who can sympathize with a nervous idealism will always find inspiration in his sincere and sustained desire to "burn with a hard, gem-like flame," and to live in harmony with the highest.